How JoJo Got Her Mojo Back

A Dysfunctional Family Saga

By

Cynthia A. King

To my mom. Every time I whined, "I'm bored," she told me to go write a book. This one's for you, Mama.

CHAPTER ONE

JoJo wasn't even through her first cup of coffee when she heard the noise coming from outside. After last night's events, she didn't have the energy or desire to talk about it. *Yet someone is coming, someone who wanted to dissect the situation in an attempt to fix it. I don't know why they came here when the problem is somewhere else,* JoJo thought. The fact that her husband didn't tell her where he was going, and she didn't ask him to spoke volumes. She heard the screen door scrape the concrete, the key in the lock and bolts turned as the tumblers unlocked the door. The door opened and heels stomped up the stairs. JoJo could tell by the sound of the footwear it wasn't one of the boys. *Oh, Lord,* JoJo thought. It was her oldest and only daughter, Abbey, who showed up for her Saturday morning breakfast with Daddy.

At the sound of the door opening, the big black dog stood up and walked silently to JoJo's side. The dog was a recent addition to the household, something Ray brought home after a couple of kids on a corner asked him if he wanted to buy her. She was for sale, and Ray bought her. Initially, JoJo was pissed. *How dare he bring home anything that would ultimately become my responsibility? Ray travels for work and won't be around to care for her. He could have called and asked me if I wanted a dog, but of course he didn't. Ray doesn't think about anybody but himself, as usual,* JoJo thought.

There was something undefinable about the dog, JoJo couldn't put her finger on it. She was a very large, solid black German Shepard. The dog decided JoJo needed her, and at any noise, the dog went right to her side and stood on high alert. She had yet to bark.

It was in her eyes. She stood next to JoJo and looked at the door. Her eyes locked on to whoever came through it with a laser like focus and evaluated how big a threat they might be to JoJo. Ray said the boys told him her name was Furry. JoJo scratched behind the dog's ears and thought, *Thank you, Furry. It's nice to know someone's got my back. I might change your name, though. I'm not sold on Furry.*

"Go lay down, Furry. It's just Abbey." She went back to her dog bed, sat like the Sphinx, and watched JoJo the entire time.

1

"Where's Daddy?" Abbey asked. She leaned against the counter, her arms crossed over her chest. "He didn't come for breakfast, and he's not answering his phone."

JoJo looked at her daughter. They were equal in height, but Abbey took after her dad. His hair was thick and red in his youth, but now resembled a rust-colored Brillo pad. Abbey dodged that bullet and had a head of naturally curly auburn hair. She had her father's blue eyes, the exact shape of his face, and his smile. In fact, she looked so much like her father JoJo fought the desire to slap her. Irrational, JoJo knew. It wasn't Abbey's fault her father was a jerk. Abbey and her father were very close, something JoJo was happy about. She was Daddy's little girl, regardless that she was in her twenties. She was glad they had each other. JoJo worried that Abbey would end up alone; she was cute enough but about as soft and tender as a cactus.

Most guys realized she wasn't worth the effort. Plenty of girls wanted to date and have sex were pleasant and friendly. Even guys Abbey wouldn't consider in high school wouldn't consider Abbey now. Her reputation as a Class A bitch got around ahead of her, and since people expected that from her, Abbey made sure she delivered. JoJo couldn't see how that made her happy.

JoJo was sad that she and her daughter had such a contentious relationship. Since birth, it seemed they were at odds with each other. JoJo would say the sky was blue, Abbey would say green and run to her dad, who would tell her it was whatever color she wanted it to be. Abbey would run back and say, "See, Mommy. You're *wrong*."

Abbey thought her mother and her views were both archaic and anachronistic, but if life had taught JoJo anything, it didn't matter how it was packaged, not much had changed since Adam and Eve got tossed out of the Garden of Eden.

"I don't know where your father is, honey. He left last night with no forwarding address. All I can say is keep calling his phone," JoJo told her as she got up to make another cup of coffee. She thought about offering Abbey a cup but decided Abbey could make her own. This was JoJo's "new." She was no longer the hostess. This place was now self-service. No longer when you pop in for a cup of coffee on a Saturday morning will there be a freshly baked chocolate chip or blueberry coffee cake. It's now BYOC. Bring your own carbohydrates. Or BYOB, bring your own breakfast.

Abbey's petty tit for tat attitude was catchy, and JoJo matched her. *You know, Abbey, I am the queen of sharp tongues,* JoJo thought. *I could cut you to the quick in a heartbeat, so watch your step.* Growing older had softened and smoothed out some of JoJo's rough edges and mellowed her humor away from sarcasm to benign remarks. Every once in a while, the wiseass JoJo used to be broke the surface and said something she'd regret. Unfortunately, that streak of harshness was still there, one of JoJo's less attractive traits Abbey inherited. It was the one thing JoJo wished could be tempered. She took her cup and sat back down. The heat of her coffee released the steam in little swirls above the liquid. She looked at the mug. She bought it last Mother's Day as a gift to herself. It said, "Fucking Mother of the Year." *Yeah, right,* JoJo thought.

"When was the last time you talked to your father?" JoJo asked Abbey.

"Last week," Abbey said. "Why, what did you do?"

JoJo bit her tongue. She was at a point where she felt she no longer needed to shield her kids from their dad's selfishness. All the lies JoJo told the kids so they wouldn't know what a jerk he was underneath his nicely packaged exterior. His plane was late. He got a flat tire. His meeting ran over. When in reality, Ray never planned on coming. Something that didn't involve his family was always in front of Ray, that demanded his immediate attention. He was famous for his "Oh, you should have told me sooner" response. It never was his fault. Now, everyone was an adult. They could make their own assessment of their parents' faults and let the chips fall where they may.

JoJo figured if Ray thought he was going to get out of the obligations and responsibilities of having a family, it might not be a bad time for her to step off as well. Her children were adults. Once again, JoJo was left to mop up somebody else's mess. Deliver someone else's bad news. Call an audible. Perhaps Abbey deserved to get hit right between the eyes and learn the realities of adulthood firsthand.

"Well, your father packed his things and moved out. He said some bullshit about a man's life. It's his turn now. Well, good for him. He can have it. I hope he marries a *Price is Right* spokesmodel. If our marriage and home life were so bad, Daddy felt his only option was to leave, well, bye. Thanks for the extra twenty pounds and the stretch marks because that's all I got out of this marriage. I told him if he left, I'm calling a lawyer and change the locks so he can't

3

just waltz back in here. His attitude was 'do what you gotta do,' and still he left. He left," JoJo added, still surprised. Surprised he had the balls to leave.

"Daddy moved out? To where?" Abbey demanded. JoJo shrugged and shook her head. "What do you mean you don't know?"

"He said it wasn't a mid-life crisis, it was a search for self and hope you'd understand."

"I can see why he wants to separate from you, you're his wife. But us? We're his family. He can't leave his family."

"Uh, thanks for the vote of support, darlin', but that's exactly what he did." JoJo was sad. Sad her daughter was so self-centered and so quick to assign blame. "Unless he contacts you directly otherwise, I don't know what to say."

"What did you do?" Abbey asked again.

"Why don't you get a cup of coffee and sit down so we can talk about it? It's a long story."

Abbey dug in. "I don't want a long story. I want an answer."

JoJo looked at her daughter as she stood against the counter, her arms still tightly crossed against her chest, her eyes squinted in anger. Abbey was so much like her dad. She wanted to know the part of the story she wanted to know. The details were of no value to her, so she didn't want to waste her precious time listening to them. She cherry-picked the conversation. It was great if you were a mind reader, but it made a normal conversation hard. It left people unaware of what holes needed to be filled in or where the pitfalls lay. Abbey tended to hold the people who didn't know what Abbey wanted to know against them. Her sharp tongue would accuse the other party of keeping her in the dark or deliberately withholding information.

"What did I do?" JoJo asked. "I got old. I went through menopause. Oh, yeah. I had that car accident that left me broken with nothing to offer a man such as your dad. He needs more than what's inside these four walls. He had lots of reasons, I'm sure, but he didn't get into them. You have to ask him for the specifics, Abbey. But I don't know why he left you or your brothers."

****

Last night, JoJo's husband Ray came home from work in an unusually good mood. His diatribe about how much he hated his job usually started before he hung up his coat. It was just a whole lot of hot air. He loved his career. Ray

4

had been working his way up the corporate ladder all his adult life and was quite content at his progress. Complaining about it let him relive his victorious moments all over again, pure ego, and JoJo would nod her head hopefully at the right moments while thinking about her grocery list. Last night, he was whistling and quite happy.

"Why are you so happy, Ray? Did you have to fire someone today? Get a raise, did you?" JoJo asked him suspiciously. She knew his moods and could read him like an old copy of the *Enquirer*. Something was up. He went into their bedroom, and JoJo followed him.

She watched him go to the closet and get a suitcase. He put the suitcase on the bed, the bed they shared and where they created three children. The bed where they consoled each other against the little earthquakes that threatened a marriage, the bed where late at night they brainstormed solutions to problems the world thrust upon them. He opened it and started to pack, still without explanation, still with a smile on his face. JoJo sat on the bed next to his open suitcase.

"Look, Ray, you really need to tell me what's going on. Where are you going?" JoJo asked.

He turned and faced her. "It's like this," he said. "It's an opportunity."

"An opportunity for what?" JoJo probed.

"A man has three phases in his life. The first third is growing into a man, the second he's a family man, and the third phase is now. He gets to be his own man. *I* get to be my own man now. It's a chance to start over. That's what I'm doing. Grabbing hold of the rest of my life and starting fresh." His face still held the smile.

"So that's what this is about," she said, pointing at the suitcase. "Starting over?' What the hell does that even mean? Where are you going to start over?"

"See, this is the beauty of it. I don't know. I don't care. Anywhere I want." JoJo stood up. "This fresh start. What about the rest of us?"

"The kids are adults now. They don't need me anymore. And you, I can't help you anymore." That last remark stung. JoJo could put the amount of help Ray gave her in a thimble, and there would still be room for more. If she needed help, she had to hire somebody.

"What about her?" JoJo asked. "You're leaving her too?" she said, pointing at the dog he rescued a week ago. "You're the kind of man that would dump a dog as soon as it's an inconvenience? How dare you. You're such an asshole. You know what, Ray? Go. Get the fuck out of here. But realize this: That door is exit only. If you go out through that door, don't bother coming back. I'm changing the locks first thing in the morning," JoJo said with conviction. "Don't fuck with me, Ray."

He looked up from the suitcase, from packing his perfectly paired and rolled socks courtesy of JoJo. Everything he put in that there was clean and neatly folded because of her efforts.

"I know. That's the point. Leave all this to reinvent myself."

"Well," JoJo said. "Good luck with that. You'll be hearing from my lawyer."

She went into the family room and chose the chair where the back faced him, the back of her head the only thing visible. The dog followed and sat at her feet. Ray called out goodbye to her, but he still left. He left. He, after all these years, thinks he's entitled just to decide to go off in a direction to parts unknown. He felt no concern, no sorrow, not even grief because that would mean he felt something as far as the death of their marriage. He didn't feel anything.

It stunned her. She knew their marriage wasn't all hearts and flowers, hell, it wasn't ever hearts and flowers. It never was. It was a mutual partnership, and she learned to love him, or most of him. He had the nerve to walk out on her when if anybody should've walked out, it should have been her years ago.

****

JoJo got up and looked around their bedroom, which, since her accident, had become his bedroom. She needed special things like an adjustable bed, room for the accessories of disability like the walker and wheelchair, so she moved into the boys' old room. *"Huh,"* thought JoJo. *Accessories used to mean purses and pearls. Now it's crutches and grab bars.* Maybe doesn't see her anymore. Maybe he lost sight of her among all this institutional crap.

JoJo lost sight of herself for a long time after her accident. When it was said and done, she lost a lot of who she used to be. JoJo worked with a therapist for a long time to reach self-acceptance. The lasting physical damage was one thing; her psyche was damaged as well. She had reached the point in her healing that the therapist decided that JoJo could have a productive, meaningful life within her limitations. Despite her limitations. Maybe Ray didn't see that, or simply what was left no longer suited his needs.

****

CHAPTER TWO

He left Friday. It was Sunday afternoon, a nice quiet Sunday afternoon, JoJo doing the Sunday crossword puzzle. Nobody bothered her, asking about dinner when it wasn't even lunchtime, shooting down every idea she had. She knew Ray did it to annoy her, just like her talking while he read the Sunday newspaper. She sat at the kitchen table, the crossword puzzle spread out in front of her. She used to have to work in quarters to avoid the massive spread into communal areas Ray always complained about. It actually was neater with him gone.

He felt being the breadwinner allowed him to pass on the domestic end of the household, which JoJo knew, and it didn't bother her. It was his inability to do reasonable things. When the garbage can got too full, rather than take it out, he would leave the trash on the counter and his dishes and coffee cups piled up all weekend, leaving her with a Monday morning mess to clean up. Well, not tomorrow. How nice. She could get through the day with one cup. Used for coffee, tea, soup, water or wine, that one cup would be the only sign anyone lived here come Monday.

The kitchen was her favorite room in the house. From her seat at the table, she did everything from the monster puzzle to paying bills. Once, her family sat around this table and had dinner. They sat here and talked about bad grades and fake friends. Their family talked about everything at this table. They had "the talk" at this table. Their friends came over and did school projects and homework at this table. There was a dent in the table where Frankie dropped a barbell. JoJo took her index finger and ran it over the blemish. When Denver was little, he took stickers someone had gifted him and stuck them the only place he could reach: the legs of the table. She tried to peel them off, but a few remained. It made her happy to have the reminder of him as a little boy. The spot where Abbey spilled nail polish remover and marred the finish, and she tried to blame it on Frankie. When asked about it, he made a face and shook his head.

Family meetings were held here. Applications for schools and summer camps were filled out at this table. Now, sunlight streamed in through the window, warmed the room, and left a spot big enough for the dog to stretch out and warm her weary bones if they were weary. JoJo couldn't tell.

The screen door clattered, the knob turned with a push, and in walked her younger son, Denver. Totally his father's son, his name an homage to the peerless John Denver and the city of Denver where Ray went to college many years ago. JoJo said if the baby was a boy, he could have naming rights, and if it was a girl, she chose. He won and named the boy Denver. *Fine,* JoJo thought. *I'll call him Denny.* He was Denny until college, where he discovered most girls preferred Denver. JoJo compromised on 'Den,' but still called him Denny.

"What's up, mom? Abbey sounded so stressed out when she left the message to be here at six. Where is she? What's going on?" Denver asked his mother. "Mom, can you make the dog go lie down? She's staring at me."

"Furry. Go get in your bed. That's Denny."

Furry stood and looked at Denny for a few seconds. She turned and went to her bed. "Abbey probably wanted to talk about your father moving out." JoJo braced herself for the deluge of questions, but only one came.

"What?" Denver said, unsure he heard correctly.

"Your father is pretending to have a mid-life crisis so he can walk away and start over with a clean conscience. Just you watch."

JoJo leaned into her son's hug hello. Being in her son's arms gave JoJo a glimpse of her desolate future, everybody grown and gone. It took all she had not to burst into tears and make this her son's burden. This was between her and Ray, and JoJo wanted it to stay that way.

The door, perhaps from being used so much, was starting to loosen up and quieted down. Her middle child, the ruminator, Frankie. Frankie made a great middle child. You could ask him something, and a week later, he'd give you his answer. He mulled things over and thought things through. Frankie drove a truck for the county and had a small house. Girls swarmed around Frankie, hoping he would use one of his few chosen words and say her name. He worked out a lot, and it showed. He was an inch or so shorter than his brother but more than made up for it in bulk. Frankie walked in and said a general "Hey," his standard greeting to them and fixed himself a cup of coffee.

Furry looked from JoJo to Frankie, decided he was good and stayed in her bed,

"Hi, Mom," he said as he took the seat next to her. "Where's Abbey? She made us come over here. If she's not here in five, I'm out," Frankie said.

"Me too," said Den.

"We don't need her anyway. I can fill you in on what's so important. I didn't have any control over this at all, just to let you know." JoJo took a deep breath and tried to hold her voice steady. "The big news is your father moved out Friday and left everything. He said he wanted to start life over. Abbey thinks I drove him away. Did I? I don't know, but I never saw it coming. He packed up and left. Your dad said he needed to unburden himself of things weighing him down, I guess part of that is me. But not you. Never you."

"Huh," said Frankie.

"That's news to me," said Den. "I never knew he was unhappy."

The noise of the doors opening had them turn towards the entrance of Abbey. Furry, too. She sensed the tension between JoJo and Abbey but didn't consider Abbey meant harm, but Furry didn't take her eyes off her for the length of her visit. Abbey ignored the dog, came in and threw her purse on the table.

"Okay," Abbey said. "Let's get started."

"Started? We're finished," said Denver. "Next time, don't be late."

Abbey was her oldest and had an impatience with life in general, humanity to be specific. Someone was always taking too long in front of her at the bank, the gas station, the green light, the grocery store. Somebody was always in her way. She expelled a breath that sounded like she had phlegm in the back of her throat. Or hawking up a loogie, as Denver said.

"What do you mean it's over? I just got here," Abbey said and tried to pull rank. She felt she got to call the shots and got angry when her brothers disrespected the birth order.

"Dad left. Everything. Nobody knows where he is. He, I guess, thinks he has the right to reinvent himself. Does he? Have that right?" Denver asked the rest of his family.

"Everyone has the right to live their own lives," Abbey said, mad they ignored her seniority and started without her. "Daddy, too."

"Yeah, but Dad promised Mom to be here. That's different. It sounds like she was just as surprised as we are," Denver said to Abbey. Abbey glared at her brother.

JoJo stayed quiet but changed her mind. "Whoever hears from him first, let the others know. Don't include me. Just get his address so I know where to send his mail and the divorce papers."

The kids looked at JoJo, their mouths agape in horror. Divorce? Them?

"You know, let your dad get a do-over. In the meantime, perhaps I'll get one myself and see how it fits. Like right now. Who wants to go out to eat? My treat," their mom offered.

The kids looked at each other. Mom's treat? Hell yes.

****

CHAPTER THREE

Ray had been gone almost a week. JoJo turned off the TV, which left the house quiet, something it hadn't been since they bought it. If someone was home, it was on. JoJo hated it, but it was just background noise like the hum of the refrigerator or the heat kicking on. The overwhelming silence was the first thing that brought JoJo to her knees.

No slamming doors. No arguing. Nobody looked in the fridge saying, "There's never anything to eat in this house." No one pulled in and out of the driveway. No FedEx deliveries for Ray. It came to JoJo that what she really was grieving was her empty nest. The kids and their friends created the noise that she missed.

Ray, not so much. He was more trouble than he was worth. His noise was just that. He was the area district manager of a large medical supply company. He managed the East Coast, so he traveled during the week. It was the weekends when he was home, he felt obligated to manage JoJo and that stressed her out. He thought it was his job to impart his expertise to make JoJo's life easier.

For example, the laundry. She would wash, fold, and put the clean towels in a basket. Ray didn't like this, he thought the basket on the floor was a tripping hazard. The folded towels should be placed on top of the dryer. Why he couldn't pick up the basket and put the clean towels where they belonged was a mystery to JoJo. First of all, he could never trip over a basket because he never went in the laundry room, and secondly, after distracting her with his sales speech for five minutes, he would leave, adding value to her life, but the basket of towels hadn't moved.

****

It was so hard after the accident. While JoJo was laid up with a back broken in three places, a fractured pelvis and a number of broken bones in her leg, she missed a critical time in her kids growing up. It was the time of so many lasts she hated to miss. Last high school ball games, last art show, last school play, last day as a freshman. Frankie was in love with a girl who had an identical twin. She wouldn't go to the Junior Prom unless Frankie found a date for her sister.

Frankie found one: Denny. It was so sweet when Frankie, Denny, and their dates for the junior prom came to see her at the hospital so she could see them all dressed up. The girls were kind of odd because they wore identical gowns but otherwise looked lovely. The nurses got a big kick out of seeing them. JoJo was released to the rehab part of the hospital.

JoJo almost missed Abbey's high school graduation. It was with the help of her sons and the rehab facility's wheelchair van that allowed JoJo out for the afternoon. It was a plan worthy of Patton invading Iwa Jima. When it was over, it was as if the incredible effort it took for her to attend was nothing. Abbey came over and thanked her for coming, but she had to go because Ray had planned a party for her at a restaurant. She kissed her mother's cheek and hurried off.

Once JoJo was strapped and Frankie drove the van back, she let loose the waterworks. Tears started to roll down her cheeks at the way Abbey treated her. Denny gave her one of the boxes of tissues he found, wondering if everybody who needed the van cried. He rubbed his mother's back in an attempt to soothe her.

"It's okay, Mom. It's okay."

"I bet me in a wheelchair needing a special van embarrassed Abbey," JoJo sobbed.

"No," Frankie said. "I bet it's because she's a real bitch."

JoJo laughed through her tears and stopped crying. She was soon back at the rehab campus and back in her room. After the boys left, JoJo considered the hurt caused by Abbey's behavior. It was a hurt only a child could inflict upon a parent. It may be forgiven, but it was a scar on her mother's heart and could never be forgotten.

****

Abbey's longtime boyfriend broke up with her before he left for college. JoJo asked Abbey to come to her bedside because she could sympathize, commiserate, and otherwise be there for Abbey. She would get ice cream. Abbey came but didn't want to talk about it. She ate some ice cream with big sighs between spoonfuls. JoJo asked her if anything else was new, at which Abbey flew into a fit.

"How could you be so, I don't know, so cold?" Abbey accused her. "Did you forget I just broke up with Dylan?" she said, her voice so loud people in the hall heard her.

JoJo was thinking about her previous physical therapy session and dreaded the next one. Learning to walk again with a ton of hardware in your back and a metal rod in your leg wasn't as easy as it sounds.

"MOM!" Abbey yelled. "You're not even listening!"

"You're right, Abbey, I am distracted, and I apologize for that. Let me scoot over and you come lay down with me so I can hold you." JoJo reached for her daughter's hand. "When I broke up with my first boyfriend, I was devastated. The first time somebody says they'll love you forever then he doesn't rock you to the very core. Dylan was your first serious boyfriend, and he broke your heart. It *hurts*. I need to respect that. I wish I could get out of this damn bed and console you as I should, but you squeeze in here and at least I can hold you. You need me Abbey, and I can't be there for you physically, so let me be there for you emotionally. Come cry on my shoulder."

"I can't fit in that bed with you. That's a stupid idea."

"Then let me hold your hand. I need to be there for you. If you feel like crying, I'll cry with you. Nothing hurts worse than your first broken heart. Look at me, Abbey. I got smashed into a million pieces, and it's nothing compared to a broken heart. I've experienced both. Your broken heart trumps my broken back, baby," JoJo said. "I'm sorry it hurts you so much. What can I do? What do you want me to say? Do you want me to trash talk him so your pain turns to anger for a bit? That, I can do. The only thing I can say for sure is you'll survive it. It may take a while, but you will. Somebody better will come along."

JoJo didn't want to say Dylan was right. While Abbey was going to a state school an hour and a half away, Dylan was going away to school in another state. He didn't want the responsibility of Abbey missing opportunities waiting for him. Dylan wanted them both to be free to experience whatever college life offered, and he was trying to be a good guy about it.

"Abbey, who knows what the future holds for you? This an opportunity for you, too. Be open to new ideas and experiences. He may come home and say he wants you back, and your response may be later dude. I've got new things in my life, and there's no room for you.' You never know what life has in store for you, Abbey. Good things. Great things."

"Oh yes, me." Abbey was her favorite subject. "It hurts so badly I can't talk about it. I love Dylan. He said he loved me. I don't know what I'm going to do," she cried.

JoJo's mind wandered once again. She wasn't listening. *Oh shit, what do I say?* Abbey stood there waiting for an answer.

"All I can say is give it time, Abbey. It hurts like hell now, but it will get better. I promise. Talk to Daddy about it. He was a young guy once, maybe he can help explain what Dylan is thinking." JoJo shifted her weight off her hip, but it still hurt. *Ray will give Abbey the necessary ego strokes she needs. When I try, the words don't soothe Abbey, they agitate her. Another disconnect on my part,* JoJo thought.

A commotion in the doorway saved JoJo. Her roommate's family. It got loud and Abby needed quiet so she could perform for maximum effect. She lost interest as soon as the competition showed up. She got up, leaned in, and kissed her mother's cheek. Abbey rubbed her mother's shoulder.

"I'll let you get some rest now," Abbey said. "I love you, Mom,"

"I love you too, baby. Try to remember what I said. It will get better with time," JoJo said. Abbey left. JoJo listened to the tap of Abbey's heels against the linoleum as they faded away.

****

Frankie was a creature of habit. He went to work, then to the gym. He took a shower at the gym so he could stop at the pub on the way home. He sat at the bar ordered dinner and exactly one beer. He was an inch shorter than Denny, but he more than made up for it with muscle. He took after JoJo's side of the family. Where his siblings had red hair and freckles, Frankie had neither. He was the definition of tall, dark, and handsome. He had been lifting weights since he was a teenager and was rock solid. The cliche "still waters run deep" applied to him as well.

He stayed at the pub, depending on who else was there. Occasionally, a girl would cross his path he thought was cute and funny. He didn't think it would be so hard to find one, but the older he got, the rarer they became.

Of all her kids, Frankie was the smartest, JoJo thought. When she was pregnant with him, they made a deal it was her turn to name the baby. It was a boy. She named him after her father, Frank DeLuca. She chose the name Franklin, the name Frank sounded too hard to JoJo's ear. Her father was called Frankie, so that worked. Ray, being the smartass he was, gave him the middle name of Benjamin. His full name was Franklin Benjamin Anderson.

Frankie decided not to go into a morass of debt to achieve his dreams. He learned how to drive those big trucks and now worked for the county as a driver on one of the outdoor crews.

Frankie had his house by his mid-twenties. He seemed happy enough, although sometimes it was hard to tell with Frankie.

He was never very chatty as a child, but he liked to make things. He built with blocks and Legos, sticks, old boards and junk he found in the woods. When Frankie was eight, he was building a fort in the woods behind their house. He wasn't supposed to use old boards, and he stepped on a nail.

It passed through his sneaker and into his foot. He didn't say anything, it was when he took off his sneakers and JoJo saw that the blood on his sock led to the hole in his foot. He had to go to the urgent care for a tetanus shot. She left Ray home with the kids, figuring how much damage they could do, but didn't want to think that through to the end, so she returned to thinking about getting Frankie to the doctor. They were lucky and were able to go right into an exam room.

The nurse said the doctor would be right in. JoJo sat in a chair while Frankie sat on the exam table, his legs hanging off and swinging them.

JoJo said to Frankie, "Listen to me; I need to talk to you." She waited until he looked her in the eye. People made the mistake of talking to Frankie without making sure they had his attention and then blamed him as a difficult child. JoJo knew her kids, and this was one of his quirks.

"Frankie. When did you hurt your foot?" He shrugged his answer. "Frankie. Was it after lunch?" He looked at her and nodded.

"Was it out in the woods? Where you built the fort?" He nodded, surprised she knew about the fort. It was supposed to be a secret.

"Did you step on a board? Some old wood with a rusty nail poking out?" He nodded again.

"Frankie, why didn't you tell me? You could get sick from a dirty nail."

"I knew you'd want me get me a shot."

"If I tell you not to go in the woods and play, are you going to go in the woods anyway?" JoJo asked him. He looked at his mom again and wondered

15

how she became so smart. Frankie could have lied and denied everything, but since that wasn't his nature, he nodded yes.

JoJo stood up and gave him a hug. He still let her hug him, he knew it made her happy. It made him happy, too, but he didn't want to admit it.

"Let's get through this shot and then let's go shopping. I've got an idea."

The doctor came in, gave Frankie his shot, and warned him to be careful where he was playing. Frankie nodded, jumped off the table, and left the room. The doctor handed her a script for antibiotics. He nodded after Frankie.

"Does he have a hot date or something?" the doctor asked, referring to his quick exit.

"It's more *or something*," JoJo told him.

****

JoJo drove a few miles and turned into a strip mall. It consisted of a bank, a drugstore, and a farm supply store. Frankie couldn't figure out what his mother thought was so special about the drugstore, but she only used the drive-thru to drop off his prescription. She pulled up and parked the car. JoJo turned and looked at her not so little boy. She sat there until he looked at her.

"You know when I asked you if you were going to play in the woods even if I told you not to, and you said yes?" He nodded.

"Well, thank you for telling me the truth. Now I know that my job as your mom to make sure when you do play in the woods you are as safe as possible. We're going here." She pointed at the farm supply store. A big sign with a tractor and a cow hung outside.

Frankie's eyes shone. *A farm store!* He wondered if there were chickens inside. He let his mom hold his hand until they got to the door, and he let go and held it open for her.

"Why, thank you," she said and smiled at his manners, proof that if you nag enough, sooner or later, something sticks.

****

A kindly old guy dressed like he used to get up at four in the morning to milk the cows approached them. JoJo talked to the man while Frankie looked around. He couldn't believe you could buy things like this at a store. Big bags of dirt and shovels, wire fencing and posts. Plants and paving stones. He was fascinated by everything he saw. His father never fixed things. *His mom proba-bly got all her garden stuff here,* he thought. *That's how she knew about this place.*

JoJo shook him. "C'mon. Follow him." She pointed at the man, so he did. They ended up in the shoe department. Frankie looked at a pair of humongous rubber boots. He wanted a pair of those.

"Frankie, I told Mr. Jim about how we just came from the doctor, and he's going to help us find boots you can wear in the woods and keep your feet safe."

As luck would have it the only brand that fit his foot was Timberlands, the most expensive boots in the store. They opened some tube socks to see how they fit. They fit fine. The thick rubber lug tread on the bottoms and the leath-er uppers gave as much safety as she could find, but they weren't done yet. She took him over to the tools. *The tools!* Thought Frankie.

Mr. Jim helped Frankie find a hammer that felt good in his hand, and then they went over to the wood. *The wood!* Frankie marveled. Mr. Jim gave him some big clear eye protection and put on his own. He picked up a nail and taught Frankie how to use the claw part of the hammer to get a nail out. He taught him what to do if he couldn't; how to pound it sideways so nobody could be injured by stepping on it, and because Frankie caught on so quickly, he was shown how to drive the nail into a board.

She left the store with an open pack of tube socks, a box of nails, a free piece of wood and one very happy boy, wearing his goggles, new boots and socks, carrying a hammer. Frankie wore those boots all summer, and as a special treat at the beginning of each summer, they went out to lunch and back to buy him a new pair for the summer. It was always just the two of them. It was one of those memories JoJo knew she'd treasure in her mother's heart forever, and hope it lasted as long for Frankie, too.

****

CHAPTER FOUR

The storm door stuck every time it opened, the frame bent just enough to catch and make a scraping noise. Just minor enough to think *why doesn't he fix this? And while he's at it, oil the hinges.* Ray was not one to take on home improvements. *You can't expect something from someone who never had it to give,* JoJo thought. *It was even less likely because Ray no longer lived here. I should probably ask Frankie or just buy a new one.* The door opened, and in walked her best friend, Julie, Ray's sister. Furry rose and positioned herself between JoJo and the unfamiliar guest.

JoJo sat at the table looking at the junk mail, the free catalogs, the town newsletter, the home medical supply company marketing, and oh, all those "Limited Time Only" offers, junk like that. She liked getting the flowers and garden catalogs. *Well, this is sooner than I expected,* JoJo said to herself. *Probably, Abbey ran right over and boohooed all over Julie's shoulder.* She needed someone to cry to, and this was right up Julie's alley.

"Um, Jo? This dog? Is she okay? She's staring at me like I'm a ham sandwich."

"Really? I thought you looked more like a pork chop. Okay, Furry. Get in your bed." The dog returned to her bed and lay down. Julie was eliminated as a danger and Furry laid her head down.

Julie came in and hugged her. JoJo thought Julie smelled good, like fresh lemons and sunshine.

"Oh dear," Julie said as she pulled away. "Let me make some coffee."

She searched through this seemingly bottomless ostrich tote bag she carried around. "Ah ha! Found it!" Julie had specific tastes for specific items. One of them was coffee.

This was from some organic ethically sourced bean, you had to order it off their website. Julie tried to be a good citizen of the planet. JoJo once looked at the box and noticed the company was owned by Maxwell House.

"Oh. Wow," Julie said and reached out to touch JoJo's hand. "I can't believe it." JoJo pulled back at her touch.

"What are you doing Julie? All touchy-feely? Stop it."

18

"I'm consoling you."

"Well stop it. You're not very good at consoling someone. You're too rough," JoJo said, rethinking what she said to her best friend. "I'm sorry. I shouldn't have said that. I'm being a real bitch, and I apologize. It's not your fault Ray left."

"Abbey made it sound like you were crying your eyes out; you were in really bad shape," Julie said. "You look okay to me."

"I got over him quickly," JoJo said. "Not really, I think I'm still in shock. I'm not mad at him. That's not true. I'd like to strangle the bastard. I still can't believe he walked out on me. On us. He just packed a bag and left with a smile on his face. He left."

"I can't believe he left. What did he say?" Julie asked. She wanted JoJo's version of the events.

"He came home from work smiling. He packed his suitcase and left. To start fresh, he said, whatever that means. He said the kids would be fine since they're adults, and there was nothing more he could do for me, so he was going out there to start the third chapter of his life.'"

"What's with this start 'fresh' shit?" Julie asked.

"I don't know. Is it possible to negate everything that happened for the last thirty years? Like it didn't happen? He can draw a line, and the past doesn't count. He can get a fresh piece of paper and start over? I guess he can because that's what he did. I'm sorry, Julie. I still can't believe it. But as to Ray, seeing you reminded me to have the locks changed. He should know better than to do this shit. I told him don't fuck with me. If he wants out, he's out. I'm going to find a divorce lawyer and put an ad on Craigslist and sell his crap. He spends a lot of money on toys. I'll start with his precious lawn mower," JoJo said and processed the idea. "Lonely Lawnmower Looking for Loving Landscaper. I like it." The more she thought about it, the more she liked it.

"You can't do that. He'll be back," Julie said.

"I told him I don't want him back. He could crawl five miles on a bed of shattered glass and show up all bloody and bleeding at my door and I still wouldn't let him in. If he threatened to drink bleach if I didn't talk to him, I'd say—"

Julie interrupted. "I get it, I get it. What are you gonna do?"

"Call a lawyer and a locksmith."

"Don't act too quickly," Julie said. "Please. Let's get Ray's side first. Do you think there's another woman?"

"He didn't say so, and I haven't seen lipstick on his collar. He hasn't been acting any different, same old asshole. He's too cheap to have an affair. Talk to him if you need to, go right ahead, but won't change anything over here."

****

CHAPTER FIVE

JoJo was best friends with Julie since second grade when Julie's family moved here. They met on the playground, playing hopscotch at recess when Julie saw JoJo start running towards the fence. Julie had just finished her turn and was standing around, so when she saw JoJo take off Julie followed. She stayed back a bit; she wasn't close enough to be in any trouble, but she got close enough to hear what was going to happen.

JoJo had confronted a group of boys she saw tormenting a smaller boy. They were a grade above her and JoJo stopped to think about who she was challenging. The bigger kid pushed the smaller kid hard into the fence. The smaller boy clung to the fence, his little fingers twisted in the links, his knuckles white from his grip.

JoJo intervened before it went any further. Julie ran to find the teacher who was supposed to be in charge, but she was deep in conversation with another teacher, telling her about a fight she had with her boyfriend. Julie looked back at the group of kids and pulled on the teacher's hand. The teacher pushed her off, but Julie kept trying to get the teacher's attention.

"HEY!" JoJo yelled. She pushed one of the onlookers into the crowd. She didn't mean to push him that hard, but like dominoes the other boys got knocked back. That act cemented her position as far as the playground hierarchy went.

JoJo stepped between the two boys. She looked at the smaller kid, frozen in place. She jerked her head towards freedom and said "RUN!" and he took off. JoJo looked up at the bigger boy and gulped. She was too mad to be afraid when she confronted the older boy.

Julie was in awe of JoJo she was so brave to get involved with those boys. The teacher finally stopped talking and looked at what Julie was trying to show her.

"HEY!" JoJo yelled in the kid's face. "I said HEY!" JoJo decided right then this kid was a big jerk which only made her madder. *He was going down,* JoJo thought.

"WHAT'S WRONG WITH YOU?" Silence. She yelled louder. "I SAID, WHAT'S WRONG WITH YOU? YOU WANNA FIGHT, I'LL FIGHT

YOU!!" She was inching towards him, and he was slowly backing up. "I'LL BEAT THE CRAP OUTA YOU, YOU LITTLE..."

"Josephine Montgomery! Here! Immediately!" The teacher called, but JoJo got right up in his face and didn't back down. The teacher came close enough to prevent the fight from escalating, Julie trailing after her. Julie watched JoJo with her mouth open. She would not back down.

"Why are you talking to me?" JoJo asked. "Talk to him. He's a bully! Ask anyone. He was picking on this smaller kid. Somebody had to do something. You weren't around. You should thank me for doing your job."

Uh-oh, Julie thought. *Not only was JoJo brave, she was crazy, too.*

JoJo was mad. People always paid attention to her, ready to punish her, but never were there at the beginning when other people started things. She always ended up on the hook. *It wasn't fair,* she thought.

The teacher put herself between the two kids. JoJo gave the boy a death stare. She figured he wouldn't start anything with the teacher there, and she wanted him to get in trouble, too.

"I heard you fighting. I heard what you said, Josephine Montgomery. This school has a zero-tolerance for bullying. *You* were being the bully," the teacher reprimanded her. The boy slipped under the radar and smiled back at Josephine's stare. That made Josephine even madder. If she was going to get in trouble, so should he.

"Come with me, Josephine Montgomery. I think the principal would like a word with you."

The teacher reached out and took ahold of Josephine's arm and started to drag her towards the entrance. Josephine pulled her arm out of the teacher's grasp.

"What about him? Why doesn't he have to go to the principal's office? If I'm in trouble for being a bully, why isn't he? He started it!" JoJo yelled at the teacher.

"I only know what I heard, and I heard you threatening to beat him up. I didn't hear him." The teacher grabbed Josephine's arm, this time with a firmer grip.

"Of course, you didn't hear him. YOU WEREN'T PAYING ATTENTION! Isn't that against the rules or something?" JoJo yelled again. "Where were you when he was picking on that other kid? How come you never see how things get started? I didn't start it, but I'm not afraid to finish it."

The teacher had enough of Josephine. "This way. Now." She dragged her inside the building, Julie lagging behind. She thought JoJo was fearless and

22

wanted to go inside to see how it ended, but the bell rang and it was time to go back to class.

JoJo sat in the secretary's office with her arms tightly across her chest. *The injustice of it all. It wasn't fair. And where is that stupid principal?* JoJo fumed.

JoJo was so brave, Julie thought. Even when they called her mom to come get her and she didn't cry at all. Julie watched from the window and decided she wanted JoJo to be her best friend.

****

JoJo helped set the table. Her mother wasn't talking. She said she wanted to wait for Ritchie, Jo's older brother to get home. Daddy was in Boston, so it was just the three of them. When she pushed for her punishment, all her mom would say was "I don't know, Josephine. From what your principal said, you were the one heard threatening another student. Fighting is not allowed. Neither is bullying."

"BUT—" JoJo started to defend herself. Her mother shot her a look that silenced her. JoJo sat at the table, kicking the table legs.

"I know all kinds of punishment for kicking my table legs. I suggest you stop unless you're interested in finding out what one of them might be." JoJo harrumphed and crossed her arms across her chest, but she stopped kicking her mother's table legs.

JoJo heard Ritchie coming in the door and got up. "Sit," her mother said, so she did. He put his backpack away, washed his hands and joined JoJo at the table. He smiled at her to signal to her he heard about the playground, and he'd help her. After everyone was sitting at the table, their plates full of the chicken casserole her mom cooked when her dad wasn't around. He hated casseroles. He didn't like his food mixed together he liked each item separate. Her mom started talking about JoJo's latest episode.

"So, Ritchie, I have a problem. Jo had some trouble today at school on the playground. She was fighting with a third-grade boy and I don't know what to do about it."

"BUT—" JoJo jumped in to present her defense, but her mom silenced her with a glance. "I know, Mom. She took on the third-grade bully and won! She's famous. Everyone knows he's a bully, but nobody wanted to go up against him.

23

He picked on the smaller kids. He had a kid pinned up against the fence, but JoJo went over and yelled at him to stop, and if he wanted to fight, she'd fight him."

"If you older boys knew he was such a bully, why didn't you say something?"

"We don't get involved with little kid stuff." He looked at his mom like she was crazy to think they would.

"Well. I heard she said she'd beat the crap out of him," her mom said.

"You did? I didn't hear that part. Good job, JoJo." JoJo smiled.

"Don't encourage her. She got sent to the principal's office for bullying. There is a zero-tolerance policy, and she violated it. The teacher didn't hear the other boy making any threats, only JoJo. What's more, the teacher that was supposed to be supervising them was talking with another teacher and not watching. JoJo felt obligated to tell the principal about it and accused her of not doing her job.

"The older boy had been picking on smaller kids all along, but the teacher wasn't doing her job to step in because she was always talking to other teachers. If that teacher had been paying attention, JoJo wouldn't be in trouble. Actually, JoJo said, 'If that teacher had been doing her job I wouldn't be here, the only reason I'm in trouble was because I had to do the teacher's job for her.'"

Ritchie looked at his sister and shook his head, half in admiration that she would go down with the ship and half at her stupidity of ratting out a teacher. Taking on another kid was one thing, but a teacher? *What, was she nuts?* He thought.

"So you saw a bigger kid picking on a smaller kid, and you went to help him?" JoJo nodded her head.

"You didn't start a fight with him, you offered to fight him for someone else?"

"Yeah," JoJo said. She figured if she was going to sell it, she had to do it now. She stood. "That's what I was trying to tell you. See, this kid, Devin somebody was picking on this other third grader. This other kid is kinda sickly, well maybe he's just little. I think he was born too soon or something. Anyway, all these boys had him against the fence. He was scared and somebody had to do something." JoJo threw her trump card. "It wasn't fair, Mom, the teacher wasn't watching like she's supposed to. It wasn't fair!" JoJo sat back to let that sink in. "I had to help him. He needed it."

"What do you mean 'born too soon'?" her mother asked.

"You know. Like Macie's brother. He had to be in that oven thing until he was big enough to go home."

"You mean an incubator?"

"Yeah. That. He had to be incubated. Probably. Maybe. Anyway, he's just this little guy. He needed back up, so I backed him up."

"Weren't you afraid of fighting this Devin? He's older than you and bigger, too."

"I just pretended he was Ritchie."

JoJo's mother was silent as she studied her daughter. "I'd like to punish you, but I'd rather be proud of you," her mother finally said. "However, the school is using you as the poster child against bullying. You have to stay after school for a week. You have to write an essay on why bullying is bad. You have to write the teacher a letter of apology, and you have to write I will not be a bully one hundred times.

"But Mom—" JoJo started.

"But, Mom, nothing. You'll do your punishment. A word of advice, not that it will do any good, but you need to learn how to keep your mouth shut. That business about the teacher not doing her job, maybe next time tell your teacher first.

"If you see a bully, tell an adult. About the kid that's being bullied, don't say things you don't know anything about. Maybe his dad's a little guy. You don't know anything about why he's small. Don't talk about other people's business. That's gossip. I'd rather you be a bully than a gossip. That's not true. I don't want you to be either. Sometimes words can hurt just as much as punches. Sometimes more. Remember that, Josephine. Enough about this."

"Ritchie, how was your day?" With this, her mother changed the subject.

No more was said, JoJo served her punishment, and tried really hard to keep her mouth shut, but she never quite got the hang of it.

****

CHAPTER SIX

The next day, Josephine Montgomery was noticed and feared, but it was short lived. Something else soon took the front page.

The mother of the smaller boy heard about it and sent Mrs. Montgomery a thank you note. Her son's name was Drew. She said, *He's a sweet, shy little guy, but new, and kids pick on him. Having your daughter stick up for him helped him. He's been able to relax a bit. That kid was making him miserable but it seems your daughter fixed it for him.*

The next time she saw him sitting alone eating lunch JoJo sat with him. New kids always had a hard time, she figured she knew enough about boys from Ritchie that she could talk to him. It seemed she didn't need to know about boy stuff. They had this popular game in common. He was two levels ahead of her. They sat together a couple of times and talked about the game. Drew gave her a cheat sheet. Other kids wondered what was so interesting and gravitated to their table. They played the game, too. He gradually found a peer group and got lost in the mix.

After that, Julie did everything she could to stay in JoJo's orbit. She outlasted the other girls. They were together all the time. As they got older, Julie had a huge crush on Ritchie. JoJo was oblivious to it all. The two girls became best friends, although they were totally different. Julie was into clothes and make up, JoJo liked to wear boy's shorts or sweats. Julie helped JoJo become a girl, and JoJo helped Julie not to be afraid to stick up for herself.

"You can't be a tomboy forever, Jo," Julie told her.

"Why not? I have a boy's name," JoJo said.

"You do not. Your name is Josephine."

"That's the worst name ever. I wouldn't name a dog Josephine," JoJo said vehemently.

Their friendship lasted, even surviving middle school. It was summer vacation, and they had a sleepover at Julie's. They were playing in the driveway, jumping rope. JoJo saw a boxer on TV, and part of his training was jumping rope. She had to ask her mom what endurance was, and after she found out JoJo decided she was going to be able to jump rope longer than anybody else.

They would have contests to see who could jump longer, and even if JoJo tried to let Julie win, she never did. She'd rather talk so JoJo did most of the jumping. Her older brother Ray was shooting foul shots. He got bored and decided to tease his kid sister and her friend.

"Hello, girls. Jumping rope, are you?" he asked.

"No. Ray, we are building an atomic bomb."

"How are you, Josephine?" Ray asked, ignoring her comment.

"Just fine, Raymond," JoJo answered. "You shouldn't stop practicing your foul shots. My brother said you stink."

Ray looked at JoJo. He's been friends with Ritchie since forever and by default, JoJo. He took a good look at her. He was going into tenth grade, and JoJo eighth. Her last year in middle school, and judged by Ray, her last year as a tomboy. Girls were definitely on his radar, and he could see her developing into one whether she liked it or not. She shot up and was a head taller than Julie.

"What are you looking at?" JoJo said, her eyes narrowed. She caught him staring at her.

"Nothing," he said. He recovered his older brother's voice. "I bet I can jump rope longer than you."

"You're on!" she yelled and threw the rope at him. "You first! Give your watch to Julie, she'll time how many you can do in a minute."

"Okay," he said. "Ready. Set. Go!"

He started out strong, but halfway through he was sweating, he barely made the minute mark. He tossed the rope back at her. JoJo knew she had him beat. She practiced all summer for this moment, and he was going down.

"Okay, my turn, ready, set, go!"

JoJo started out slow, but at the point where Ray started sweating, she sped up. At the one-minute mark, she started jumping rope backward, then she reversed and started cross-crossing the rope. Ray watched her kick his ass. She just kept going.

"Okay, okay," Ray said. "You win. Show off." *Just try to do that when you get some boobs,* he thought. "You're a girl, you're supposed to be good at jumping rope," he said, justifying his poor performance.

"Oh, no, that's not true. Mohammed Ali jumped rope for endurance. Maybe you should try it. Maybe it'll help you make your foul shots. Endurance," JoJo said and tossed the rope at him.

"Come on Julie, let's go inside and get a drink." She looked at him. "See ya, wouldn't want to be ya, Raymond."

"Later, Josephine." He really wanted to kick her ass but thought he might kiss her instead. He was in high school. She wasn't. He must really be bored to think about her like that. It would be about as fun as kissing a two-by-four. He decided to keep shooting foul shots. He went in later to take a shower, but the girls were in Julie's room with the door shut. He forgot about JoJo as a girl. She was just his best friend's punk ass sister.

****

CHAPTER SEVEN

The next time Ray had a chance to really look at JoJo was at the eighth-grade graduation. He sat in the audience waiting for his sister to get her award for "Academic Achievement in French." After that, hopefully they'd walk, and he could split. He looked at all the kids onstage who were bored out of their minds. He saw JoJo in the back. She was up there with the boys, close to the end of the riser. He watched her thinking she was turning into a pretty girl who would probably be a babe when she settled into her looks. He was watching her and saw some commotion near her.

Some boys started pushing and shoving, just goofing around. Somebody made the mistake of pushing a kid into her. The next time it happened, JoJo switched places with the boy. When it happened again, she returned the shove, once again harder than she meant to, but hard enough to knock two kids off the end, in front of the guidance counselor. The counselor pulled her off the riser and the two boys took her place. While the guidance counselor was giving her a lecture about her bad behavior, trying to impress upon JoJo she was growing up, and she needed to behave as such. JoJo tried to explain what happened, but the counselor's voice got louder.

JoJo's did too. They were off to the side arguing. They started handing out the diplomas, unaware of what happened on the other end.

Ray missed Julie getting her award, he watched JoJo and the drama over there. They were moving through the class at a pretty good pace when they called JoJo's name. JoJo didn't hear it, and the line stopped. The guidance counselor realized it was JoJo's turn and pushed her down front to get her diploma. The gym erupted yelling and screaming, "Yo, JoJo!" Nobody knew who started the chant, but the bored crowd picked up on it and continued as she walked as if her feet were stuck in molasses. Ray watched as she dragged herself across the stage to pick up her diploma. She finally reached the principal and took it from his hands.

The crowd was still making a lot of noise, at which point JoJo acknowledged the audience with a grand bow. The gym erupted again. Maybe it was because she bowed or because she looked like a proper lady from the knees up, but from the knees down she had more than a few bruises scabby knees and wore the rattiest sneakers she owned. One of the teachers came over, grabbed her arm and dragged her off stage as she continued to bow.

****

He saw her at Julie's graduation party the next day. She was sitting alone at a picnic table, her look grim and morose. She had her chin propped up on her fists, her elbows on the table.

"It can't be that bad, I mean, leaving that behind," Ray said, "but I think your real problem is the immediate future. How bad is it?"

"Eh. Not so bad. Can't leave the yard for a week. But you'll come over. Julie can too. We'll get Ritchie and shoot hoops."

"I have a job this summer. But yeah. Maybe," Ray said.

"Huh. That's right. He's getting a job too."

"Are you playing soccer? Basketball?" Ray asked her.

"You know I don't play well with others. Oh yeah. Apparently, I have to talk to a therapist about my so-called problem with 'Authority Figures.' The thing is the tennis coach from the high school was there. He came up and asked if I knew how to play tennis. I said no. He said, 'Want to learn? You'd be great. We really need someone like you. Someone who'll attack the ball.'"

"Yeah. It's so obvious, how could we miss this? You playing tennis. Put all the endurance from jumping rope to good use," Ray teased, and she smiled.

"Yeah, right," she said. "I really kicked your ass, didn't I? I wonder where that went," she said about her jump rope. "It's gotta be here. Or there must be one at my house."

Julie came over and took JoJo. He noticed she was barefoot. He looked up and caught her eye. She looked at him over her shoulder, smiled, and waved. Ray felt like all the air had been sucked out of him. He looked down to see if his chest had collapsed. *Oh, fuck. I think I'm crushing on my sister's best friend. She's not even in high school yet. I'll be a junior, and she'll only be a freshman. Close, but no cigar. She's like my sister. My little sister. I really need to get a girlfriend, a real one, not some dopey kid.*

Summer came and the guys had their job. They worked as laborers for a landscaping company. It was hard work, and they got their muscles the old-fashioned way. They had to stop mid-August for football practice. They reported for practice in the transition between boys to men, taller, meatier, and hairy. They smelled a lot like men. Whenever one of the guys drove the car smelled like B.O. JoJo finally said something about it.

"You guys really stink. It's soaking into the upholstery. It's awful. If you ever want to drive some girl around, you better use some deodorant. That little pine tree," JoJo pointed at what was hanging from the rear-view mirror, "it's not cutting it. You could have a forest hanging from there, and it's still gonna stink in here. Geez, take a shower once in a while."

Julie and JoJo took the bus a lot.

****

Football season came and went. JoJo and Julie still remained best friends although their interests diverged. Julie was into musical theatre, and JoJo was becoming a good tennis player. She had mastered the fundamentals and just needed practice. The coach was right about JoJo.

He, like everyone else, tried to dial her back. She was in great shape and there were times when she connected with the ball and skimmed the top of the net and past her opponent in a blur, and other times she missed it completely.

Ray saw JoJo in the halls but always in a group of freshman girls. Every once in a while, they would make eye contact in the halls; she would smile and go back to her friends. Ray and his friends were all starting the college evaluation process and it was always his plan to go out west for school. Colorado. Denver Colorado.

****

CHAPTER EIGHT

The summer going into tenth grade was busy. Everybody worked, the girls worked scooping ice cream at the local ice cream shop, Coney Island. A rite of passage for entering the workforce; they hired anyone as soon as they got their working papers. It was a popular spot for high school kids to hang out on a hot summer night. She scooped so much ice cream JoJo thought she'd have carpal tunnel before school started.

One evening, Ray and Ritchie brought a couple of girls in the class ahead of theirs out for ice cream. It was a hot night, and the girls felt like they served everyone in town twice. She saw Ritchie at the window and yelled at him, and he yelled back. Ritchie had grown up, or maybe JoJo had, but he acknowledged her in public now. She handed the customers—one a kid with his head shaved except for an impressive mohawk, and the girl he was with, she wore black nail polish and black lipstick—their hot fudge sundaes and change. She looked down to wipe her fingers on her apron, then called out, "Next!" She looked up and saw Ray.

"Hi, Ray, what can I get you?"

"Hey, JoJo. Long time no see. How've you been?"

"Good, although I think I'll need my arm in a cast by the end of the summer."

Ray didn't say anything and looked at JoJo. He was surprised at how grown-up JoJo got while he wasn't paying attention. As much as JoJo would hate him telling her, she was a very pretty girl. She was straddling adolescence and adulthood, and when she finally settled into her looks, she'd be a knock-out. JoJo looked at Ray with a raised eyebrow. "Your order, Ray? There's a line behind you."

"Where's my sister?" Ray asked, cutting his gaze away from JoJo.

"My brother. She got all flustered and ran in the back."

"I wish you'd get all flustered over me," Ray said and smiled at her.

JoJo looked at Ray. *Did he just flirt with me in front of his date?* she thought. *No, of course not.*

"Hah! That's a good one! Your order?"

JoJo fixed Ray's order. She could feel the back of her neck turn red and if she wasn't flustered before she was now. Julie came out of the back and ran into JoJo. She handed the order to Julie.

"Help me. My window. Your brother," and pushed her that way.

"Here's your ice cream. Let me get the total."

"What happened to JoJo?" Ray asked his sister.

"Phone call, I think," she said. "Here's your change." Later, while they closed, they finally had time to talk.

"What happened to you? Why didn't you want to wait on my brother?"

JoJo ran her finger down the closing chore list. "Ray? I think he flirted with me in front of his date."

"Who was he with? The blonde cheerleader or the renaissance faire reject?"

"It had to be the cheerleader. I didn't see any Stevie Nicks knockoffs tonight."

"Really? You think he was flirting or goofing around with his best friend's little sister?"

"Ah, he was just goofing around," JoJo decided. "He wouldn't be interested in me. I'm too young. He's going to be a senior."

"Your brother's a senior. If he asked me, I'd go out with him. Lots of seniors date sophomores."

"Ew. I think Ray looks at me like a punk kid, just like I look at him like your annoying older brother. Why would he be interested in me? If he was interested in a girl, I'm sure there's a whole lot of girls who'd be glad to help him out. Besides, I beat him in foul shots. He's never forgiven me for that."

"There's a weird vibe around you two. It could happen."

"Ew," JoJo repeated. "Maybe if a brick fell off a building and knocked me out so I had amnesia it could happen."

They finished the checklist and locked up. They waited for Julie's mother to pick them up, but she was ten minutes late as usual. It was still hot out. They were sweaty and sticky from the day, and the dust from the gravel parking lot had plenty of places to creep into and stick. Two headlights pulled into the lot and the girls walked to the car, but Ray was driving. They got in the car, Julie in the front seat. She put the air on high and angled the vents towards her.

"Hey," JoJo said. "Quit hogging the air."

"How long are you girls alone?" Ray asked them.

"Just an hour. The owner takes the money home when he leaves at nine, so there's not any money in the store. We clean up and close at ten."

"So, two girls who aren't even old enough to drive home are stuck here all alone?"

"Yeah. So?" JoJo said, unimpressed.

"It's not safe." Ray said. "What if someone wanted to rob you? Not everyone knows there's no money there. Maybe if there's no money, they'll decide to take it out on you."

"We can drive, we have our permits," Julie said.

"Julie. Not good enough. Does Mom always pick you up? Is she always late?"

"Yes. JoJo's dad drops us off, Mom picks up. And is she late? Always."

"What days do you close?"

"Tuesdays and Thursdays, and Sunday afternoons," Julie said.

JoJo interrupted, "We don't close on Sundays."

"It's not very safe," Ray said as he pulled out.

One evening, Julie had to leave early but promised to be back later to pick her up. JoJo closed with the new kid. He rode his bike. When he saw the headlights from JoJo's ride pull in. he took off. JoJo ran over and opened the back door yelling up to the front seat "You missed that new kid, Julie. The one from...oh hey, Ray, where's Julie?"

"She ran late. Here, sit up front." She jumped in.

"You didn't have to come. I could have called my mom."

"I had planned on it. I didn't know Julie wasn't going to be here until after. I was going to be out anyway, so I figured I'd swing by. I haven't talked to you in ages." He turned the car off and asked her if she ever had a boyfriend.

"No. Not really," JoJo said, shifting in her seat. "Why?"

"Has Julie been kissed by a boy?"

"I can't answer any questions about her, Ray."

"How about you? You ever been kissed by a boy?" Ray asked.

"Well, I know it wasn't man," she said. "I don't know what the big deal is, it was a lot of fumbling around in the dark. I guess we'll figure it out."

"You could kiss me. I have it figured out," he offered.

She was going to be a sophomore and he was a senior. That's pretty close, just for one kiss, he rationalized. He convinced himself it wasn't too creepy.

"Really? You would do that for me?"

"Yeah, I really would."

JoJo slid over and leaned over the console. She had her eyes shut, a smile on her lips. He leaned in and gently kissed her, not like some horny boy would, but by a boy on the cusp of manhood. He explored her tender mouth gently, trying not to scare her, but when he felt her mouth move against his, he lost it and pushed her away. JoJo looked at him and touched her lips. She smiled and said, "I see."

They sat back, and each digested what happened in the moment. It wasn't that JoJo had never been around boys, it was inexperience on her part. She knew how things were supposed to work, but all that storybook and fairytale crap was just that. Crap.

She decided it was just one big lie people told each other so the human race didn't die out. Kind of like if everyone else thought it was fantastic, you'd keep doing it saying it was fantastic, even if it wasn't but you'd end up with a baby and do your part for mankind. Ray's kiss was the first time she ever kissed back. She didn't know what to do but her lips sure did.

Ray felt guilty. He manipulated his sister so he could be alone with JoJo. He knew she was inexperienced, and soon enough she'd figure it out. Everyone does, just at different speeds, but by the time you graduate high school you usually end up with at least one broken heart. He wanted to kiss her in the worst way.

Ray wanted to be the guy that showed JoJo how it was supposed to be, the first guy to make her heart flutter, the first guy so she'd remember he was the guy that caused the light bulb in her head to go on, but what he didn't realize how the whole thing would boomerang back on him. Ray knew he thought he had a thing for her years ago, but that was probably an aberration caused by the fact she was always hanging around with his sister and a girl is a girl. What he realized now was that never it faded. He figured that was so long ago, untended love withered on the vine and died. Except it didn't.

"What's the matter, Ray? Are you sorry you kissed me?" JoJo asked him.

"Uh, no. Are you?

"No. I want you to kiss me again."

"Some other time, maybe," he said.

He looked at her. What he wanted to do was throw her in the back seat and make out with her until they were both hot and sweaty. JoJo was just so new and shiny. So untarnished. He didn't want to be remembered as the guy who stole all that and broke her heart. He would be gone a year from now and unsure when he'd be back. Let some other guy do that to her. He started the car.

"Here. Let me bring you home before they start to worry."

They drove in silence. He pulled into her driveway and said, "Here you go."

"Aren't you going to walk me to the door and kiss me goodnight?" JoJo asked him.

"No. Why would I do that? I didn't take you out on a date."

"If you asked me out, I wouldn't say no," she told him. "Well, I'm not going to, so go."

"Why don't you want to kiss me again?"

"Kissing leads to other things. Things I don't want to happen. Things I don't think you're ready for."

"You don't get to decide that for me," she said and got out of the car. She went to the driver's side door and opened it. She pulled him halfway out of the car. She grabbed his head, kissed him, and in spite of himself he responded with heat and lust. She came back with a little heat of her own. She let go of his head and he almost fell out onto the driveway.

"You don't know what you're missing, Ray. Thanks for the ride," she said, laughing to herself. *Poor Ray. It's so easy to yank his chain.*

He watched her walk to her door. She turned and waved before she went inside. She was like a walking stick of dynamite. He envied the guy who would light that fuse. He just didn't want to be the guy when it blew up in his face.

****

August came and football practice started. JoJo rarely saw Ray. She wondered in the beginning if she did something wrong or if she did something right that scared him away. Rather than waste any more time pondering this, she filed it under blips, things out of the ordinary she couldn't explain. He came with the blond cheerleader once after practice, and JoJo waited on them.

Ray said hello to her with a big smile. JoJo wasn't sure what that meant, so she said hey and got them their cones. It usually worked where you gave the ice cream to the person who ordered it, and that person passed it around to the others. JoJo gave the cheerleader her cone personally, mostly to get a good look at Ray's girlfriend. She was cute with her blonde hair and an upturned nose. He occasionally gave her and Julie a ride home when they closed, but it fell back on Julie's mom. Ray must have talked to her because she was there by nine-forty-five.

****

CHAPTER NINE

JoJo was in tenth grade and focused on tenth grade things. JoJo was determined to get her license, and she needed her dad to teach her. Ritchie was really busy doing things seniors do, so he was no help. Her mother was the world's worst driver, and for insurance reasons her dad had her take driver's education.

JoJo had to take it on Saturday because of tennis. She was playing year-round, and it made her a much happier person. She was turning her frustrations into results on the court, and that settled her down. She was glad she had tennis, Julie was really boy-crazy and Jo could only tolerate it for so long. Julie was very happy growing up, into fashion and make up and guys.

"You know, JoJo, it's happening to you, too," Julie told her. "What is?"

"Growing up. You already have boobs and getting your period. You can't be a tomboy forever."

"Gross. That's disgusting. I'm the same person on the inside. Why do I have to change?"

"Biology requires it. You have no choice."

"What do you know about it anyways? You flunked science."

"Well, you didn't. You know exactly what's happening to you. We should go to the mall and pick you out some nice outfits."

"Tee shirts and jeans are just fine."

"If you want people to think you're just some old plain Jane. If you want guys to notice you, you have to give them something to look at."

"Any guy I catch looking at me I'll give them a black eye."

"Sooner or later, JoJo, you'll notice somebody and want them to notice you. It'll happen. I guarantee it."

"Well, don't hold your breath."

****

JoJo spent one day with Julie stalking upper class guys and thought if she had her racquet in her hand she would smack Julie upside the head. What a waste of time. She did go to the Homecoming game and then to the gym for the dance for about ten minutes, just enough time for Julie to ditch her. JoJo called her mom to come get her and waited outside. It was the perfect evening for homecoming. A crisp sunny day for the game, a cool evening for the dance. She saw Ritchie and Ray come in with their dates.

Her brother actually acknowledged her and said hello, and she said hello back. Ray told them to go on ahead, he wanted to talk to her.

"Leaving so soon, JoJo?" he asked her.

"Yeah. I'm not in the mood to have some sweaty douchebag grind all over me." Ray laughed at that. "Where's my sister?"

"Probably somewhere under the bleachers making out with some random dude," JoJo said. "She's into upper class men now she's a sophomore. It's nothing new. When she comes up for air and can't find me, she'll call me at home to make sure I got there."

"What about you, JoJo? No upperclassmen for you?" Ray teased.

She shook her head. "Just you, Ray, just you." She didn't know why she felt compelled to tease him, but it was probably because it made him so uncomfortable. Ray took a step backward at her answer but didn't speak; he didn't know if she was kidding or not. He never got a chance to ask because her mom pulled up.

"Gotta go, Ray, my mom's here. Try not to sweat all over your cheerleader."

She waved as she walked away. This time she just got in the car. She looked over her shoulder to see if he was still watching, but she couldn't help it. She peeked and knew because he was still standing there.

Julie got a job at the mall and dated on weekends, so JoJo didn't see her that much. They still hung out at school and on breaks. Julie had one of the lead roles in the school play and spent a lot of time rehearsing. JoJo achieved her goal of getting her license but had to share the car with Ritchie, so she never drove. Once Ritchie left for college, she would get the car. Yeah, she would miss him, but she wanted the car more.

****

A junior named Brandon Bridges noticed JoJo playing tennis. Rumor had it JoJo was going to be playing on the boys' team, she was getting that good. The girls' team was mostly made up of debutantes who didn't want to break a nail, JoJo frustrated with their lack of a competitive agenda. The boys' team was made up of, well, boys, who by nature didn't like to lose. Brandon was on the boys' Varsity team, he knew who JoJo was, and she was good enough he wanted to check out the competition. Brandon didn't know why he wasn't aware of her sooner, she was smoking hot and a hell of a player. He caught her on the way into the girls' locker room and approached her.

"Hi, my name's Brandon Bridges. I play on the boys' Varsity team. I would like to play you and see if you're as good as everybody says you are."

"JoJo Montgomery," she said. "But you already know that."

"Are you Ritchie's sister?"

"Yeah, but you probably already know that, too."

"So, are you going to play me or not?"

"Don't you know?" she asked him. "You know everything else."

"Yes. Court 4. Wednesday afternoon, three-thirty."

"Sure, I'll play you, unless you're the kind of guy who gets pissy when a girl beats him."

"No," he said. "I'll let you beat the pants off me. Gladly. But I get to return the favor." JoJo laughed at that.

"Okay, sure. Wednesday three-thirty, court 4."

"It's a date, then."

"No, Brandon Bridges, it's a match. See you Wednesday," she told him and headed inside the locker room.

****

She called Julie to see if she had last year's yearbook. Julie was into all that crap. She wanted to check out this Brandon guy. Julie wanted to know if Ritchie was going to be home.

"Yeah, after practice I guess," JoJo said.

"Okay, I'll come over after dinner. My mom's not using the car." Julie had her license, too.

Julie came over with the yearbook. After checking that Ritchie was nowhere on the first floor, they went up to her room. JoJo hadn't bothered to upgrade her childhood bedroom it's been the same since fifth grade. She taped things that interested her over old things that interested her, so underneath the current rock star was a teen idol. Julie redecorated her room every two years right down to a fresh coat of paint.

They sat on her bed, Julie combed through the yearbook. She found his class picture, he would have been a sophomore last year.

"Him? Him?" Julie questioned her. "Yeah, but he looks a lot older now."

"Here. Chess Club. Kinda nerdy. Mathletes. Definitely nerdy." Julie dismissed him. "He's a dork. You can do better than that."

"The only thing I want is to kick his ass. Here. Look at the spring sports. There. Varsity tennis." Jo pointed him out.

"That's the same guy? He grew a lot. He's cute. A sophomore on the Varsity team? He must be pretty good." His stock went up in Julie's eyes.

"We're playing Wednesday. You should come to watch me make him bleed."

"I think that's the only reason you're interested. You just want to slap some guy around," Julie said.

"That's right. You don't want to miss this." JoJo smiled, the thought of taking down Brandon Bridges excited her.

"Show some mercy, Jo. He's gotta come to school the next day."

****

The courts are behind the football spectators' bench, not very visible to passersby, meaning if you were there it was on purpose. The exit for the boy's locker room was located near there. Every once in a while, there was an epic battle between two good tennis players. Those who knew Jo knew she was really good, and those that knew Brandon knew he was really good, so different types of people showed up plus the regular jocks.

They started just a warm-up volley. Every so often, Brandon would zing one by her and her head would follow the noise, but she let him do it. Just when he decided she was overrated, she exploded. JoJo took every shot at her like it was personal and returned it with a fury unleashed. She read his body language and could predict by the way his feet pointed where he was going to hit the ball. Her eyes never left him.

Brandon decided *this a fucking girl for Christ's sake.* He tried to take her down, but he couldn't. They just pounded back and forth. It never ended up in an actual game. The battle over who was going to serve first wouldn't stop. JoJo had the ball in her hand and looked at him. He looked awful, all red blotches and sweaty. She threw it to him. He caught it. The spectators applauded.

41

Ritchie and Ray came out of the boy's locker room and watched the tennis courts.

"Hey, Ritchie isn't that your sister?" Ray asked. "I'm glad we play lacrosse. Your sister's a beast."

Brandon and JoJo sat on the bench panting and sweating. They drank water and cooled down.

"Why'd you stop?" he asked her, still taking big gulps of air.

"I got thirsty," she panted.

"Can I give you a ride home?"

"Yes," she said.

"Want to go out for pizza sometime?" he asked.

"Yes."

Julie was right. It did happen to her. That was how JoJo fell in love.

CHAPTER TEN

Brandon Bridges was tall. He was thin with an athletic build, not an ounce of fat on him.

He had sandy-colored hair that was thick and threatened to get in his eyes. JoJo thought his sandy brown eyes were gorgeous, so different than her own dark brown ones. He had long, dark brown eyelashes that ringed his eyes, so long JoJo wanted to put mascara on them, but he just laughed at the idea. He laughed a lot, he made her laugh a lot, too, even if they couldn't figure out what exactly was funny. She thought he was so intelligent he was a straight A student in all the AP classes. JoJo thought he was perfect.

Thank goodness he was Julie approved. A lot of the time the three of them hung out when Julie was between boyfriends. It seemed that Julie had changed her philosophy. She wanted a boyfriend like Brandon Bridges. He spoke JoJo's language. They had all these inside jokes.

Brandon Bridges was polite. JoJo's parents trusted Ritchie, and Ritchie said he was a good guy. He was a Mathlete. He had credentials; Julie wanted a boy-friend with those. A regular guy who did geeky things who would worship her, but one seems elusive.

JoJo was Brandon's dream girl. Smart, athletic, beautiful, he could not believe his luck. She was gorgeous with her thick dark hair and mysterious brown eyes. She had long limbs and lean muscles; she looked strong and healthy. Her skin was olive-colored that turned brown in the sun. He thought she was exotic with her dark brown hair she always wore in a ponytail. Her smile was radiant and she was quick to laugh, and he loved the sound of it. Brandon tried to make her laugh as often as possible. Why no other guy picked up on her was beyond him. Her brother was cool, too. They would go to her house and do homework every day after school at the dining room table. They occasionally found them-selves in the house alone and they would have these intense make-out sessions that were almost everything but. She decided to talk to her mom.

"I know you probably won't like to hear what I'm going to say, but I think I want to get on birth control," JoJo said to her mom.

"Brandon?" her mom asked. "You haven't known each other that long. Are you sure you're ready for such a big step?"

"Yes, Mom. I'm almost seventeen."

"Yes, yes, you are, but not quite. It's hard for me to get behind this, you're both so young. Well, big steps require big talks, so have a seat. I'm going to assume both of you are new to this, so you have got to promise me something. Always use a condom. That's absolute, a non-negotiable. Even if you are on the pill, accidents happen. Protect yourself at all costs. If he doesn't do this for you, think about that says about him.

"What kind of guy would put a girl he cares about in jeopardy? Either pregnancy or sexually transmitted diseases, would a guy who supposedly loves you put you at risk? Think long and hard before you do anything. Ask yourself, is it worth it? Is *he* worth it?

"If you want to go on the pill, go down to Planned Parenthood. Make Brandon go with you. If you want to do adult things, you have to act like an adult, which means being responsible, him too. He has to be willing to be responsible. How he treats this is how he really feels about you. If he's not willing to actively participate, that's a red flag for sure. I wish you'd wait until you're seventeen. I'll take you if you wait. Right now, I still think you're too young.

"I was seventeen once, too. I'm going to tell you something I have never told anyone and I'm not sure I want you to know, but if you do grown-up things, sometimes you have to pay grown-up consequences. When I was seventeen, I had an abortion," her mom told her.

"What?" JoJo said, stunned. "You what?"

"I had an abortion." Her mother's eyes looked inward. "I was in high school, my first boyfriend. I was so in love. Mike O'Brien. I thought this was it. We were going to be together forever. The promises you make in the heat of the moment aren't necessarily realistic. The things he said to me. I still think he meant them. I refuse to believe it wasn't real.

"I believe he did love me. I mean, how could I love someone so much I would have done anything to be with him? How could he not feel the same way about me? I thought I was ready. All I'll say is the first time you fall in love, it's real. It's not puppy love. I'm not going to minimize the way you feel. The way he feels. It's real. It's stronger than anything. You can't deny it. What can I say?

"I was seventeen, inexperienced, and blind. I saw what I wanted to see. I got pregnant. I freaked out and told him. He freaked out. Suddenly, it was what was *I* going to do? *I* was the one in trouble, not him. There wasn't a 'we' anymore. He asked me how much money I needed to get an abortion. He said he was sorry, but he was too young to have a baby. He was going to college on a basketball scholarship. That was his plan. Not this. If I had the baby, I would have to do it alone. I couldn't wrap my head around something conceived with such love as a bad thing.

"Maybe I should have thought about the fact I got pregnant in the backseat of his father's Buick. "He wanted me to get an abortion. He offered to pay for it, but that was it. He didn't even offer to take me. What did he expect me to do? Look in the phone book under 'Abortions'? They were illegal back then. I walked home from school.

"He couldn't get far enough away from me. I came home, and I couldn't even go into the house. I was so scared I just sat on the front steps and cried. I was practically in hysterics when my mom came home. I told her the whole story from the front porch. I couldn't go in the house. I wouldn't go in the house. I didn't belong there anymore. I was all alone.

"Grandma just hugged me until I exhausted myself. She asked me what I wanted. I kept saying I didn't want to do this alone. 'Do what?' she said and told me to stop saying I was alone. She was there. 'Don't think about that fuckhead Mike, he already got what he wanted, and he wasn't man enough to face up to the consequences of his actions,' she said. 'Quit saying you're alone. I'm here. I'll help you. Do you think you're the first seventeen-year-oldwho ever got knocked up because they believed some horny high school guy who told them they'd love them forever?'

"I decided I was too young to be a single mom. I had dreams of my own. Grandma said she'd take care of it. She made a few calls to people who called some people who gave her the name of somebody who could help. Remember, abortions were illegal. They were still done, but you couldn't just ask around. I think communication was done in pieces, on purpose, so nobody had all the information so legally nobody could incriminate anybody else. One lady took the call, another found someone, she'd pass the name on, this one set it up and passed the info to someone else it, the next lady called Grandma with the specifics.

"Grandma drove me, paid for it, and didn't tell my dad. Get this: Grandma told me to bring the dog. It was done at a veterinarian's office. The vet's wife was a midwife, and she did it early in the morning before office hours. I'm not sure he even knew. It was done in a clean place, with sterilized equipment. I wasn't too far along. She put some stuff up there, and I miscarried. It hurt like hell, but was over quick. I had it done on a Friday of a long weekend. I was back in school next week. I saw Mike and said don't worry about it, false alarm, and I never spoke to him again.

"My mom was so good to me. I was so sad. Everything I thought about life to be true was a big lie. I felt so guilty about the abortion. I felt guilty about feeling relieved about the abortion. I felt guilty about my mom not being able to tell my dad.

"Finally, Grandma told me to move on. You made your choice, accept it, and move on. You made a mistake, and you handled it. That's life, she said, get used to it. When she died, she took my secret with her. I could pretend it didn't happen, but it did.

"I'm telling you so maybe you can learn something from it. I don't know. Maybe if someone talked to me like this, I wouldn't have punished myself for years. I'll tell you something else. When I met your dad, it was one of the first things I told him. I liked your dad a lot. I didn't want him to fall in love with damaged goods.

"Daddy laughed at me. He loved damaged goods, he said, if that what I was, but he didn't think so. He told me to stop defining myself by one event. Live and learn, he said. He sounded a lot like Grandma. Then he bought me the biggest hot fudge sundae ever with two spoons, and I finally understood what made love real. But don't ever think you're alone, ever. So I can't endorse it, but I can't stop it, can I? I just ask there be no closed doors, including your room when I'm home. I wish you'd wait, Jo. I really do. Even just six months. What happens when I'm not here I can't control? Always use a condom. I love you, JoJo. Just be smart, whatever your choices. Make them wisely, and if you need me, I'll be here. I love you."

"I love you too Mom," she said, giving her a big hug. JoJo couldn't picture her mother in such a position. It was hard to think she once was young, in love with a guy who dumped her when she needed him the most. She squeezed her mother her harder, feeling sorry she had to handle a broken heart and an unplanned pregnancy at the same time. *Fuck that Mike guy,* JoJo thought. *What an asshole.*

I'm hugging my little girl for the last time, her mother thought as JoJo hugged her tighter.

****

It happened over spring break. He went away with his family, but he had to return on Friday for his college prep tutor on Saturday. Friday night he was home alone, and she went over. They were both delirious with the thought of and the act of sex. He wanted to do it in his room, saying he wanted to wake up and smell her on his sheets. At this age all the fumbling in the dark was unbuttoning and unzipping. He had a small light on; soon clothes came off and JoJo realized this was the first time they saw each other completely naked. The first time she was ever naked with a guy, too.

"Oh my God, you are the most beautiful thing I've ever seen," Brandon said, awe in his voice. He ran his fingers over her naked body. "Oh, please," he mumbled into her neck. She took him in her hand and caused him to orgasm.

"What? Why did you do that?" he asked, embarrassed it took about two seconds. "Now you don't have to worry about it," JoJo explained. They made out for a bit, his hands constantly roamed all over her naked body.

"Now?" he asked.

She rolled onto her back and opened her legs.

"Now," she said and reached for him. He fumbled a bit when he put on the condom. She guided him in the general direction, instinct took over and he found his way. He pushed into her but stopped before he was fully inside.

"Do it," she whispered, "do it now."

She raised her hips and pulled him down to accommodate him. He pushed through and made a noise low in his throat. He pumped against her a few times and came. He lay on her for a minute and then rolled off her. He was flat on his back, silent. He pulled off the used condom.

She looked at his face and touched his cheek.

"Are you crying? Why are your eyelashes wet?" she asked him, surprised.

"Because I think that was the most beautiful thing that could ever happen to me, and I don't think I'll ever love anyone more than I do you right now. Why are you crying?"

47

"Because you are."

"Stop it."

"You stop it."

****

CHAPTER ELEVEN

JoJo never played tennis on the guys' team. She never knew why. After the exhibition with Brandon, the subject was never brought up.

His parents belonged to the Country Club. JoJo always felt uncomfortable there. She wasn't exactly from the wrong side of the tracks, but they ran with a whole other class of people. They were friends with the parents of all the rich kids in school, but JoJo was straight-up middle class. She was always afraid she'd use the wrong fork or make some other glaring mistake.

They won the mixed doubles in a tournament. That was the one place at the club she felt comfortable—on the tennis court—like she was an equal. Brandon played for fun, but sometimes they really got into it; it wasn't in JoJo's nature not to go for the throat, and he would laugh. He also had a part-time job there, bussing tables.

JoJo felt deep down his parents didn't like her; there was always this undercurrent of standoffishness when she was there. Like the time his father found them studying at the kitchen table. He told Brandon he didn't want them in the house alone.

"You have a problem with us *studying?* You're crazy. Come on, Jo. Let's go to the library." He grabbed his stuff as well as hers and she followed him out to his car. "Geez, I don't know what's wrong with them. Sorry about that. They're nuts."

"They don't like me, Brandon. I'm not one of those cotillion cuties they would prefer your date." Brandon said she was imagining things, that's how they always acted.

One day, his mother came back early, and they were in his room watching TV, sitting there on his bed. His mother walked by and saw them. She called for Brandon to come out into the hall. JoJo could hear the conversation, almost like his mother wanted her to.

"Brandon, this is not acceptable. You know you're not allowed to have that girl in your room."

"What's the big deal? We're just watching TV. The door is open. You should trust me more," he pushed back.

"Of course, I trust you. I don't *trust* her." his mother said loud enough to make sure it was overheard.

"I don't know why you don't trust her. I love her."

"You're too young to know what love is," his mother told him.

"I'm older than you think," he said back to his mother in a voice JoJo didn't recognize, hard and firm. "You have no idea what I know." He came back in and said, "Let's get out of here."

They drove around and he parked the car at the canal. He looked at her.

"I'm sorry about that. I wish you didn't hear it, but it sounded like she wanted you to listen to it. If she's got a problem with us, she should speak to *us.*

"My whole life they decided everything. My friends. Tennis. Summer camps. Activities. It never really bothered me, and to be perfectly honest, I never thought about it. But I'm growing up. Hell, in a little while I could join the army and roll up in a tank. I could join the circus. I don't need their permission. Or I won't, soon enough. Like you. They don't get to pick my girlfriend. They don't get to choose who I love, and I love you." He picked up her hand and kissed it. "I love you."

"I love you, too. Brandon. But I'm worried." She started to cry. "I don't understand why they don't like me. What did I do wrong?" He reached over the console and dried her tears.

"Believe me, it's not you. It's me," he told her. "I think they resent the fact that they are losing control. I want a say in my life. I'm older now, and if you did anything it was you who opened my eyes to the fact that the world is a great big place with lots of things to experience.

"I guess I'm considering things differently than I did before. I look at things now that I just used to swallow whole without any thought. Maybe they think you're dangerous to the status quo. You are a dangerous girl, JoJo, putting crazy ideas in my head. Ideas like I can think for myself. Ideas like I can think at all."

They were always together. Her parents were concerned as well. Her mom kept a running dialogue with her about young love, not to discourage her, but just to keep the lines of communication open should JoJo need it. They went to his junior prom. They looked so good together.

He was tall and lean, with sandy brown hair that kept getting in his eyes and a sweet smile. He looked so handsome in his tuxedo. She was dark, her Italian side prominent. Her dark brown hair, which she always wore in a ponytail was styled in a becoming updo. He loved her dark brown eyes, and the crystals of her prom dress accentuated the sparkle in them. She loved his soft brown eyes, she thought they made him look sweet and kind. They only had eyes for each other.

The semester ended, and graduation weekend arrived. Brandon went with her family to see Ritchie graduate he came to his party afterward. Julie and Ray were there, too. Ritchie had tons of friends and the party was very crowded. Brandon went with Julie to look at Ritchie's display of school accomplishments, but he hurried back to JoJo. They sat together amid a huge crowd but only had room for each other.

Ray's party was the next day, it was one of the few times JoJo went anywhere without Brandon, he had a family function he couldn't miss. It was the same group of kids from Ritchie's party, just different relatives. JoJo had been around Julie's family since forever, so she pretty much knew everyone. Julie left to go talk to someone, and JoJo momentarily sat alone. Ray slid into the spot Julie vacated.

"Hello, stranger," he said. "You grew up while I wasn't watching."

"It was bound to happen sooner or later," JoJo said. "Besides, look at you. High school graduate, college bound. Go west, young man."

"That's me. Colorado, here I come. You gonna miss me?" he asked her. She looked at him with her big dark eyes, evaluating the thought.

"I suppose so. Who am I going to double scoop Rocky Road for when you're gone?"

Ray looked at JoJo. She really had grown up. She had a steady boyfriend. It was only a year ago he kissed her, but he could tell she matured a lot. He could tell she wasn't a kid anymore, he would bet money she wasn't a virgin, either. Ray felt a sudden red hot streak of jealousy. Where was that skinny twerp anyway? He stood up before he said anything he would regret.

"Well, JoJo, I think I might miss you a little bit. I leave in two weeks. If I don't get a chance to see you, well, this would be goodbye. Goodbye, JoJo. I'm not sure when I'll be back. If I'll be back."

JoJo looked at him.

"I can't believe you are such a drama queen, 'goodbye and farewell.' Like you're not coming back. Like you'll get lost in the Rockies or something. You can't mean that. You'll be back to visit," JoJo said.

"Probably. Who knows where you'll be, though."

Ray looked at her like he wanted to kiss her, but he walked away. Sometimes she just infuriated him. He wanted to grab her and shake her by the shoulders. Ray wanted her to be a little sad at his leaving. He wanted her to show some emotion towards him, he wanted her to say, "Don't go so far away. I'll miss you." Anything. All he got was attitude, like "See you. Don't let the door hit you in the ass on the way out."

JoJo spent the summer going into her junior year back at the ice cream stand. Julie wanted her to get a job at the mall, but JoJo would rather stay where she knew the routine. A no brainer. She didn't need to work at the mall to know she didn't want to work at the mall.

Brandon still had a job as a busboy in the dining room of the Club. She played tennis with Brandon, but mostly for fun. Every once in a while, he would get competitive and push her, she stopped playing and started playing for real. Brandon loved when she got into her game. JoJo usually won because she had that edge that wouldn't let her lose. They could play at the club his family belonged to, but JoJo preferred to play at the high school. She felt like she was being watched all the time when they played at the club, and they had more fun in the smaller setting and the best time when they were alone.

His parents were at work during the day, and he worked evenings, so when they wanted to have sex, it was usually at his house. Afterward, they would lie next to each other and talk quietly about nothing. He would absentmindedly touch and stroke her. JoJo loved this part best. It was hard to tell where he stopped, and she began as if in dreamland.

Real life intruded. One night, he came home to find JoJo's bra hanging from the doorknob to his room. It wasn't there when he left. His mother must have found it and put it there to send him a message. He knew what they were implying, and he didn't care what they knew. If they knew, so what? Brandon didn't bring it up and his parents didn't either, but he could feel tension for days. His mother didn't mention the condom wrapper she found under his bed until later.

His parents had always assumed he would be a legacy at his father's alma mater, pledge the same fraternity, attend the same law school, and eventually join his father's firm. One day, they sat him down to plot out the rest of his life; they wanted to schedule a college visit during the summer before tennis camp. They were surprised at his response.

"No. I don't want to go all the way to California for college. I want to look at schools on the East Coast." he said, using his new hard and firm voice.

They were stunned.

"How long have you been thinking about this? Why didn't you tell us?" his father demanded.

"For a while now. I didn't tell you because I knew you'd act like this. You never even asked me if I wanted to be a lawyer. You just made a lot of assumptions over the years I never thought through. Now I'm thinking about things *I* might want. *I* might want something different."

"It's about that girl, isn't it? She's pressuring you to stay here." his mother said.

"She's not telling me anything other than to do what *I want. What will make me happy,* and I didn't say I was staying here. I said on the East Coast. Yeah, it would be closer if I wanted to come home. So what? It's not like I'm planning on coming home every weekend. California was your dream, not mine."

"This is totally unacceptable. We have a visit scheduled later this month, and you're going. That's non-negotiable." his father told him. The Brandon he had been conditioned to be was too strong. He didn't want to displease his parents, so he agreed.

"I'll go. For a visit. As long as I can look at some east coast schools."

His parents sensed his newfound voice wavering. The old pliable Brandon was still there. If they could get him away from JoJo, this conflict would disappear. He was only acting like this because of her. He told JoJo about the conversation.

"I only agreed so they would quit pressuring me. It doesn't mean anything."

"It's your choice. Go. Just make sure it's what you want," JoJo told him, but deep down she sensed storm clouds on the horizon and said so.

"Don't make more out of this than it is." He kissed her. "Hey. I love you. I always will."

He went to California for a long weekend. His parents exerted a subtle pressure on him. They knew if they came directly at him, he would dig in with resolve, so they came at him sideways. Brandon was happy; his parents weren't browbeating him with college out there. They presented it as an option. He was afraid they would double team him out there once JoJo wasn't around. When he was with her, he believed he could do anything, but when he was away, he doubted himself. All he did his whole life was please his parents, now he was straddled between childhood and burgeoning adulthood. He felt secure in neither.

Brandon had a two-week tennis camp he attended every summer. He decided not to go. His parents knew he didn't want to be away from JoJo that long. He finally caved after JoJo told him to go.

"Just go already. Up your game," was her advice.

****

CHAPTER TWELVE

He went to camp, and she scooped ice cream. JoJo was concerned he never called. She had an uneasy feeling in the pit of her stomach. Something was wrong, but she didn't want to admit it. Maybe it was the reception. But you'd expect him to send a letter or carrier pigeons, something, anything, but nope. JoJo waited. Finally, the day he came home she went over there. His mother answered the door.

"He's in the kitchen. We've been waiting for you." JoJo ran to hug him only to have him push her off.

"Here, JoJo," his mother said. "Have a seat and listen to him."

"No. What's wrong Brandon?" JoJo asked, alarmed. She could sense what was coming.

"Tell her, Brandon. Tell her your plans." his mother urged him.

"Um, I am, I have changed my plans. I'm not coming back to school here. I'm going to Midstate Prep in Connecticut. I'm moving away. I'm breaking up with you." His eyes were focused on a spot over her head.

"What?" she asked, dumbfounded.

"It's better this way," he said. "We were way too serious. We are way too young to be so involved in each other's lives. It's better this way."

She couldn't help it, she started to cry. "*No*. I don't believe you. You love me, Brandon. You said so. You *have* to." She stopped talking and blinked back the tears, willing herself to stop crying. "Look me in the eye and say you don't love me anymore. Tell me to my face. Tell me you don't love me. Look at me. Tell me," she pleaded.

"I don't love you anymore," he said, looking her in the eye. He looked panicked, like a cornered animal, his eyes wild and pleading. *You have to go. Please go. I can't handle this. I can't love you anymore*, she saw in his eyes. The look in his eyes frightened her. He looked afraid and scared about what they would do if she didn't leave.

JoJo tore her eyes away from his. The look in his eyes scared and saddened her. She looked at his father, standing next to him. He looked at the floor,

55

avoiding her gaze. She looked at his mother. She stared JoJo down, daring her to challenge them.

"How dare you? How dare you break him like that!" JoJo screamed at his mother. "Your own son! You're positively evil! Brandon, I'm so sorry you're caught in the middle."

"He did what you wanted. He looked you in the eye and told you he doesn't love you anymore. Now leave. It's over," his mother said.

JoJo was too shocked to react. She didn't look at him. He said he didn't love her anymore. Even though he told her he would love her forever, he couldn't take back what he said. What's done is done. He didn't love her.

"Well, you win," JoJo said to his mother. "You got what you wanted. Admit it. You never liked me anyway. I hope it was worth it, whatever it cost him. I hope you feel guilty every day for the rest of your lives. He was the nicest, sweetest person I ever met, and you ruined him, you bitch. *You crushed his soul.* Remember that. Every day for the rest of your lives, you live with the fact you had to sacrifice *him, his spirit,* to get what *you* wanted. You crushed him to win. I wish I was as evil as you think I am because I'd burn down your house with you in it!

"It's over. I get it now, and I'm leaving, but you are two of the worst people on the face of the earth. I don't know how you sleep at night!" JoJo said and ran out the door. She slammed the door as hard as she could.

JoJo went home. She got to the front steps and collapsed, bawling like a baby. She had this ache in her chest like she had a heart attack; she had to use the lining of her jacket to wipe up her snot. *It's not true, it's not true,* she couldn't stop thinking. The snot and tears ran down her face, and she no longer bothered to wipe them up. That's how she was when her mother found her later that day, her head on her knees sobbing.

Her mother brought her inside, cleaned up her face, grabbed the tissues and brought her to the couch. She sat and had JoJo put her head in her lap on top of a towel. Her mother let her cry all afternoon. She figured Brandon broke up with her and JoJo was beyond devastated.

"His parents. He looked me in the eye and told me he didn't love me anymore. It was tearing him up inside," JoJo kept saying. "He said he didn't love me. He doesn't love me," she said between sobs. "I looked him in the eye. He wanted me to let him go. He looked desperate, Mom, like an animal caught in a trap. He's not the kind of guy who could survive if I fought with his parents. It was in his eyes, Mom. Dumping me was his only option. He was so sweet. Gentle. Kind. He's sensitive, Mom. I hope they didn't brainwash that out of him."

"I understand their fears," her mother said. "I think they figured out he might be sexually active, and it flipped them out. If he got you pregnant, he would stay with you. He loved you like that, but it would derail their vision for the future. Even if you're on birth control. I thought you guys were too young to be so serious, but I had no argument to make. You guys were responsible. Your grades didn't slip. Maybe they had no confidence in his ability to manage his life. I'm so sorry, baby. I am. Cry all you want. I'm here, Jo. Daddy and I love you. We'll help you."

"I had to let him go, Mom. I had to. They made me. They made us. I think instead of going to tennis camp, they took him somewhere. They beat on him so hard it was gonna kill him inside. I had to go to save him, Mom. How could they do that to their own kid? Didn't they even know him? Didn't they get how sweet and gentle he was? That he couldn't handle this? How could they do that? They were willing to destroy him to keep him away from me?" She started to hiccup.

"What was so bad about me they were willing to do all this to break us up? What was so awful about us being happy? Because we were. I loved him, and he loved me. How could they?" JoJo sobbed to her mother.

JoJo grieved the rest of the summer. She quit her job. She quit the tennis team. She stayed in her room and sobbed. Her mother just held her as she cried. Julie wasn't allowed over the first week. Even then, JoJo wouldn't talk. Julie was floored. How could his parents break them up? They belonged together. JoJo finally came out of her room, her eyes deep wells of sadness, but older, wiser, and tear free. When asked about Brandon, she just said he moved to Connecticut.

****

CHAPTER THIRTEEN

Her experience with Brandon left JoJo emotionally exhausted. She spent so much time, energy, and emotion trying to process everything it left her numb. JoJo stopped eating and lost weight. She just got up and went through the motions of living, but it was just an act. She spent most of her junior year in a fog; it was only after winter exited and spring came that JoJo started to feel better, or rather, feel anything at all.

She started to smile again and go out with Julie on occasion. She finally accepted sometimes love wasn't enough. She wasn't strong enough to fight the feeling that somehow, they failed. Two love drunk kids were no match for two adults who thought they knew better. She hoped Brandon forgave her. She hoped it was easier for him to move forward. She didn't mean to destroy him. His whole life changed because of her. She felt terribly guilty about what loving her cost Brandon.

****

Senior year started and she went to school, but her experience with Brandon left her hollowed out somehow, like who she was wasn't good enough. JoJo never questioned herself or her bulldozer of a personality before, but now she doubted everything she thought she knew.

She had study hall with the group of jocks. The jocks were these guys who were interchangeable. Didn't matter what sport, they just changed jerseys depending on the season.

One of them approached her. Apparently, this guy was in her history class and asked to copy her notes.

She looked through her books and found the right papers. She looked up and handed him her notes. "Here you go." She went back to her book. She looked up again, and he was still standing there.

"What?" she asked him.

"Got a pen?" he said. She looked at him and smiled.

"Would you like some paper, too?" She noticed he held in his hands just her notes.

"Yes. Do you mind if I sit here when I copy them?"

"As long as you don't ask me to copy them for you."

"Would you?" he asked her.

"No," JoJo said and went back to her book. She looked up a while later and he was just sitting there, looking at her.

"What? Study hall's almost over and you haven't copied a thing."

"I know. I was distracted. I always thought you were pretty, but you're not."

"I'm not?"

"No. You're absolutely gorgeous. Hiding in plain sight."

"What does that mean?"

"It means you don't make any noise and just keep your head down trying to be as unassuming as possible. All somebody has to do is get within five feet of you and your anonymity disappears. I just wanted to get within five feet of you."

"Huh. I hope it was worth the trip. I need my notes back. You had no intention of copying them."

"Not true. Let's stop by the media room and make some copies." He handed back her originals after he did.

"Thirty dollars. Ten a page," she said.

"Can I get that to you? Can I give you a ride home?" he asked.

"No. I have my own car."

"Could you give me a ride then?"

"How could you give me a ride home if you need one yourself?"

"If you said yes, I'd find a car. But it's not a problem. You have the car. I'm glad I didn't waste time worrying about it," he said.

"You make absolutely no sense at all. All that tackling from football must have scrambled your brain. I'm not going to give a ride to someone I don't know. You're crazy."

"You know me. We went to grade school together, Josephine Montgomery." She looked closer at him.

"One of the Alexes. Mullin? No, Smith. Alex Smith?"

"No, Josephine Montgomery. I am an Alex, but not one of those."

"Winstead?"

"You're running out of Alexes, Josephine Montgomery." She looked closer.

"Burton. Alex Burton," she said with certainty.

"Well, sure. It's the only one left."

Alex Burton walked JoJo places. He always seemed to be outside the door when classes changed and would walk her to her next class. He knew her schedule and walked her to her car. He made no move beyond getting inside that five feet. JoJo didn't know why he suddenly appeared in her life, and she didn't really care. She had had no emotional resources to deal with him and figured he'd get bored and go away. If he was looking for more, the well was dry. He wasn't going to find it here.

Julie had been a great friend to JoJo. She knew all about what happened with Brandon, and Julie was there. She spent all her free time that junior year as JoJo's shadow, waiting to catch her friend if she fell. Julie was there when Brandon's family put their home on the market, and she was there when they sold it and moved away. Julie watched her friend fade away in front of her. She was pissed at the Bridges and the trauma they caused JoJo.

There was one point before they sold the house Julie went over there and pulled into their driveway. She sat there in her car trying to figure out the best way to tell them what a couple of assholes they were. Julie was ready to fight on JoJo's behalf, and she wanted to give it to them with both barrels. She knew Brandon and knew what they did wasn't right. But much like JoJo, she knew it wouldn't do any good and might hurt her friend. She changed her mind and backed out of the driveway.

Julie would wait with JoJo while she healed. She wanted JoJo back. Fuck the Bridges. Maybe they destroyed the relationship, but they weren't going to destroy her friend. Julie knew the only thing that would help was time and distance. Julie had to wait until the experience was far enough in the past that JoJo was able to poke her head out of her gopher hole and look around. It took almost her whole junior year, but it happened. JoJo smiled again. She laughed more than she cried. Julie never left JoJo's side.

Julie was waiting by JoJo's car one afternoon looking for a ride. JoJo walked to her, her escort Alex Burton at her side.

"Hey, Jo, can you give me a ride to work? I don't have the car today. Oh, hello Alex. Is JoJo giving you a ride somewhere?"

"Maybe. I haven't asked her yet. I'm trying to figure out what kind of mood she's in today."

"He's full of shit. I don't know if I have my own secret service agent or stalk-er." JoJo looked at him. "Do you want a ride somewhere?"

"Yes."

"Where?"

"Let's give Julie a ride to work and I'll tell you on the way."

"Don't you have classes? I leave early on Wednesdays."

"You don't need to worry about my schedule. You do need to worry about Julie getting fired because she's late again," Alex said.

"Okay, sure." JoJo popped the locks open. "You get in the backseat," she told him. He hopped in and Julie sat up front. JoJo drove Julie to the mall.

"What time do you need me to pick you up?"

"You don't need to. My dad's coming," Julie said as she got out. She left the door open for Alex; he moved to the front seat and closed the car door.

"Okay, Alex. Where can I take you?"

"Do you want to go shopping? We are at the mall." Alex asked her.

"No. I hate shopping. Where to?" JoJo said.

"The canal. Let's take a walk. I know you know how to walk. I've seen you," Alex said.

"The canal? A walk? Whatever for? Besides, you have to go back to school," she told him.

"I am cutting class the rest of the day and hanging out with you."

"Don't you think you should have asked me about that first?"

"I know enough about you, Josephine Montgomery, to know you would have told me no and bug off."

"How come you always call me by my full name anyway?"

"It's a beautiful fall day. Let's take a walk on the canal and I'll tell you." She looked at him. He looked back.

"Okay. I'll play," she said. JoJo drove them to the canal. She parked the car, and they got out and headed for the path along the canal.

"You're right about one thing," she said to him. "It is a beautiful day."

"I'm right about a lot of things, Josephine Montgomery."

They walked a bit in silence. She looked at him out of the side of her eye and he was walking beside her, completely unruffled looking happy just to be there. After a while when she couldn't take it anymore. They came to a bench. She pointed to it.

"Uncle," she said. "You win. Sit."

He did as he was told. JoJo sat next to him.

"What gives?" she asked him. "What do you want to know?"

"You're the one with all the questions. What do *you* want to know?"

"Why do you use my full name?" she asked him.

"That's a good place to start. That goes way back to elementary school. That's what they called you when you got in trouble. I used to hear over the PA, 'Josephine Montgomery to the front office please.' Or 'Josephine Montgomery you sit up front where I can see you.'"

"You remember that?"

"Oh yeah. I remember lots of stuff." He smiled when he said that.

"Like what?" JoJo sounded scared.

"I remember when the new kid was getting bullied by that dick Devin Carter and you stood up to him. You said if he wanted to fight, you'd fight him, and then I heard 'Josephine Montgomery get over her this minute.'"

She smiled at the memory. "Yeah, that was me. Devin Carter was a bully, and somebody needed to take him down, but all you guys were too chickenshit to do it. He really pissed me off. Anything else?"

"I saved the best for last. Remember when we had eighth-grade graduation, and they were giving out the awards? The kid next to you kept bumping you because the kid next to him was pushing him into you, and you got mad and switched places? You were ready. When he pushed, you shoved him so hard you knocked a couple of kids into each other and one of the Alexes fell off the riser?"

She smiled again. "Yeah."

"That Alex was me. I was on the floor when the teacher said, 'Josephine Montgomery, get over here right now!' The teacher was bitching you out. They called you down to get your diploma, and you didn't go out. The line stopped and finally the teacher dragged you down and pushed across the stage, and you walked like your feet were in quicksand. Then the crowd went wild, you bowed, and they had to yank you off."

"Oops. Sorry."

"I remember you played tennis, and you played some guy from the boys' team. He tried like hell, but he couldn't beat you. You wouldn't give up." Instead of smiling at that memory, she burst into tears.

"I'm sorry. I'm sorry. Oh God, I'm sorry," she said and cried harder.

"Hey, Hey," he said and wrapped his arms around her.

She was embarrassed and cried harder. He just held her as she cried. She used both her sleeves to wipe her face and they couldn't absorb any more moisture. JoJo started to panic. She pulled away and pulled up the hem of her shirt to wipe her face. When she ran out of shirt she looked dazedly toward her car. He could tell she was going to bolt so he grabbed her and used his sleeves to wipe her face. JoJo stopped crying and pulled away.

"I'm sorry. I think I ruined your shirt with snot."

"That's okay. It's my brother's. I also remember you dated the guy pretty seriously and I know his parents made him break up with you and sent him away to military school."

"Yeah. Pretty much. I guess his parents thought we were too young to be so involved with each other. They had a problem with the amount of time we spent together. My mom said they probably thought I'd get pregnant and ruin his life. I never thought we were too young to be happy. I really don't know what to think about it. When you brought it up, it surprised me. So, why did you bring it up? To see Josephine Montgomery cry?"

"No, I'm sorry I said that. I just wanted to see if you were waiting for graduation so you could go find the guy and marry him. You could track down anybody nowadays, but it sounds like he hasn't reached out. That probably hurts the most."

"No. The last time I saw him I asked him to look me in the eye and tell me he didn't love me anymore and he did. I saw in his eyes he couldn't love me, and I had to let him go. So, I did. It just sneaks up on me sometimes how raw it still is. How about you? Anyone ever break your heart?"

"Yeah. Well, no. Not like yours. You lost something that was real. I only lost the idea of something real. I went out with a girl in tenth grade, she went to St. Agnes. We were pretty tight, or at least I thought. She dumped me when a senior asked her out. Blindsided me.

"She kept me around because I worshipped and adored her. I guess I was good for her ego. After the fact I found out she was into this other guy all along."

"What a bitch," JoJo said. "If I ever have a chance to do it over, I think I'd skip tenth grade entirely."

"I hear you there."

"I have to thank you, though."

"How come?" he asked.

"First of all, you acknowledged I lost something. Hearing the words, you lost something from somebody means they believed you had it in the first place. Second, it's lost. Gone. Even if he showed up here tomorrow and said run away with me I couldn't. Getting over him was the hardest thing I ever had to do in my life. But he asked me to, so I did. Saying it out loud means I really am over him. Tears aside."

"Ready to walk some more, JoJo?"

"No Josephine Montgomery?"

"Not now. We're friends now. You've forgiven the Alexes for being such jerks and making you miserable all those years ago. I'll quit while I'm ahead."

"Who said I forgave them? They were awful. I better not run into Alex Mullin. I have a score to settle with him. He'd eat his lunch and then told the teacher I stole his lunch money. Oh, and we forgot that other Alex, Alex Reeves."

"Yeah, him. Let go of all this crap. Make room for something else," He advised her.

"That's what I need to do. Make room for something else. Which Alex are you again?"

"Burton, Alex Burton, JoJo."

Alex Burton was a jock. He played the sport d'jour, depending on the season. He didn't care that she didn't care about sports. It was football season, so he played football. He asked her to come to the game on homecoming. She didn't have to go to the dance.

"It would mean a lot to me," Alex said, "to have you there." She went with Julie, who was thrilled to have her back from the dead. She liked Alex. So did her mom. Her mom was concerned about how quickly the attachment formed between them. Why did JoJo have to go all in with a guy so quickly? It's like an instant boyfriend. But she picked such good guys. Alex was dedicated. He hit the weight room every other day and met with a conditioning coach. It kind of made JoJo miss tennis.

They negotiated an exit plan. He was going away to school in the fall, papers done, checks written, and two-a-days scheduled for August. Each would consider the other as their plus one until August first, at which point the relationship ended. Focus turned elsewhere. He had it all figured out and she spent most of last year in an emotional coma. She had half assed applied to four schools her guidance counselor recommended. She got in two. Number three and four.

He came over to see her. Sometimes, he brought food. All that training made him hungry.

Her father liked to cook, and he liked to eat. Her dad, who tried to never interfere, liked Alex. Football. Meat. Beer. Except Alex was too young to drink. JoJo doubted he'd waste the calories anyway. Now, a pork chop was another story.

They talked openly about him leaving, he wasn't shy with his plans.

Graduation came, she and Alex went to parties. It was a no-pressure relationship. JoJo had no fight left in her, he realized that and respected it. He was very kind to her. She needed that; he was a healing salve on her battle-scarredheart.

They went to Julie's party, which had been in the works for weeks. JoJo didn't want a party, but Ritchie did come home and the four, plus one, went out to dinner and celebrated them both. His family did the same.

Julie was in her element. So was Alex. He didn't stick around and crowd her, he brought her and checked in on her periodically and brought her home. He was out in the crowd now. JoJo sat at a picnic and talked to people as they passed by her.

Somebody came up from behind and whispered, "Congratulations graduate."

She turned and gasped, "Ray! You're home!"

He sat across from her with a funny look on his face. "What's wrong with you?" she said.

"Nothing. You look exactly nothing like Josephine Montgomery," he said. "How have you been? I haven't seen you in ages."

"Pretty good. Going to SUNY Albany in the fall. You? Did Colorado measure up? Everything you dreamed about and more?"

"Yeah. This is my first trip back. Lots of changes. I just can't believe you grew up. You look beautiful. I've been waiting for this day my whole life."

"What day is that?"

"The day I can finally pursue you and make you mine!"

****

65

CHAPTER FOURTEEN

"Hah! That's a good one!" JoJo laughed at Ray. "Me and you! As if!"

"What?" Ray said sharply. "What's so funny about that?"

"Well, if it's true it's kinda creepy. Waiting for some little girl to grow up so you can hit on her? That's creepy."

"That's not what I mean, and you know it! I just meant I'm surprised how an obnoxious little kid grew up to be such a beautiful girl."

JoJo looked at Ray. He grew from a skinny beanpole to a mature man. His flaming red hair had darkened a bit, but his blue eyes still had that spark she remembered.

"Relax, Ray. I was just kidding. So how does it feel to be home?"

"Different but the same."

"Can't wait to get back?"

"I didn't think I would want to be in a hurry but yes, I can't wait to go."

He wanted to hear her say something like, "Oh, too bad you can't stay longer," or, "Oh, I wish you could stay," some sort of protestation that she cared, words he'd been waiting for forever to leave her lips.

Instead, she looked at all the guests for him and commented, "This party has everyone here. There aren't many left to see. You probably could leave tomorrow," she observed. She couldn't help it. JoJo grew up poking fun at Ray, and old habits die hard.

He grew up while he was gone, too. Some might even consider him handsome, but JoJo couldn't help but revert to her immature twelve-year-old self around him.

Huh, thought JoJo. *Who would have thought Ray would grow up into a nice looking man? He grew beyond his zit-faced, scrawny self into a man. A good-looking man.*

"You'd like that, wouldn't you?" he said.

"What? Why would I care? What is wrong with you?" JoJo asked.

"Nothing. Never mind."

****

Alex came over to see if she needed anything. He asked her if she wanted to leave soon and said hello to Ray. Ray looked at Alex and wondered what place he occupied in JoJo's life. He obviously was an athlete; he was built like he spent all his free time lifting weights. Alex walked away and said he'd be back in a bit.

"You really work quick, don't you?" Ray said to her.

"Again? What the fuck is wrong with you?" JoJo said back, a little more harshly.

"Him. The jock. Last I heard you were going to die from a broken heart."

JoJo felt the hot tears spurt between her eyelashes. *Why is Ray being so cruel?* JoJo thought. *Maybe I'm not the only that reverted back into the annoying personality of my childhood when we see each other.*

Maybe she didn't die from a broken heart, but she certainly wasn't living with one. If it wasn't for people like his sister and Alex being there when she was on the verge of an emotional suicide, who knew what she would have done? Losing Brandon like that. Whatever happened to puppy love? It was Great Dane love. Why did it feel like she lost part of her soul after he left?

Why care about anything if it was only going to be ripped away from you with no warning? She obsessed over it constantly, going in circles, trying to figure out where she failed. JoJo couldn't help it. She survived. With time, her friends and her parents, JoJo was still here.

She accepted it and moved forward. It didn't break her. And now, fuckhead Ray brings it up like that?

JoJo stood up, beyond pissed. "Fuck you, Ray! You asshole! I hope you go back to Colorado and stay there! How dare you, Ray! Fuck you! I hope I never see you again!" she screamed.

The noise of the party was hushed as JoJo screamed at Ray. All eyes were on them, watching them, trying to figure out what was going on. JoJo's face became red the more she yelled. He enraged her. He sat there, stunned and embarrassed. *God, it felt good yelling at him,* she thought. It was so much better than crying.

She stopped when she realized they were the center of attention. JoJo looked up and saw everyone staring at her, and she looked for the quickest way out of there. She was ready to run when she found Alex on one side of her and Julie on the other. Alex had his hand on her arm, waiting for her to move, when Julie got in Ray's face.

"Jesus, Ray, what's wrong with you? You think you're going to come back here and stir shit up and leave? Go harass someone else. Leave JoJo the fuck alone!" Julie yelled at her brother.

She stepped in front of Ray to block him from JoJo's line of sight. If he only saw her a year ago when she stopped eating in an attempt to make herself disappear.

"You're such a dick, Ray! Why don't you just get on a plane and get the fuck out of here, NOW! Nobody wants you here. Alex, take JoJo home."

All of a sudden, the voices started back up; people figured the excitement was over, and the party resumed. Alex took her by the arm and escorted her out of there, holding her back so she couldn't run.

"Walk out of here like you're the winner," Alex told her. "Fuck him. It now looks like he didn't get what he wanted from you. Use it. Let's go."

She got in his car, her face still red, and started to shake uncontrollably.

"What? Are you okay? Jesus, you're scaring me JoJo. Give me something," Alex said. She reached for his hand.

"Take me somewhere, Alex. I don't want to go home. Let's get some ice cream and go to the canal."

That's what they did. They ate their cones in silence. It was a while until she spoke. "Alex, I need to ask you something, and I want the truth. Why did you come over to me in study hall that time? Why?"

He looked at her. It was late afternoon, and the sun was low and bounced off her, bathing her in a golden light. She looked all soft and beautiful.

"I was in your homeroom junior year. I couldn't believe it when they called your name. I couldn't believe that was you. I was looking for the girl who took on the bully, instead, I found the shadow of Josephine Montgomery. You looked so broken down, defeated and blank. What happened to you? Somebody needed to save Josephine Montgomery. She was going down for the third time and not even putting up a fight.

"I asked Julie about you. She told me what happened, that she was trying her best to hold you up. You were so skinny. I watched you fade away and that broke my heart. You made it through the year, and by the end of the year you were at least smiling every once in a while, so I thought you were going to be okay.

"Senior year started, you were in my history class. The outside looked better, but I could tell the inside something wasn't right. You looked better, but it was just a front. You weren't better. So, I decided to help you. Or at least try. I talked to Julie about it. She had run out of ideas on how to help you and thought maybe I should give it a shot. So that's why. I wanted to save Josephine Montgomery."

"Huh," she said. "I collapsed internally. I couldn't get out from under the weight of my depression. I figured that's the way I was going to be. Just sleep-walk through life. Julie helped so much. She kept the world away from me, but she couldn't do it forever. So there I was, stuck. I thought something inside me died. A part of me was gone. I tried so hard to find it, but I didn't have the energy to look anymore. I was all set to live my life as the ghost of Josephine Montgomery.

"I couldn't get out from under it. Then you come along. You helped me. I guess I just needed a really strong jock to push that weight off me or else drag me out from under it. But it worked. Most of Josephine Montgomery is back, so I really, really thank you. There's still a piece missing. I wanted to see if maybe you'll help me a little more."

"Anything," Alex said. "What do you need?"

"You have to be sure you can do it, though. I don't want you ending up where I was."

"What? Tell me. Let me decide."

"Remember how you said that girl kept you around because you worshipped and adored her? I need some of that. My ego needs some of that. I need to know I am still worthy. Still attractive. Still desirable. Are you a virgin?" JoJo asked him.

"Excuse me? Did you just say what I think you did?"

"Yeah. Because if you are I'm offering to remove it from your sexual resume."

"What?" Alex said. "What?"

"I'm looking for validation. All my drama happened when I was a kid, really. I'm looking for validation as a woman. I'm looking into renegotiating our agreement. I'm throwing sex into the mix. If I ask you to fuck me and tell me how wonderful and beautiful I am, could you do that? I mean, no strings attached. You don't have to say you love me because that's not what I need.

"I need positivity. Affirmation. I'm finally over Brandon; that happened to some other girl a long time ago. I don't want to complicate your life. I know you need to concentrate on football. I don't want to break your heart. It would ruin your season and I'd hate to see you benched because of me," she joked. "I'm asking you this because I know you would never hurt me. I feel safe with you, but I don't want to fuck with your head and mess up your life."

"So, you're proposing I have sex with you, tell you how gorgeous and desirable you are, and just walk away? The only thing I can't do is fall in love with you, and this is something you need me to do?" he clarified.

"Yeah, that's what I'm saying. It expires on August first. That can't change."

"What about you falling in love with me? What if that happens?" he asked her.

"I'll be zero for two and probably become a nun."

"There is no way I'm letting Josephine Montgomery become a nun. So yes. I'll start now. Josephine Montgomery, who is one of the hottest girls in town wants me? That stunning, sexy piece of ass wants to be adored? I'll adore the fuck out of her. She'll get body slammed with adore."

She looked at him and smiled. "Yeah. Like that."

"How soon do I start? I have tomorrow evening free if you're into it."

"Does it involve a car?" she asked him.

"Only for transportation."

"Don't you want to test the product before you commit?"

"I'd love to, but did you have in mind?"

"Here. Let's go over to that picnic table."

She pointed to a table alone and off to the side. They went over to the table and JoJo positioned herself sitting but found he was too tall. If he sat on the table and she got between his legs their lips met just about perfect. She measured while he sat with her standing between his legs, just waiting. She looked at him and smiled.

"I truly have to warn you. I don't know what's going to happen. I have a feeling I'm going to devour you like female spiders do after they mate, they eat them. I think for a long time it was easier to feel nothing. Now, I'm out to prove something. I'm feeling something strong. Like a volcano. Like I'm going to erupt or something."

"What are you trying to prove?"

She stepped forward and grabbed his neck and placed her cheek against his, her mouth to his ear. "That there's nothing wrong with me. There never was. I'm older, wiser, stronger. I'm going to use you up. While I was in my emotional coma, I grew up and around my body. It's new to me, and I want to test it out. This who I am now. You ready to feel the power?"

"Why do you think I have a conditioning coach?" he said.

He kissed her with a passion that was like a category five storm out over the gulf. The sea raged and swept away any childhood fantasy of love. What was left he could have all he wanted.

She had a moment of reason and pulled away. *Fuck it,* she thought. *I'm going back in and let him try to swallow me whole.* It was like every nerve ending on was on high alert and the warning system was broken.

They broke apart, each breathing quickly and heavily. He looked at the surprised look on her face.

She touched her lips and said "Wow."

"Wow? You said wow?"

"Yeah," she said like she was in shock.

"Get back here," he said and pulled her to him. "I'm not done. You were supposed to be speechless."

He was a very good kisser, content to kiss her and watch her squirm. She finally pulled herself away from him. "Holy shit!" escaped from her mouth.

"Still talking," he said and pulled her back. This time, he took possession of her and released her when he thought she had enough. "Well?" he asked her.

"Um," was her answer. He slid off the table and took her hand. He started towards the car, walking close to her. He opened the car door, seated her and shut the door. He went around the driver's side and got in. She looked at him, still mute.

"Josephine Montgomery has the softest lips I've ever kissed," Alex said to her. "She's a ten out of ten, and she wants me. I'm the luckiest guy on the planet." He put the car in drive and took her home. He held her hand all the way and walked her to the door.

"I am picking you up at six tomorrow and taking you out on a date. Be ready to leave the house, and be ready to stay out late. Or up late. I've been adoring you, but I haven't worshipped you yet. Be ready."

He smiled and let go of her hand. He winked at her and walked back to his car. He didn't pull out of her driveway until she was safely in the house.

JoJo went inside, still in awe of what happened to her. Ray making her mad was the best thing that could ever have happened to her. Finding her temper also allowed her to find her voice again. Yelling at him touched some reserve in her JoJo never knew she had left.

She was going to use that and rebuild herself. Poor Ray. He was probably joking, and she told him to fuck off. That's something Josephine Montgomery would do. She doesn't need to look for a new Josephine Montgomery. The old one was just fine, buried but not dead. Digging herself out was going to be fun, she thought, thinking of Alex.

Alex called her at nine o'clock the next morning to confirm.

"Do you think I developed cold feet overnight?" she asked him, laughing.

"Could be. I just wanted to make sure. We have a whole month to put you back together. I don't want to go too quick and cause any more trouble for you."

"Not enough time to stick in a toe. It's the deep end or nothing. But we need to use condoms. I'm not on anything."

"So the deep end with a life jacket? I can work with that," he said.

He came over promptly at six, sat for a bit and visited with her dad. He got up, looked at her and said, "Ready?" She got up and grabbed her jacket.

Her mother said, "Going out two days in row? That's new."

"Yeah. I know." JoJo smiled. "See you later."

They got in the car, and he said there were three options. "Dine out. Eat in. Or eat in the car."

"Where's eat in?"

"We have this small apartment added on. My grandma lived there for a while. I moved into it for the summer. It's off the kitchen, but there's a separate entrance. And cable."

"Let's go there," she said.

Since he was training, he needed to eat more. He usually had a sandwich this time of day. That's what they decided to get and bring back to Chez Alex, a nod to his seventh grade French teacher. He explained it was an inside joke. She didn't care. Casa Alex, a nod to her Spanish teacher. After they finished, he went around and lit a bunch of candles.

"Atmosphere," he said. He clicked on the TV and invited her over. "Let's make out like a couple of high school kids and see where it goes."

She sat next to him, and he put his arm around her. She then watched him become enchanted and totally slack-jawed at some National Geographic special. After a bit, she took the remote out of his hand and turned the TV off. He looked at her and dove on her.

"Looking for something?" she said.

Alex grabbed her and flipped her around so suddenly she ended up on top of him.

"You," he said. He put her on top for a reason. Alex wanted her mouth to seek him out and feel every twitch of her body.

"Weren't you All-County Wrestling or something?" she asked, held in an odd yet painless position.

"Yes," he told her, "Varsity when I was in tenth grade. I was good because I have brothers and, well, guys like to prove who's stronger. I remember my mom yelling, 'Take it outside, boys' all the time. They wanted me to pick just one sport and devote myself to it, so I picked football. Figured I'd have more options—enough about that. I have to figure out what position I want *you* in," but he didn't move.

He figured he'd let her call it. She wanted him to feel the power. She needed to deliver it first. Frustrated he was only just kissing her back, she sat up and pulled her shirt off. She started kissing him again. He ran his hands over her bare back and there was power in her goosebumps.

"Oh, lord," he said and flipped her beneath him, but it was too late. Her body was a living, breathing thing and already moving beneath him. He picked her up, carried her over and tossed her on the bed. He pulled off his shirt and joined her.

"Oh," she said. "You're built like the rock of Gibraltar." Her eyes glowed at his muscles. He laughed at the comparison, flattered. She ran her hands over his chest and shoulders. "Nice definition. You're quite the specimen." She ran her hands over his back. "Holy shit. I am speechless now."

"Thank you," he said, and his face reddened at her compliment. "It's not why I do it, but, yeah, well, it doesn't hurt this is the result."

They lay on his bed on their sides and faced each other. She ran her palm over the muscles of his upper arm. He looked at her breasts in the delicate black lace bra. He reached down and unbuttoned her jeans.

"Are you wearing matching lingerie?" he asked as he tugged at her jeans.

"They're the same color," she said. "Besides, I'm too young for lingerie. Brings to mind martinis, cigarettes, and stockings with the seams up the back."

"Tell that to Victoria's Secret. Very nice," he said into her belly button.

He kissed around there for a while until he heard her giggle. He blew raspberries on her stomach, and she started to laugh. Alex grabbed her pulled her on top of him and unhooked her bra. JoJo must not have realized that happened when she sat up her bra fell down and exposed both her breasts. She looked down in shock and froze. She felt this overwhelming urge to run and looked to the door. Alex felt the tension in her and looked at her face as it looked at her boob. He had to bring her back, and soon.

"Hey, JoJo, over here. It's me. Over here," he said and shook her leg. She blinked a couple of times and swallowed.

"Oh, um," she said in a high breathy voice. "I don't I think I..." She stumbled over the words.

"Here," he said and wrapped his arms around her. "Talk to me," he said gently.

"Sorry I'm panicking, and I don't know what to do," JoJo whispered.

"Relax. I need to worship you first, anyway. Lay back down. Close your eyes. Breathe." Alex told her quietly. "You don't need to do anything but listen." He started at her wrist. He gave her little kisses and murmured against her skin words like incredible, beautiful, soft, gorgeous. He ransacked his SAT vocabulary. Alex worked his way inside her elbow, and she gave a little laugh.

He kissed her neck, behind her ear whispered sweet things and she melted into him. Alex kissed her along her collarbone to the base of her throat. He kissed down her chest to the base of her sternum. He looked up at her and smiled. JoJo smiled back, took his hand and placed it on her teardrop shaped breast, the nipple hard against his palm. Alex lightly ran his palm over her. If she wanted more, she had to come get it. JoJo pulled his mouth up to hers and turned towards him.

"I'm all yours," she said into his mouth. That was all he needed. He gave her the best he had, and he could tell it was more than enough by the way she trembled and clung to him afterward. *I guess you don't need to be in love to have mind-blowing sex,* JoJo thought.

"You okay?" he asked her.

"Yeah. More than okay. Can I talk to you? Well, I know I can," she said. "It's about feelings. I fucking hate feelings, but I need to talk about this, and I'm worried about your feelings. I don't want it to come out wrong and hurt you."

"As long as you're not going to tell me to take you home, I'm fine. What's on your mind?" he asked her. "You don't want to leave, do you?"

"No, far from it. I just want to figure things out and want to bounce a few things off you. Maybe if I say things out loud, I can release their hold over me."

He rolled over and grabbed her. Alex laid on his side and gathered her to him. He spooned her, maybe she could speak clearer if she wasn't looking at him. JoJo didn't need to see him, she needed to feel him.

"Shoot," Alex said after he was sure she was comfortable. "Well. Will it bother you if I talk about the past?"

"No. I don't think so. If it wasn't for what happened to you, I doubt we'd be here now."

"I guess I want to think out loud," JoJo said. "Stop me if you don't want to hear it."

"I don't care. I love the sound of your voice. I could listen to it all day."

She adjusted herself so she sank into him. "It's like this. All that shit with Brandon happened when I was so young. It seemed perfect like we were the same person split in two. We never had a fight. We were each other's first. First love. First partner. I was sixteen for most of it. Tenth grade. He left in August before my junior year. What if that was it? What would have happened if nothing happened? Would we be together today? I'm not sure. We had a lot of growing up to do. Would we have grown in the same direction? It was so innocent, so pure. Was that even realistic? Was it like that because we were so insular? There was the whole world going on around us, it was bound to intrude sooner or later.

"Maybe his parents were right. Maybe we were too young. The way they were willing to sacrifice me to save him was unforgivable. It wasn't my fault he loved me. It wasn't my fault we seemed so perfectly matched. Maybe they just could have let the relationship run its course and see what happened. I have a feeling if we stayed together, the real Josephine Montgomery might have shown up and started pushing him around.

"I don't want to make him sound like a wuss, but he was much more, I don't know, sensitive? Delicate? Then I was. That's what bothered me. His parents were brutal. He wasn't the kind of guy who challenged things; he wasn't a fighter. Brandon was so sweet and kind. His parents felt I was so dangerous they physically had to move him someplace far away. They had to sell their house and move?" She started to feel tears start to form, but instead of crying in silence, she rolled over to face him. "Could a naive barely seventeen-year-old girl be that bad? Was I that bad?"

"Are you asking because you want to know what I think? Or posing some what ifs?" he asked her.

"Originally, it was just to vent, but now yeah, I want your opinion. Say whatever you want and don't be afraid to tell me what you really think."

"Okay, JoJo. I'll be honest, or as honest as I can be because I am biased. I think you're perfect just the way you are. First of all, no seventeen-year-old girl has enough strength to destroy anybody unless she's carrying an Uzi. Love is not supposed to be used as a weapon, from what I understand, and that's all you had to work with, so no. You were not bad. He wasn't bad.

"The way his parents handled it was bad. You were just a young, inexperienced girl. They almost wrecked *you, not the* other way around. Looking back on it, they probably should have talked to your parents and all of you should have sat down and discussed it. He was going to be a senior, y'know, that's not that young. What would have happened if instead of letting you go, he stood up to them and told you to wait for him? That he would find you wherever you were and to hold on? But he didn't. If he didn't have the strength to fight them, how were you supposed to? I can only give you a male viewpoint, I'm sorry if it sounds harsh.

"Why didn't he throw down for you? You may not think he was weak, but I might. Maybe he was in over his head and didn't know what to do. Maybe they ambushed him and didn't give him a choice. All I know is you shouldn't have had to destroy yourself to save him. The fact that you were going to do that says more about how strong you are than anything else. You thought if you carried the burden he wouldn't have to. That doesn't make any sense. But that's past and that's where this all belongs. Leave it there. As an outsider looking in all I can say for sure is that you are not bad. You never were, so stop that line of thought. Immediately. You are this really great person who deserves whatever you want."

He took his finger and touched one of the tears that escaped her eyes. He brought his wet finger to his lips and then touched hers.

"Really, JoJo. You're finally able to get far enough away from it to look at it differently. None of it matters anymore. I'll fuck you five times a day if that's what needs to be done if that's what it's gonna take for you to believe in yourself. If I have to fuck it out of you, I will. Let go and make room for some new things. Have you even thought about school? How new all of that shit's going to be? I'm leaving. You're leaving. Let go, JoJo. Let go of all of it," he recommended.

She put her face next to his and whispered in his ear. "Yes. Fuck it out of me," she said in what she hoped was a sexy voice.

"So JoJo wants to talk dirty? You need more than that."

"I know. I need more than one word. I need to get creative."

"First I need to eat something." He said and got up to look in the fridge. "You want anything?"

"Do you have any popcorn?" JoJo said. "You can eat the other half of my sandwich if you want."

Alex took it out of the fridge. "It's a start." He opened a few cupboards. "Nothing. C'mon. Grab a shirt." He picked one up and tossed it to her. "Here. This is clean. Follow me. The popcorn is over here," he said, pointing towards inside the house.

She just wore her bottoms and his shirt. They went down this short hallway to a door that entered into the kitchen. It was dark and quiet. "My parents' house. Vacation," he said.

"I need to use the bathroom. I have to pee," JoJo told him.

He found the popcorn and pointed her towards the bathroom. JoJo came back into the kitchen when she was finished and found Alex talking to a guy she thought must be his brother because they looked a lot alike. She walked through them and said "hello" to the other guy. She tried to pass but Alex put his hand up on her shoulder to stop her as the microwave beeped. He took the popcorn out and poured it into a bowl. He turned to her and said, "Here. Take it with you. I'll be right back."

She went back to his place and sat on the couch looking for something to watch on TV. She found a channel that played old sitcoms. *The Mary Tyler Moore Show* was on, and she started watching.

He came back and from behind her and said in her ear, "Hungry?" He sat next to her with a plateful of food.

She laughed and laughed again at the amount of food he had.

"We just ate. I feel sorry for your wife. She better like to cook. And weigh five hundred pounds." Her measly sandwich was dwarfed by leftovers of some sort.

"It's fuel," he said and cleaned his plate. He brought the dirty dish to the sink. He brought back two bottles of water, gave her one, and started eating the popcorn.

"You're still hungry?"

"Hungry for you," Alex laughed.

"Who was that in the kitchen? Your brother?" JoJo asked.

"That was my older brother George. He's your brother's age. I think your little exercise here is working."

"What do you mean?"

"He felt the power. When you left, he said, 'Dude, you're banging JoJo Montgomery? How did that happen? You're so lucky.'"

"What did you say?"

"I am lucky. Do you have any popcorn stuck in your teeth? I do. I'm going to go floss. I'll leave it out for you."

She went after him into the bathroom and flossed. JoJo came back and he was getting that guy getting lost in the sports zone with a glazed look on his face. She sat on his lap, straddling him, and cut off his line of sight to the TV.

"Hey," he said and pushed her aside, only to pull her back. Alex looked at her and smiled.

"Yes? What do you want?" he said to her.

"Attention," she answered, kissing him. "Yours. All of it."

"I want to go very slow. I have the opportunity to celebrate every square inch of you, so sit still. Move, and I may have to start over," he warned her.

Alex found it odd he had never considered her cute. She had so many adjectives to describe her, stunning, gorgeous, beautiful, a knockout, but never cute, when that's exactly what she was. She was giggly and funny. JoJo had very brown eyes, so brown they sometimes look black. Her dark hair was always in her eyes, and her skin so creamy he thought he could pour it into a cup of coffee, but she was so freaking cute. Alex told her so.

Alex said she was like a flower opening up. Every petal was more beautiful than the last. She didn't know if this was true or not, but he was so good at slinging it she felt that way. JoJo laid on her back on the couch while he was on his knees on the floor kissing every square inch of her, found every word he could think of that meant incredible and mumbled it into her skin. He stopped everywhere and concentrated between her legs with his hands, his mouth in her ear telling her wonderful things. Her body took over and started to let go. She bucked and ground into his hand and was mumbling back into his neck.

Alex grabbed a condom and pulled her down onto him. He placed both hands around her waist and forced her into his rhythm, but she wanted to follow her own. That delicious conflict near about made her scream and he wanted, by God, he wanted to make her scream. Alex could feel her reach her climax by her moaning and rocking, her legs shaking. He considered leaving her on top, but when she started to make noise he decided no, he was going to drill into her good. He flipped her onto her back and plunged in as far as he could go, and she called out his name. "Alex...oh Alex...Alex...Winstead!" She yelled as she came.

He collapsed next to her and said in her ear. "It's Burton, JoJo. Alex Burton."

"I know that. Alex Winstead was black."

"Very funny, JoJo. Very funny."

****

Every woman should have an Alex Burton, some man to take a month out of his life to worship and adore her, she thought. It was only two days, but she felt lighter than she had in ages.

They had exhausted themselves sexually. There was nothing left, only fumes to carry them further, but they were content to sit on the couch and watch a movie. They didn't talk much, but they still touched each other. She had her hand on his leg or her head on his shoulder. He had his arm around her or held her hand. JoJo fell asleep halfway through the movie; he woke her when it was over.

"Hey," Alex said, jiggling her awake. "You ready to go home?"

"No. Can't I stay here?" JoJo mumbled.

"Won't your mom care?"

"No, I'll call and tell her I fell asleep watching a movie, and you'll drop me off in the morning. I'll tell her the truth."

"Sure, as long as I can drop you off around eight-thirty. I have to be at the gym by nine. Let's see if we can find a toothbrush for you. I can't guarantee I'll have one. I don't entertain much."

After looking through a few drawers, he managed to find one, and she went off into the bathroom.

She came out to him, putting a clean pillowcase on one of the pillows. He handed it to her and went into the bathroom himself. He came out and saw her standing next to the bed.

"What are you waiting for?"

"You," she said shyly. "I don't know what side you sleep on."

"The side next to you," he said. He pulled the covers back, grabbed her, and threw her on the bed.

"It's kind of a turn on, you know," JoJo told him.

"What is?" he asked.

"The way you pick me up and toss me around. It's very you Tarzan, me Jane."

"Don't be grabbing me under my loincloth," he instructed her.

"You have to ask first."

"Get comfy," he said, got in, and pulled the covers over her. She shifted around to get comfortable, and he filled in beside her.

"Alex? Can I ask you a question?"

"No, Josephine. It's time to go to sleep. We have all month to answer your questions."

"Okay. Goodnight, Alex."

"Goodnight JoJo. Sweet dreams," he said and threw his arm over her waist.

She wasn't sure she'd be able to sleep with someone, let alone next to a guy. It must not have been a big issue for her because JoJo fell fast asleep and didn't wake until he shook her shoulder the next morning.

Alex dropped her off on his way to the gym. He walked her to the door and kissed her goodbye, but she told him he was going overboard.

"The deal was for sex, not a boyfriend," she said. She found it hard to look him in the eye in the light of day.

"What's the matter, JoJo? Are you embarrassed?" He smiled and took her hand.

"I must be. I'm such a freak in the sheets at night, I'm finding it hard to reconcile it with myself during the day. It's like maybe I shouldn't be doing this, maybe I'm not cut out for such, I don't know, such—"

"Pleasure?"

JoJo immediately blushed and felt hot. She glanced up at the sky, avoiding his gaze.

"JoJo, look at me."

"I can't. You've seen me naked." She turned her head away. "Sorry."

"So? You've seen me naked. It's a wash," Alex told her. "It's a little late for that. I've seen it all and you're the eighth wonder of the world."

He stepped forward until there was no space between them. He took her in his arms and tightly held her.

"I've seen it all. I can tell you how many moles you have on your back," he whispered in her ear. He felt her twist in his embrace like she was trying to make a break for it, but her struggle was half-hearted. JoJo leaned into him instead. She lifted her eyes to meet his and smiled.

"I guess you have. How many?" she said to him.

"Many what?"

"Moles."

"I'm not telling. I need a recount to be sure. You don't want a temporary boyfriend that's fine, but I might think of you as my temporary girlfriend," Alex said. He felt her stiffen at that. He kissed her head and let her go.

"Relax, JoJo. It's all good. I'll call you later."

****

She enjoyed her coffee and the sunlight coming through the window. She was alone with her thoughts digesting the past few days. So much had changed, she had changed, she felt like she had each foot in a different room. Not quite one or the other. She went from a confused kid to a maturing woman overnight. She didn't even look the same. The haunted look in her eyes had morphed into clear eyed optimism.

She didn't even care that he might be using her purely for his own reasons. Complete access to her was easier than going out searching for girls.

Her mother came into the kitchen and looked at JoJo, smiling to herself. Her mother came over and gave her a hug. Her mother held on to her and didn't let go. JoJo disentangled herself from her mom's embrace.

"Mom? Mom? What's wrong? Are you okay? Why are you crying?"

"Oh, JoJo, you have no idea how happy I am. I can't believe it. I have been holding my breath for the past few years, waiting for you. Waiting for you to break, for you to do something, for something to happen. I was afraid your experience with Brandon broke you; you were so young. You gave up living because you found it too painful. You were so young to go through something so emotional, another reason why you shouldn't have gotten so serious.

"As hard as it is to believe, nobody ever died from a broken heart, but I was worried about you. You were so young I wasn't sure you had the skills to cope. I was afraid every time I looked into your eyes, there'd be a sadness that never left. Everybody said give her time, she'll get better, but you didn't get better. You got worse. You stopped eating."

"You knew about that?" JoJo asked.

"I'm your mother. Of course, I knew." Her Mother looked at her and frowned. "The guidance counselor said you needed to talk to someone, but you wouldn't. Julie wanted to help but had no idea what to do. Alex offered to help. I just said 'sure'. A guy caused this mess; maybe one can help clean it up. He's doing something right. You seem happier."

"Alex's helping me get my confidence up before I leave. He's giving me a crash course in my awesomeness. Alex is so kind to me, Mom. He's worried I'm not taking it seriously enough, going away to school. He's taking me shopping to get stuff for my dorm room. Now he wants me to call my roommate. His big old jock self is just so comforting," JoJo said, blushing.

"Your father and I couldn't see how you'd make it to college. We doubted you'd go.

"Geez, Mom. Don't be so melodramatic."

"You can say that now. You scared me something awful."

****

CHAPTER FIFTEEN

Alex came over that night and hung out for a while, watching TV. When he was leaving, she walked him to his car. He asked her if she was busy the next night, hoping she was free to come over. JoJo was so he said to expect him there around six, and they said goodnight. He didn't leave until she was safely inside.

The next night, Alex came inside, talked to her parents for a bit, and left when they decided to get dinner. Alex decided on a pizza and a large salad. They called and ordered it from her house and went to pick it up on the way back. JoJo laughed at him for ordering a salad.

"Why didn't you get wings?" she asked him. "A salad won't fill you up."

"I don't just eat to eat," he told her. "I eat quality food. Wings are gross. The reason they taste so good is because they are primarily fat and grease. Besides, anytime I've ever seen you eat you always have a salad. I've never seen you eat a wing."

"That's right. I don't eat wings because you're right. They're gross, and I do like a good salad. I'll even eat a bad salad."

"It's just fuel, JoJo. It's a means to an end."

They returned back to his place and ate. They used paper plates so clean-up was quick and easy. He asked her if she wanted to watch some TV.

"Not really. Do you mind if we just go lie on your bed and talk?"

"Do you know any guy who'd say no to that?" Alex asked her.

"No, but it's because your bed is way more comfortable than your couch. Can I wear one of your shirts?"

"JoJo, no need to ask. Do what you want. My chez is your casa. I need to go brush my teeth, though. I'll be right back."

JoJo was waiting at the door when he came out, she wanted to brush hers, too. She wore one of his tee shirts and he hoped just her underwear. When she returned, he was waiting for her in bed, shirtless. JoJo hoped he kept his boxers on, but it didn't really matter. She was going to join him regardless. She slid under the covers and into his arms, relaxing into him. JoJo made a few sounds of contentment but otherwise didn't speak. Alex remained silent, waiting for her to start, but she didn't talk. He turned her on her side facing away from him and tucked in behind her.

"What's on your mind? What did you want to talk about?" he asked the back of her head.

"I want to talk about you."

"Me? Why?"

"I guess I wanted to talk about what makes you so, I don't know, so disciplined? Was your father in the Marines? You always brush your teeth after eating. You floss. Religiously. You've got me doing it. You have a set schedule. You're conscious of what you eat. It's like you're on a path and you never deviate from it. How do you know? How do you know this is the right path for you? Have you ever said, 'fuck the gym, I'm sleeping in today'?"

He laughed at her. "I'm an Alex, one of many Alexes. I needed to figure out what I could do to separate myself from the pack. I wasn't the smartest Alex or the most handsome Alex, but I was a tough Alex. Maybe because I have three older brothers who were jocks, I was good at sports. I was a fast Alex, probably because I was always being chased by one of my brothers who wanted to pound the shit out of me. But okay, there's a lot of fast Alexes, so now I needed to separate myself from them. That's where the gym comes in. After sending my three older brothers through college I don't believe there would be any money left to send one more, so I figured my best shot was a football scholarship. I became a fast, strong, tough Alex who understood the game. Good enough to get the scholarship, now the goal is to keep the scholarship, play for four years and not get hurt. I have no illusions of playing beyond college. I'm going for a business degree."

"That's pretty impressive. You know what you want, and you figured out how to get it. I'm trying to find the most useless degree I can. Can you major in Latin?"

"I don't know. Can you speak Latin? Does anyone speak Latin?" He laughed at her.

"Maybe 13th century Medieval Literature? How does that sound?" she asked him.

"Sounds awful."

"Well, I'll figure it out," she said. Alex gave her a squeeze.

"Yes, yes, you will. I have a question for you. Who is Josephine?"

84

"What? I am."

"You have to be named after someone. Nobody picks the name Josephine out of a baby book."

"No reputable baby book even has the name Josephine in it," she joked. "I am named after my grandmother, Josephine DeLuca. My mom wanted to honor her mom. 'Nobody will ever love you like your mom,' she told me. DeLuca women are tough; If you say you are going to do something, you better do it, or else you faced an angry DeLuca. Nobody wants to face an angry DeLuca. I remember the original Josephine telling me about smacking my grandfather with a wooden spoon if he stepped out of line, and I'm not sure she was joking. My dad only went along with the name Josephine because he wanted to call me Josie, after the outlaw Josie Wales, one of his favorite movies. That was all fine and good and lasted about a week. My brother was learning how to talk and called me Jo, JoJo, and that stuck."

"Josie. The outlaw Josie Montgomery. That's not bad. Are you an outlaw, JoJo?"

"Not really," she said as she turned to face him, "but maybe you could talk me into doing something still illegal in a few states right now. Amoral, even."

"I was worried I'd corrupt you. It looks like I should worry about you corrupting me."

JoJo ran her fingers through his wiry sandy brown hair. It was on the longer side and looked shaggy. He had freckles across the bridge of his nose. His eyebrows were thick and darker than his hair. He had dark blue eyes that were very dark for being blue, not a cornflower or sky blue, but a blue that only existed deep in the ocean. He always had a smile on his face that seemed to get bigger when he saw JoJo. She pushed his hair out of his face and smiled at him.

"What's that for? The smile?"

"Your forehead. It's white. Doesn't match the rest of you."

"I know. I need to get a haircut soon. It'll be obvious then." He laughed.

"You need to do it soon otherwise it'll be like that for your college ID."

"Maybe I'll get it cut after," Alex said.

"I need to disagree with you," she told him. "You might've been the handsomest Alex." He flushed a deep red. She put her cool palm on his cheek. "Maybe."

Alex smiled and said, "Definitely the luckiest."

85

"Oh, you want to get lucky? Do you?" JoJo teased him. "Yes. I want to get very lucky. Please?"

JoJo was the aggressor now, trying it out to see how it fit. It felt good to be in control, she thought. No more letting the world push her around, it was time to push back. Alex was strong and liked to move her around for his satisfaction. He would pick her up and toss her around. JoJo decided to do the same verbally. She wasn't strong enough to push him around, so she told him what to do and didn't say please. Alex was more than happy to do what she demanded. JoJo even threw a condom at him and told him to put it on.

Even though she was eighteen, she considered herself sexually immature; her experience with one guy two years ago seemed irrelevant now. JoJo wasn't sure what the future held as far as men and relationships, but she had a man right here whose sole purpose was her satisfaction, and she was going to take advantage of it. God, the thrill of it all.

The fact that he was built like a small mountain didn't hurt either. This time, she collapsed on him. She growled contentedly in his ear, her turn to massage his ego. She said out loud every wonderful thing about him she could think of, as well as some things she wanted him to do to her and things she'd like to do to him.

"Ooh, JoJo wants to talk dirty." He said.

"JoJo wants to be dirty," she answered him. "JoJo wants to do dirty things with you. To you."

"Let me know when you're ready to start."

"I think I need a nap first," she confessed.

"I'll be here when you wake up," he said as he tucked her in around him.

He fell asleep shortly after she did, and they both enjoyed a power nap. JoJo woke him up by breathing in his ear.

"What the—?" Alex woke, waving his hand around his head. He looked at her. "Was that you?"

"I'm getting lonely," JoJo laughed.

"That's why I'm here," he said as he grabbed her and pulled her on top of him. "Where do you want to start?"

"Everywhere. Now pleasure me," she said, and he obliged.

They lay in his bed in the dark. She found it easier to talk to him if he wasn't directly looking at her, but she didn't realize she was such a clinger. After the intense sex she needed to be in his arms. She wondered if it was because after sex she was at her most vulnerable, it was hard to fight when she felt completely exposed. She clung to him like Velcro, but he didn't seem to mind.

"Yes, JoJo?" He asked her. "What, Alex?" she said to him.

"Whenever you're quiet, it means you're thinking about something. After you think things through you like to talk. So, what do you want to know?"

"I think I shouldn't think so much," JoJo explained. "I don't need to know everything."

"Now you have to ask." He told her. "If it's none of your business I'll let you know."

JoJo had her face on his chest and her leg flung over his. She ran her fingers over his ab muscles, hard and defined. "Well, okay, how did you learn to do all this?"

"What?"

"Sex. I'm no expert, far from it, but how do you know exactly what to do and where to do it?" She asked him.

"Why, JoJo, you don't know?"

"No. Was I absent the day they covered it in health class?"

"You may not realize this, but you tell me. If I touch you and you shiver or moan, it means you like what I'm doing. If you reach for the remote, it means you don't and try something else. Since my work ethic is hardwired, no matter what I'm doing I have to do it to the best of my ability. But porn and practice help."

"Practice? Who do you practice with?" JoJo asked. "Wait a minute. None of my business. You don't have to answer that."

"I'll answer it. You know how my parents are away? We have a lake house up north, and we'd spend summers up there. There's a girl who had a thing for my brothers, or the two older than me. She rotated through them, and when they stopped going up as much, she turned her attention to me. She was pretty experienced and kind of bossy. She'd say, 'not there, not so hard, faster, slower,' you get the idea. But it reduced the learning curve."

"Huh. Thank goodness for your work ethic. I feel something, though. I was wondering if you feel it, too."

"Feel something? I feel a lot of things. I feel like this experience will be one of the highlights of my life. I feel like I might be in over my head with you. When

I'm with you it feels like an earthquake or a freight train bearing down on me, and I'm helpless. It's out of my hands. Being with you is magic. Pure magic," he told her. "What do you feel?"

"I feel lucky you came into my life. I feel I'm not sure this is the right word, but a certain tenderness for you. It doesn't matter what happens in the future. What I feel is so true and pure I think I'll carry it with me forever, even if I never see you again. I want to thank you for being there for me."

"Ah, JoJo, I feel the same way about you. You're very special to me, and I think the memory of you will last forever."

****

JoJo rolled over, placed his face between her breasts, and held his head there. She could feel his eyelashes brush her skin. He could hear her heartbeat, and when he listened closely, he swore it thumped out his name, "A-lex, A-lex." She held his head there until he sighed into her skin.

"Look, JoJo, this has to stop. Feelings might be getting a bit deep."

"What? I'm confused. I thought we were talking about how special this is."

"It is, but I think we've taken this as far as we can. The goal of this whole thing was to get you back in touch with yourself, to prove to yourself that you weren't damaged. I didn't realize how close to the surface you were. You didn't need me to prove anything. You already knew, you just needed help proving it to yourself. So you're there. You have the power. I'm scared shitless of the power. You have enough power you could light up the whole eastern seaboard. I can't say no to you. I'm afraid I'll report to practice in a body bag, and the thing is I don't care. I got where I am because I'm disciplined. I can delay gratification now for better in the future, but I can't when it comes to you.

"Jesus, Josephine, I'm a horny red-blooded guy. I'm not going to say no when some chick throws herself at me, especially not when some gorgeous, incredible girl sticks her tits in my face."

"Could you look at perhaps burning all this energy on lust now is taking away the desire for it in the future? You'll be so sexed out when you get there you won't be distracted by girls and can focus solely on football?"

"You make it sound so easy," he said and brought his hand up to cup her breast. He teased the nipple until it was hard and teased him back. It didn't help that JoJo turned her body slightly, so it was millimeters from his mouth.

He looked at it and the internal struggle was visible on his face. Youth and hormones ended the winner.

He stood up, grabbed her, and threw her over his shoulder. She let out a squeal and said, "What are you doing?"

"I'm going to fuck you. You're drunk with power, JoJo. I'm going to take advantage of it, and I have to fuck this out of you, too. Maybe if I bang you enough you won't want to have sex ever again, or at least until you graduate. That's all you need, walking around campus with this power. Guys are gonna hound you. Restraining orders will need to be issued. If I was smart, I'd take you home immediately and run the other way, but I can't. My fucking work ethic won't allow me not to finish something once I start it. It looks like it's going to be a busy July, JoJo."

He brought her back to his room and tossed her on the bed.

"Didn't you want to spank me? My ass was right there," JoJo said as she laughed.

"Not a bad idea," he answered and tackled her on the bed.

****

Alex took her home and told her he wasn't going to be around the next few days; he had a few things to take care of, and he'd give her a call. JoJo said sure, she wanted to catch up with Julie. He walked her to the door but didn't kiss her or leave.

"What's up?" JoJo asked him. "You seem like you have something on your mind."

"I do, but I haven't quite figured it out yet. Look, JoJo, I need to have some space. I think I might be becoming obsessed with you. Maybe see each other every other day. I need a little room to think. I count the minutes until I see you. That scares me."

"I wouldn't worry about that," she said to him. "I think maybe you're just feeling guilty. After all, you weren't raised to treat women like sex objects. You were raised in a nice family and to be respectful of others, including women. You were raised to be a gentleman, not some asshole who treats women like they're disposable. Maybe the fact I treat you like a sex object is the problem."

Alex smiled at that. "I'm a sex object. Me."

She laughed. "Stranger things have happened," she said, and she kissed him. He kissed back with hunger on his lips. Kissing her was a prelude to all the other things they did, and her kiss held the promise of a garden of hedonistic delights. Alex really had to go because if he stayed any longer, he would throw her on the ground and fuck her until her until his dick fell off.

"I gotta go, JoJo. Now." He let go of her and hurried to his car before he felt the power and his resolve melted like chocolate in the noonday sun.

JoJo sat around with her mom for breakfast, sometimes lunch and usually dinner but she didn't mind. She should have gotten a summer job but didn't. Her dad cooked dinner but didn't view it as a chore. He was a foodie, he loved all things food related. The PeeWee Herman cookie jar. His special wok pan. Mr. Montgomery always wanted to open a restaurant. He worked for about a week in a restaurant one summer helping out a friend and decided the restaurant business was for young people, people who could stay on their feet for hours on end and liked to stay up late.

He went back to his office job. Mr. Montgomery had no audience for his symphony of tastes, so JoJo and her mother had to eat these rich dishes. Alex came over and ate the leftovers. Mr. Montgomery finally found the perfect person in Alex to talk about his meals. He could talk endlessly to Alex about it solely as a consumer of food. The consistency of the demi glacé. The texture of the potatoes. Were the green beans green enough? Almond slivers not too thin? They would go on for hours.

****

She called Julie to check in and see how she was doing, and Julie said she was going to call her to see if she wanted to go to a party out at Red Pond, a local party site. This was probably their last party there. Once you move towards college this was one of the first traditions dropped. JoJo went and had a good time, plenty of people were happy to see her. JoJo looked across the bonfire and saw Alex. He saw her but didn't smile, and she didn't smile back. The flames blew up with a gust of wind, and once they settled, the airborne embers rode the air currents of heat upwards. When the fire died down and she could see where he was, the space was empty.

He called the next morning to make sure she got home okay. "Yeah sure," JoJo said. "I looked for you, but you left."

"What are you doing for lunch? I'd like to see you."

"What happened to you wanted some space? I saw you last night. I left you alone."

"I know. I didn't like it," Alex said. "It's stupid to put any more restrictions on this. It has an end date we are both aware of. It'll go how it goes and then end. Let's just enjoy this. I don't know if I'll survive it, but what a way to go."

"As long as you don't suffer a groin pull you should be fine."

Alex picked her up and had already stopped for lunch. Three submarine sandwiches. He wanted to eat at first, but he looked at her and pulled her into the house. He took her to the couch, said, "Come on," and pulled his shirt off. Next, he pulled her shirt off; they lunged for each other in a tangle of sleeves and limbs and tongues.

"JoJo," he said as he panted, "you are the most amazing woman I'll ever meet."

"You can't say that," JoJo told him. "You'll meet a whole bunch of women, all kinds of women, you've got the rest of your life. I can't be your peak. There's so much more ahead for you, including identical twin Swedish foreign exchange students."

He wanted to tell her she was the peak he could never do better than her. Alex knew she was wrong for him at Red Pond when he wanted to go over and pound whomever she was with. Being with JoJo was a full-time job. He needed a girl who didn't dominate him or his thoughts, but man, this summer with JoJo Montgomery consumed him, and he couldn't stay away. Again, clothes were scattered everywhere, and their naked bodies were fused together with sweat.

"What's today's date?" he asked her. "Is it August yet?"

"Not yet, Alex."

"I know. It's only lunchtime. I'll bring the sandwiches over." He jumped up. "What would you like to drink?" he asked her from the kitchen.

"Water's fine," she yelled as she picked up his shirt and put it on. She put on her undies and waited for Alex.

"Hey," he said. "That's my shirt." He handed over her sandwich, still in his boxers.

Alex sat down with his pile of sandwiches and gave her a bottle of water. They ate in silence, eating for him was just one more item on his to-do list. She respected his dedication and didn't bother him. She marveled at the way he just devoured those sandwiches. He caught her looking at him.

"What?"

"You have quite the appetite," JoJo told him.

"I do. Let's find out what you'll need to bring with you to school and do some shopping."

They spent the afternoon in Target, wandering the aisles. He put things in her cart he thought she needed or said she needed. He told her she should take advantage of someone who moved two brothers into dorms and had a certain expertise in this area. They laughed at each other. Alex kept saying it was stuff she needed because they were moving in together.

He took her home and carried her packages inside. Mr. Montgomery was home and glad to see him. He had a new dish he wanted to try, and Alex was the only one who would give him an honest appraisal of the recipe. Alex sat in the kitchen and indulged her father's passion. He stayed, ate, and reviewed. After which, he left and said he'd talk to her soon. He didn't want her to bother walking him to the car, and he drove off.

****

CHAPTER SIXTEEN

Alex called her later that night to say he was going to only be able to see her in the evenings. He found his dedication to training was influenced by her and he was slipping. JoJo understood completely.

"That's one more thing on the plus side. No pressure," Alex said.

"Hey. Focus. If you come, come in time for dinner. He keeps shoveling food at us and we can't take it anymore," JoJo reminded him.

"If you can't seduce me you want to feed me."

"Something like that," she said. "Come when you can. I'll see if he's set a menu, and you can pick out when you want to come over."

"Maybe we could walk the canal."

"Love to. Let me know."

Alex took a step back and she let him. JoJo thought he was one of those peel the band-aid off slowly kind of people, so he was detaching himself from her in little bites. They were physically together a few more times, but each time less intimate. He came over to say goodbye to her folks and thank Mr. Montgomery for all the calories, he was grateful for everyone and thanked her mom for putting up with him.

Alex asked JoJo to do something a couple of evenings before he left. She said sure. They went directly to his place, the mood a little deep and heavy.

"I won't be able to see you after tonight. All my time is committed before I go." Alex sounded kind of dazed. JoJo realized he needed a dose of self-confidence.

"Come on. Let's go lie on your bed and talk." He followed her into his room, or his room for the next few days and took a spot on his back. She lay on her side and traced the outline of something on his chest, and he'd have to tell her what it was she drew. The first couple were easy, a football and a cup. She outlined a heart. Alex grabbed her wrist and looked into her eyes, unsure what she was trying to tell him. After a few minutes she spoke.

"I have a few things I'd like to say to you. You spent a lot of time this summer helping me believe in myself again. I think what you need now is a pep talk."

"What?" he asked, surprised.

"You. You need to believe in yourself. You are smart, fast, and strong. There may be other Alexes, but not like you. They're not built like you, they're not as strong or fast as you, and they're not as smart as you. They don't understand the game like you do. You earned that scholarship. Never forget that. You're good. Real good. Get ready to play football." JoJo whispered in his ear.

"Could we do it one more time?" Alex asked. "I wasn't going to, I wanted to detox from you slowly, so I didn't go into withdrawal. I can't pass this up. This could be the last time or the last time for a long time. I'm going to miss you. You make me feel strong and invincible."

"You *are* strong and invincible. Fuck me, college boy," she commanded him. "Let's light this candle."

"Then shut up and quit telling me what to do," Alex ordered her.

Instead of a final blow-the-roof-off the place goodbye, it was quiet and sweet, tender and gentle. They both whispered words of encouragement to the other. By the time they were done they were both feeling good and strong and able to take on the unknown.

He took her home and walked her to the door.

"This is the last time we'll do this," Alex said and held her fingers.

"Yes, but you have other things you have to do."

"I don't know what to say. I can't say what I want to."

"Remember you're on your path, follow it," JoJo told him. "Someday, if we end up on the same path, who knows? But right now, you have a vision. That's where you should spend your energy. It's showtime. As for me, you spoiled me. I'm never going to find anybody like you. You have to go your way. I'll go mine. If it wasn't for you, I doubt I'd even have a path. I'd be home hiding under the bed. This is good. It's the way it's supposed to be. I wish you much success on your path. Be sure to enjoy yourself, Alex. You need things besides football."

He gave her a sweet kiss on the lips. "Goodbye, Josephine Montgomery."

"Goodbye, Alex Burton."

She watched him get into his car. He stayed until she was safely inside and then pulled out and drove away. She watched him from the door and felt the earth move beneath her feet. There was a shift happening to all of them. JoJo feared the hole he left would be too painful to fill, but she was going in the opposite direction changing everything herself. No Alex, no Julie.

****

JoJo's parents loaded her up and drove two hours east to her school, a state school, one of many. Freshmen arrived two days before the rest of campus returned. JoJo figured everyone was in the same boat. Nobody knew what they were doing so they all were pretty much equal. She had to be there by four on Thursday for freshman orientation. The next couple of days were filled with all kinds of activities designed to break the ice and acclimate the new students. She decided to have an open mind and do what was asked, as much as she wished she could stay in her room and read.

Her roommate was six feet tall and two hundred pounds. She wore denim overalls with rips everywhere, a black leather motorcycle jacket, and Doc Martens. She wore her hair spiky with bleached tips. Her name was Stacy, but she wanted to be called Stace. They hung out that first night wandering the campus, checking it all out. Stace was on the hunt for a guy. Not just any guy, one that was boyfriend material. They decided to go all out and fully engage in college life and see what happened.

They participated in every stupid mixer; they even went to the Science Club. They got into this ridiculously pretentious debate about whether there was life on other planets and alien life forms which might have made sense if she was high, but she wasn't. Her roommate thought she was hardcore because she was edgy, but these guys were intense. They bypassed edgy years ago.

There were clubs all over to cater to all sorts of special interests. What made you a loser in high school was embraced by others here. Science Club was open to all, especially pretty girls.

Stace had four guys ask for her number.

****

"Well, that was unexpected," her new roommate said.

"Yeah. It almost makes me wish I paid more attention to the periodic table of elements." JoJo said. "We should really do that, go to a new club like once a month. Something from the bulletin board. Something we would never do."

"Chess?" suggested Stace. "I saw a sign for that. Do you know how to play?"

"I think I know how to set up the board," offered JoJo.

"Let's try that next. Maybe some cute guys play chess."

95

They made their way downstairs where the Resident Authorities requested they meet.

They convened the freshman. They were playing SUNY trivia to introduce the class to their new surroundings. Stace won a prize, a navy college hoodie for knowing who the dean was, of all things, and Stace only knew because JoJo fed her the answer. They left and wandered around the dorm for a while but decided they were too tired to explore anymore. They had all day tomorrow and went back to their room to get some sleep. Both found it hard to unwind from the excitement of the day or the lumpy mattress they talked late into the night.

JoJo was happy with Stace. They became instant best friends. She was a little more worldly growing up on Long Island and spent many weekends exploring the city. She was tall, buxom, big assed and spiky haired bleached blond. She was loud and funny and gave people a lot of shit if they were in her way. She didn't mind taking the lead if JoJo got uncomfortable being out front. At Science Club it was just a meet and greet, but four guys wanted Stace's number, and it didn't matter to them her grasp of science stopped after the apple hit Sir Isaac Newton on the head.

After orientation, they bummed around some more. All the rest of the campus was due to move in on Saturday and Sunday, so they had plenty to look at in the cute guy department.

Sunday night they sat at dinner somewhat subdued; classes started the next day, and both were a little nervous. JoJo talked to Julie earlier to see how she liked school, and Julie had the same butterflies in her stomach. She wasn't too fond of her roommate. She treated Julie like an interloper when they were both in their room.

Julie had a right to half of the room but her roommate didn't see it that way. If Julie left even to get a soda from the machines her bed was covered with this other girl's shit. Julie told JoJo if the girl touched her closet space, she was a dead woman, and JoJo found that believable. She called her parents and checked in. She was finished with her calls. JoJo sat quietly after using the phone.

"What?" Stace asked her. "Homesick already?"

"I have someone I want to check in with but I'm not sure I should," JoJo said. "We said goodbye when he left a few weeks ago and I haven't heard from him, which was fine. That was the deal. He go do his thing and I do mine. He has a football scholarship and that's his priority."

"You didn't tell me you just broke up with somebody. Your high school sweetheart?"

"Only after dark," JoJo answered.

"What?! That needs explanation, JoJo," Stacy demanded.

"Well, we made a deal. He spent July trying to increase my self-esteem and for his trouble I let him fuck me," JoJo bluntly told Stace. She thought Stace didn't deserve to be the only badass in the room.

Stacy sat up. "You? You? Little Miss still waters run deep? No way. Prove it."

JoJo went through the photos in her bag. There were just a few of Alex and only one of the two of them, but it was a good one. Julie gave it to her. She was sitting at a picnic table, and he was standing next to her, his tee shirt in one hand, the other hand on JoJo's shoulder. She was looking up at him laughing.

"This guy," JoJo said and passed the picture over to Stace.

"This guy? The guy with no shirt on? Holy fuck! He was your high school boyfriend?"

"No. He was just a guy who thought he could help me. Just a good friend. I compensated him with sex. His body was unreal. I was very lucky to have someone like him in my corner. But yeah. He was a good friend when I needed one. Ugh. I can't believe I said it out loud. I should call him."

JoJo dialed his number. He answered after a few rings. "Hello?"

"Yes, hello? I'm calling for Alex Reeves. Is he available?"

"No. Are you particular about which Alex? My name's Alex. Alex *Burton.*"

"He's there? Alex Burton? He's my favorite Alex anyway. How's he doing?"

"He's exhausted. He's too tired to talk to anybody but JoJo Montgomery."

"I'll get her. Alex Burton? That you?" she asked. "How's it going? Football kicking your ass?"

"And how. You were right. I'd be too tired to have a girlfriend. I sure enjoyed it, though. I have the memories. I'm glad you called and adjusting to college life isn't too hard for you. I was thinking about you and hoped you were doing okay. Sorry, I didn't call. I thought I'd have more free time, but it's booked solid. We're booked solid."

"I understand. Just checking up on you. No need to worry about me. I think things here will be fine. Play smart, Alex, don't get hurt. Take care of yourself. Goodbye, Alex Burton."

"Goodbye, Josephine Montgomery."

JoJo quickly adapted to college life and Stace filled the spot Alex vacated. It was an almost seamless transition. If he came home for Thanksgiving, she'd be at Stace's. Stace came to JoJo's for Christmas and met her brother and his new fiancée, Jordan.

It was a surprise to everyone, but it seemed they lived together anyway so at least he put a ring on it. *How noble,* JoJo thought. JoJo had to leave on the 26th to be back at school for an experimental theater production they participated in, Alex arrived on the 28th for New Year's and missed her by a few days. He was sorry he missed her and left a message that said as much. She responded, "Next time," but there never was.

After freshman year JoJo and Stace stayed on campus for the summer and got a sublet.

They planned on leasing it for their sophomore year. They got jobs, she at the bookstore and Stace at a group home. Soon, the event that ruins most female friendships occurred. Stace met someone and fell in love. She looked high and low for a boyfriend, and eventually she found one.

It happened just like that. She met someone at the library, went to a coffee shop and by the end of the afternoon they finished each other's sentences. JoJo wanted to gag.

"Look," Stace said. "I know you wanted to live in the dorms, so why don't you just go ahead and get a single? Mike's going to take your room here."

"This the first I'm hearing about it. I thought we were leasing this place and rooming together sophomore year," JoJo said, confused.

"We were, but since Mike will be around here all the time, I figured you'd rather not deal with all this. Just get your own place."

"It's kinda late notice to get a single," JoJo told her. "You are kicking me out of my own room for him. You are picking a guy over *me.*"

"It's not like that."

"It's exactly like that."

"Well, do you mind?" Stace had the nerve to ask.

"Well, I wouldn't stay here now," JoJo told her and walked out.

She went over to student housing. She begged for a single. They had very few left but since she wasn't a freshman and she could put the deposit down now, she could have it. She notified her mother of the charges.

"Are you okay?" her mom asked her. "This was really sudden. Did you know about this beforehand?"

"No. I'm stunned, but I guess I'm not surprised. That's what we did most of the time; try to find her a man. But the way she said it was in my best interest to leave. How dare she? Technically she should have moved out and in with him, but it was easier to cut me out. Julie always had a boyfriend and the guy had to date both of us. I don't know, Mom. I have to start over making friends. I only hung around with Stace last year."

"Are you going to be all right? That was a shitty thing to do to a friend."

"Yeah, mom, I'll be okay. I guess I have a pretty good idea of what I need to do for myself here, anyway. I'm here to get an education, not make a ton of friends, and I have a single, so I won't be stuck with a freshman roommate. I'll be fine. I'm good at making friends." JoJo assured her mother. "I'm excited. My own room. This is brand new enough. I'm looking forward to this."

"Some advice. Pick better people," her mom said. "I bet it's hard to find better people. Don't give up. They're out there."

JoJo had really grown up a lot. When she saw Stace she was friendly but distant. Stace had finally come up for air and realized how far away from her JoJo had evolved. She missed JoJo and found her getting pizza for lunch.

"Oh, JoJo," Stace said. "Where have you been? I've missed you."

"You do?" JoJo responded. "Do you really? We don't have much in common anymore. I don't think we ever did, once you found a boyfriend. Anyway, I'm late for study group. Call me sometime, maybe I'll be free." JoJo turned and walked away.

One thing she had finally learned is people are ultimately in charge of their own choices. She stopped internalizing everyone else's actions. If JoJo thought about it, the main thing she felt was loneliness. She had made some friends, some good friends, but it was almost like she suffered delayed homesickness.

Last year she experienced everything new with Stace. Now she had to rediscover it all over again alone. JoJo missed Julie. She missed Alex. She felt so far away from everyone. She wanted to graduate and be done with school. *It's too bad*, she thought to herself. *Everyone else considered their high school and college days were the best time of their lives. Not me. Every year I get a little bit lonelier.*

****

99

JoJo came home for the summer. What many kids figured was the absolutely lowest entry position to be had, working at Coney Island scooping ice cream, JoJo was ecstatic to have the job. She was the oldest employee on the summer crew, and the owners paid her more because JoJo figured out the schedule and saved the owner the headache. She ran on autopilot, it was a no brainer. She looked up to see who was next.

"May I help you?" she asked the next person.

"Why, if it isn't Josephine Montgomery!" someone said.

"Oh. Hey. Alex! How are you? Home for the summer?" she asked him, momentarily stunned. She hadn't seen him in a couple of years. He smiled that smile that she thought he smiled just for her, but she realized that he just had a great smile.

"What can I get for you?" JoJo asked and smiled back.

"JoJo. I just want to introduce you to my girlfriend, this is Kate Behnke. Kate, an old friend from high school. This is JoJo."

"Hi, Kate, nice to meet you. You picked yourself one of the good ones here." She gestured at Alex. "What can I get you?" She passed their order through the window and waved off his money. He protested but put it back in his pocket when she said she did it to welcome Kate.

"We don't want her getting a bad impression of your hometown," JoJo said.

****

The fall came and she returned to school. She met someone her junior year, they dated but nothing came from it. They liked each other okay, but it gradually fizzled out. He did a semester in Italy and found someone new. JoJo found she didn't miss him too much.

She went through doing her work, kept her head down, and made it through her junior year. JoJo seriously debated not returning home for the summer, she thought she couldn't possibly go back there and scoop ice cream one more summer, but Ritchie was getting married, and she was a bridesmaid, so she had to return.

Julie was home this summer for a bit. She stopped going to school. She hit the nanny Powerball Jackpot. Her nanny job was for two little girls. Their parents were a couple of famous rock stars and lived a vagabond rock and roll lifestyle. Julie watched them while their parents went on tour. They toured often.

Julie homeschooled them into bright, engaging girls. The parents had the storybook well behaved children with absolutely no effort. The girls liked to learn about everything so they said intelligent things the parents could brag about even if they had no idea what they were talking about.

Their parents were proud of them in public, grateful Julie was able to counterweight their influence and groom them to be polite and have manners. Julie wrote her own ticket, and the parents were eternally grateful for Julie's influence. She had the month of July off. JoJo and Julie hung out like they did in high school, in their childhood bedrooms.

"Yeah," Julie said. "These girls are no effort at all. It's like they'll grow up to be Republicans or something. That would be the only way to rebel. Be clean. Live clean. The parents had their own freewheeling life of drugs and debauchery. The next time we go to Bali I'll tell them I hired extra help and you come. Pick a subject. Tutor them in that. We'll have a blast."

"Let me get through this wedding and I'd love to. I hope it's not too bad. I won't know anyone."

"Ray's the best man, you know. You'll know him," Julie informed her. "Oh. Yay."

"He asks about you," Julie teased JoJo. "Every time I see him. After all this time, JoJo, he still asks about you."

"I wish I understood the dynamics of our relationship. We have this rubber band thing going on. I go back and forth with him. Sometimes I enjoy him, I'm glad to see him, but then he pisses me off and I never want to see him again. I think I sorta had a crush on him at one time when I was growing up. I think he thinks I still do."

"Well, do you?" Julie asked.

"Now? Ew. Like I said before, yay. What's wrong with him? He only knows me as Ritchie's little sister. I don't even remember having a conversation with him," JoJo lied, not unimpressed and maybe a little a little flattered he still asked about her.

"Well," Julie pointed out, "if you married him, we'd be sisters."

"I'd rather my parents adopt you," JoJo told her.

"I think you should reconsider Ray. There's always been some weird tension between you two. Maybe he's grown up and he's not such a dick anymore. Perhaps you've grown up a bit and you're not so annoying."

"Huh," said JoJo. "Ray? I don't know. The last time I saw him I was furious at him."

"See? He inspires emotion. It's negative, but it could change,"

****

Ritchie graduated and became an accountant, working at his father's firm. He had gone to school out of state and traveled a bit, but it seemed home was the best choice to live and raise a family and here he was, back where he started. He was going to marry the very pretty Jordan Meeks. She was a teacher, her first year as a second-grade teacher happened to be here. She was from a small family, and they decided to hold the wedding here. JoJo thought it odd she was willing to settle here. *How boring,* JoJo thought. *I guess when you fall in love you'll live in an igloo if that's what he wants.*

The wedding weekend came, and the first time everyone was present was at the event was the groom's side hosted, a rehearsal dinner. It was outdoors and held at a winery. The actual rehearsal was at a church with a long aisle. It was a very traditional ceremony, with an impressive display among the stained-glass windows. JoJo thought, *wait a second, Ray's supposed to be here.* She looked around and saw him. JoJo smiled because she was glad to see him, she was glad to see anybody. He interpreted he was the cause of her smile, the result of finding him. He made his way over.

"JoJo! How are you? You look great." He exclaimed with a kiss on her cheek. He took her hand but backed up, giving her a wide berth.

"Ray!" She squeezed his hand, signaling her joy. "You'll look so grown up in your tuxedo."

"You, too." He laughed. "I have to go up front now, but we'll catch up later."

The rehearsal was uneventful, and it was on to the party. It was a beautiful evening for the outdoor wine bar. She was standing off to the side with her glass of wine when Ray approached.

"I'm here to make small talk and otherwise entertain you," he informed her.

"Well, thank you for that," she said back.

"I have to tell you, JoJo, how gorgeous you are. I can't believe it's you. You beat me at jump rope. That still hurts," he remembered. "You really were something, JoJo."

"What happened? Did I die?" JoJo sounded peeved.

"Relax. I don't know the present-day JoJo well enough to know if she's still really something," he explained.

"Oh, she's something all right. She's really something," JoJo said. It felt good to be the center of someone's attention, even if it was only Ray.

Ray spent the evening tending to her every need. Whatever she needed, he got it. He laughed at what she said whether it was funny or not. He switched seats with someone to sit next to her. He got her more wine which made her silly and giggly.

She told him she couldn't drink anymore if she wanted to be functional the next day, so he got her water. He leaned into her all evening, and he didn't leave her anytime to speak to anyone else. He gave her a ride home. He walked her to the door, wished her goodnight and left.

The day of the wedding a suite of rooms was reserved for them at the hotel for the girls to prepare. She had her nails, hair and makeup professionally done. Her dress, the color of champagne, altered to fit her like a second skin. The dress was sleeveless, and as a gift to her attendants Jordan gave them all these boho chunky necklaces that popped against the muted colors of the bridal party.

JoJo liked Jordan just fine but decided she might actually grow to love her because she picked that jewelry. JoJo knew she was going for understated elegance and that jewelry was anything but. It was big, chunky and a statement that Jordan wasn't as vanilla and white bread as everyone assumed. JoJo looked at her reflection in the mirror, stunned. That girl who looked like a model was her. *What a waste,* she thought, *looking like this and nobody to admire me. Well, Ray. There is Ray.*

****

The wedding went off without a hitch, not a cloud in the sky nor a raindrop dared ruin the day. The reception had a great band and an open bar held at the golf course. The poor groomsman she had been paired with got trampled on by Ray in his attempt to romance JoJo.

She had a couple of glasses of wine and that may be how Ray found a sliver of an opportunity to flatter and dote on JoJo. They went outside to watch all the frat bros wrestle each other on the putting green. Ray was never more than a few feet away from her. He had learned a bit about women since he saw her last. He could feel her craving for romance, for JoJo to be the center of someone's universe.

The reception was a raging success. JoJo had a bit more to drink than usual, but not an obnoxious buzz but a "whoops, I think I stood up to soon" buzz. She had misplaced her shoes, rather somebody moved them. They started to hurt her feet during dinner; she took them off and they were missing. JoJo looked under tables while Ray watched. She went into the coat room and bent over, looking for them when she knocked her head and stumbled. "Oof," she said, but somebody caught her. It was Ray. She started to giggle and being a bit tipsy may be the only explanation for why when Ray kissed her, she kissed him back.

****

She pulled back for a second; her mind went *whoa*, but Ray held her tight. JoJo was filled with longing for someone. Someone undefinable. Someone like Alex. Someone who was lonely like she was. Someone to share inside jokes. Someone who would tell her to relax, it wasn't her job. Someone to take care of her. Someone to build a life and family with and someone to keep her company. *Was that too much?* She thought, but Ray hit that nerve when he kissed her again. Maybe what she wanted was right in front of her, or maybe she was just drunk, but when Ray kissed her again, she kissed him right back.

Someone called Ray. It was time for the toast. He ushered JoJo towards the dining room, but she veered off.

"I have to go to the bathroom."

"You're not coming in to hear my toast?"

"I need to go now. I'll be right out. I'll hear your toast."

She left him standing there when another usher called him inside. He went to the head table and made his toast glasses raised, and champagne sipped. Ray saw her in the back with a glass, but he didn't know if she heard his toast. He was mildly annoyed. JoJo didn't have to use the restroom right that second. She could have held it.

JoJo caught a ride home with her parents, it was long after cake and coffee. Ray wanted her to stay but she passed. More than once, Ray wished she'd at least think about him and what he wanted first, but she didn't. Sunday afternoon he stopped over to say goodbye to her family and her specifically. He asked her to walk him out, so she did.

"I just didn't want to say goodbye in front of everyone," Ray confessed. "I just wanted to say I really had a great time at Ritchie's wedding because of you. Thank you, JoJo. You are so beautiful. Such a sweetheart. Maybe our paths will cross again. I hope so."

He kissed her cheek and left for the airport. His behavior confused her. He wasn't his usual pushy self. He was content to leave it where it was. That wasn't like him at all. Maybe she wasn't the only one that grew up.

The summer ended and the senior year started. It seemed time sped up, graduation and employment were on a collision course right in front of her. She attended a number of career fairs and decided on a position as customer service representative at a medium-sized company. It was located outside of Boston. She knew a girl from Boston, she had planned on returning there after graduation so they located a flat they could afford close to public transportation.

****

CHAPTER SEVENTEEN

Graduation came, and that was that. Four years gone by in a poof! It wasn't like high school where you spent the summer in one long goodbye, in a holding pattern waiting for the next chapter to begin. After she graduated college, she spent one week at home and then off to Boston. Her roommate was a nurse and worked odd shifts so they rarely saw each other. JoJo liked Boston the only problem was she was lonely. She didn't know anyone in Boston. JoJo worked in an office full of women. It seemed they each had someone in mind for her. Just like her freshman year in college, she decided to be open to new experiences, even one involving an unfamiliar man. She didn't have any opportunities at work to come across eligible men and she was at the mercy of her office mates.

There was Jason Burke, Melanie in accounting's stepson. He went by Burke. He was very nice looking, in wonderful shape. He was in training for a triathlon, the hallowed Iron Man. He obsessed over the menu and the caloric intake. Burke obsessed over her caloric intake, too. JoJo went to a gym to work out for the health benefits but was by no means committed to the level he was. He tried to encourage her to get more into it, Burke extolled the virtues of a runner's high. JoJo remained unmoved. She ordered chocolate cheesecake for dessert. They only went out once.

Bridget, in administrative support candidate was her divorced son Oliver. He moved home after his divorce. His wife kept the house, the kids, half of his 401k and his dog. He couldn't afford two places, so he had to move back in with his parents. He had a government job as a drone at the federal building downtown. They met for a drink after work. He was there before she was, early enough to put away two martinis. He had two more while she had a glass of wine. He was going to call a cab and go to another bar and invited her to come along but she passed. JoJo wondered if after he paid his bar tab he'd ever have enough for his own place.

She met Colin on her own. She was bringing her garbage can to the curb as he was walking his dog, a golden retriever named Molly. He introduced himself and asked her to come and walk his dog with him. He promised Molly was a good girl and knew how to sit and stay. JoJo thought he was funny. They walked by her flat a couple of times a week and invited her along. JoJo thought he was kind and sweet, he had possibilities.

He also had a couple of kids with a few different women. Usually, his phone rang two or three times, and he spent their time together on the phone with an enraged ex because he was late with his child support. Too much for her, and they parted as friends. She decided to take a break from dating. She joined a new gym and went to the library often. She kept herself busy and overall considered herself happy.

She wished she had a yard, even a crummy yard. She could grow succulents in the tiers, filled in with topsoil, should she ever get out of Boston.

****

JoJo got a call from Ray. He was in Boston on business and hoped she could make time to meet him for dinner. JoJo was so excited to deviate from the everyday grind she enthusiastically said yes. If Ray misconstrued her delight at his invitation as her delight that he was the man who issued it, she was unaware. JoJo was in a good mood, smiling, warm and inviting. She met Ray at the restaurant. They greeted each other with hugs and cheek kisses.

The hostess showed them to their table and took their drink order. They laughed and chatted about small inconsequential things. The drinks came and she left the menus. Ray and JoJo ordered, and things quieted down.

"What brings you to Boston, Ray?" JoJo asked him.

"Sales conference. Trade show. Boring corporate stuff. How's Boston treating you?"

"Oh, all right, I guess. The job's fine. More than fine. I never figured I would move back home if given a choice," she confided. "But I think I would. I'd like to bring donuts over to my parents and have coffee on a Sunday morning. It's probably different for you. You've been gone a lot longer, so you're used to it. I know companies want you to relocate so all you'll know is work, and that's all you do."

"You're not wrong," he admitted.

"You probably made a ton of money in real estate. You're rich," JoJo said.

"Again, you're not wrong," Ray repeated.

"Why are you here? Why aren't you on an island somewhere marinating your liver in top shelf booze?"

"I'm not finished quite yet with the business side of things. I'll see where it takes me." Ray talked a lot about his business, and she nodded her interest in the right places.

His voice was soothing and warm. She could listen to it all night, but she remembered she had to be up tomorrow. She abruptly stopped him. She enjoyed dinner, but she had to go. She had to be up early in the morning for work. "I'm sorry, Ray, I completely forgot how long you've known me. I was always 'Ritchie's little punk sister,' I wish I could stay longer, but I can't. Next time. For sure."

"Oh," said Ray. "I come here every once in a while, so maybe next time." He got up and helped her stand. "Let me walk you out front," he said and took her arm. Ray waited with her until the cab came and opened the door to help usher her inside. She looked up to thank him; he grabbed her and gave her a long kiss goodbye. He waved as the cab drove away and took her home.

Huh. Ray. That's a good one. she thought. *It's good to see him, though.*

They had a few additional meet ups. JoJo didn't consider their encounters as dates, but she was deluding herself if she thought Ray felt the same way. They were dates to him, and she knew it.

The next time they came across each other was the following Christmas at Julie's house.

The family had an open house on Christmas Eve. Ritchie and Jordan were there, and Julie's flavor of the month. She never showed up with the same guy twice. This guy's name was Jake and was a poet. He had that hipster corduroy blazer with leather elbow patches and scraggly facial hair.

"Hi, JoJo," Ray said. "Merry Christmas."

"Merry Christmas to you, Ray," JoJo wished him.

"You look lovely as always." Ray had a big grin on his face. "Here, JoJo, let me get you a glass of wine."

He hung around her the rest of the evening; he made sure her glass was never empty. JoJo got loose and giggly and kept touching Ray. He liked her like this. Otherwise, she was too uptight and needed to relax. Now her smile was big and her embrace wide, plenty of room for him. Ray brought her to the doorway and pointed up towards the bundle of greenery.

He grabbed her hands. "Mistletoe," and he kissed her until she forgot who was doing the kissing. Ray let go of her hands, and she threw her arms around his neck. It just felt so good to connect with someone, someone who wanted to connect with her. JoJo kept kissing him even though it was Ray.

Things have changed a bit since that Christmas party. She went back to Boston, and Ray went back to Denver. She received an occasional email from Ray, not very often the only difference being she was more likely to respond. Ray forwarded on to her a lead for a new job. The company he worked for had two divisions, consumer products and medical products. He was on the consumer side, and the job was on the medical side, but her customer account experience might make it a good fit for her.

JoJo just wanted to get out from behind her desk. This job required her to travel a bit and gave her a car. It was also more money and the opportunity for team-based compensation bonuses, so if the team did well, she did, too. JoJo wasn't sure about it, but she certainly had nothing good going on where she was, so she took a leap of faith and changed jobs.

It turned into a good move for her, she could afford to move outside the city and get her own place. It was a nice flat in an older established neighborhood. She should probably have investigated a complex that catered to a younger crowd, but she had a front porch in the shade of a maple tree perfect for reading a book on a hot summer day. It was located in an old mansion on Main Street that got carved up into rental units before the historic registry could deny them the ability. She had the front bottom one bedroom, unit 1A. JoJo loved it. She liked her new job.

Meeting new friends still wasn't any easier, but having her own place to putter around filled in any time she was feeling lonely. Ray texted her he was going to be in Boston at the end of the month, and he knew she'd moved. He was hoping to drive to where she was so he could see her new place. Sure, was her answer, nobody had seen it yet and she wanted to show it off.

He pulled up and got out. It was the one on the bottom with the cascade of flowers down the porch. It had a very small patch of yard up front. No other house had any flowers. It looked like a sad little neighborhood. Her house was the only one that offered any hope. Ray went up the stairs and rang the bell. He heard the door unlock and then it opened.

"Ray! Welcome! C'mon in." JoJo smiled and opened the door, letting him in. He crossed over the threshold into the living space. It was nice and bright. An eclectic display of many genres decorated the place and he could see she touched everything and had a say in where it was placed. JoJo looked happy here. He told her so and was glad she was happy.

"There's a nice little place for dinner a few blocks over, and it was a beautiful night, so we really should walk," JoJo suggested.

It was a nice night for a walk, and she put her arm through his. Ray hugged her closer on the walk home, and even though it took half a bottle of the house red, she invited him in. She let him come in, and she let him stay. JoJo woke up with a splitting headache. She rolled over and looked at Ray and decided that was a problem she'd worry about a few days from now. All she could do now was elbow Ray until he woke up.

"What?" he mumbled, "what is it?"

"I'm calling in sick." She grabbed some sheets, tucked herself in, and thought, *I hope this is a bad dream; I hope when I wake up, this headache is gone, and so is Ray, and I hope I don't vomit,* but she passed out for a while and fell back asleep.

****

JoJo awoke sometime later to the smell of coffee and the sound of bacon frying; she must have been past the vomiting stage because she woke up hungry. JoJo also woke up naked. She looked on the floor for her sweats and a tee shirt, got dressed, and went to brush her teeth and hopefully remove the fur that coated the inside of her mouth. She went into the kitchen to see what Ray was cooking up, literally.

"Hey, Ray, what are you doing? Don't you have to go to work?" JoJo said.

"It's Saturday, Jose. We don't work weekends. I'm cooking you breakfast before I go," he said as he pointed to a chair. "How do you take your coffee? Let me get you a cup."

JoJo sipped her coffee and watched Ray. He looked quite comfortable in the kitchen. He was making pancakes because he remembered she didn't like eggs.

JoJo studied him. What exactly was Ray's purpose? Was he looking to score with her or something more? Ray already scored last night, so if that's what he wanted, why was he still here? Why was he so happy?

"What's up, Ray? You're in an awfully good mood," JoJo probed.

"Yes, yes I am," he answered. "You know how you get something in your head, and over time it becomes exaggerated, and then you finally achieve it, it's often a lot less than you thought?"

"Yeah, I think so." Such deep thought made her nauseous.

"Well, that happened to me. I realized something I desired for so long came true, but time didn't diminish it, in fact it's way better than I ever imagined."

"Oh," was all JoJo said.

Her headache made it hard to process what he was saying, but she knew deep down he was talking about her. He placed a plate of bacon in front of her and smiled. In spite of herself she smiled back. She picked up a perfectly cooked slice of bacon. Ray. Good old Ray. *Hang in there, Ray. Be the last man standing,* she thought. He brought the pancakes and syrup over and took the seat across from her.

"Feeling better?" he asked her.

"Yes, but you didn't have to make breakfast," she told him.

"I wanted to. Pancakes and bacon. Your favorite, JoJo," he said proudly.

"Yes, Ray. Yes, they are. Thank you," she said. "I hope you're hungry because I can't eat all this."

"Thank you. I think I'll be able to make a dent in it," Ray said.

It was a very pleasant breakfast, Ray was an engaging guest. He talked, asked questions to pull out answers from her, and avoided uncomfortable pauses. She took another look at Ray from a more mature perspective, as a woman would a man. Ray was attractive, or rather, not unattractive.

He was about six feet tall with a broad back and strong shoulders smattered with freckles. He had a nice smile and thick rust colored hair. He was a redhead when he was younger but had aged out of it in adulthood. He had good bone structure and a strong jaw. He looked healthy like he took care of himself, and by extension he would take care of you. He'd probably be a great dad. JoJo was trying to remember why she disliked him so much when she was younger. She thought of all the guys that teased them growing up, Ray might have been the cruelest.

He cleaned up the kitchen and swept the floor.

"You really know your way around a kitchen," JoJo said admiringly.

"Capable bachelor," he responded. "I have to run and catch my flight. I really enjoyed being with you JoJo. Every minute of it," he told her as he grabbed her and kissed her goodbye. *His kisses needed work. He comes on too strong,* she thought.

111

They fell into a routine. Usually, one Friday each month he would come and fix her dinner. After the kitchen was cleaned up, they'd take a walk, usually holding hands and head back inside her house, and they watched late night TV. She worked on kissing with Ray, she was teaching him to slow down. Once he got the hang of what she was trying to impress upon him, it was like a light bulb went off.

Ray discovered the pleasure of a kiss. A kiss in and of itself was a thing of beauty. It was not step 1 in 'the how to get laid' handbook. JoJo taught him tenderness and patience, something he needed to learn if he wanted to kiss her. Ray's prior approach to kissing was something that needed to be crossed off the list in order to advance to the next level of intimacy when in reality it was a roadblock. It was the emotional buy-in to the next level. If a girl isn't impressed by the way she's kissed, not much else will impress her.

JoJo found men altogether confusing. Alex, who was so into her he didn't care what kind of prior experience she had, was willing to scrap everything he knew to be on the same page as her, whereas Ray thought his rules were written in stone, and it was the obligation of the woman to accommodate them. This concerned JoJo. He was inflexible in many areas. She thought about her being alone at home, him the boss at work meant he probably thought he'd be the boss at home, too. *That's got to go right there,* she thought, *and soon.*

In the morning, Ray and JoJo often made slow intimate love, after which he'd cook breakfast. Initially, the first few times, her judgment might have been impaired by alcohol, but with her guidance, he turned into a thoughtful and generous lover. Ray had a thoughtful and funny side; he used to rip cartoons he thought she'd find funny out of magazines and bring them home to her and stick them on the fridge. Ray would always be there on Friday night. Ray clipped recipes he thought they could try. JoJo enjoyed the feel of a man next to her; he would leave without her prompting him to go. She helped to dial back his personality; he sometimes forgot he wasn't trying to sell her something. Same in bed.

Ray just needed not to come on so strong. Over time, JoJo developed a tenderness for Ray. He knew he had a tendency to steamroll his agenda, and JoJo softened Ray. She went with him to important family functions, and it was nice that she was already familiar with his parents and sister. Her family felt the same about him.

The natural order of things dictated either their break-up or an evolution to a deeper level.

She convinced herself it was love. With her guidance, Ray developed into a proper boyfriend. JoJo still needed to point out where he went over the line, he to his credit, attempted to modify his behavior to make her happy. That was really all he wanted, Ray said, to make her happy.

When he proposed, he gave the ring to the manager who put it on a piece of chocolate cake. The staff came out singing "Happy Birthday." She was confused, it wasn't her birthday. When she saw the ring, she gasped. Ray got down on one knee and asked her to spend the rest of her birthdays with him. Sometimes, Ray could be a real romantic.

JoJo took a look around her life. She was almost thirty, she lived alone, and it looked like that would be the trajectory of her life. If not Ray, then who? Nobody else was lining up outside her door. If she was going to get a family, if she wanted to build a life bigger than herself, she needed a partner. JoJo was lonely, she knew it would take some work to get Ray into proper husband shape, but he was willing, and the love he had for her showed out of his eyes, so she said yes.

She wanted a small, intimate wedding. Ray didn't care. He just wanted to marry her. They went to the courthouse and held a big dinner afterwards. Julie was her witness. Ritchie, his. If her mother felt bad that JoJo didn't give her the big white dress mother of the bride moment, she kept it to herself. Personally, Mrs. Montgomery wasn't overly fond of Ray. The word smarmy came to her mind. She thought JoJo settled, but she kept her feelings to herself.

They had a certain problem about where to live. She figured things wouldn't change, nothing about his life was changing, why did she have to upend hers? Ray was happy he locked her down and said she could live anywhere she wanted. Ray said they'll know when it's time to change things, so he mostly lived with her on weekends. He still kept his place with all his things because her place was pretty small, and he wanted to not make a big deal out of her giving up her place. She loved that little apartment, and it made her happy. Ray, despite his pushy and aggressive behavior, wanted above all else for JoJo to be happy and content with the things in her life.

The company they both worked for was undergoing staff realignment and a change in management philosophy. It was decided to bring both market segments under one roof. Ray received a huge salary bump and moved up the food chain, management wise. Unfortunately, now they both worked for the same division in the same company. Human Resources considered since she now directly reported to Ray it was a violation of policy. It wasn't true she directly reported to Ray, her boss's boss did, but ultimately required a separation agreement that meant JoJo had to accept a severance package and resign.

She was furious and wanted to sue, but she found out she was pregnant. Since it didn't matter where he was based as long as it was in the Eastern US, he moved her back home. He didn't want her to be alone, especially with a new baby, since his travel schedule was heavy and erratic. Having her mother nearby would be a huge help. He was glad things happened like they did. Ray believed she would sue the company and cost them their jobs if being pregnant hadn't distracted her.

****

JoJo found herself leaving her home, her little apartment, her favorite place in the world, the place she always felt safe and happy, with apprehension. She found losing her job to be a sock in the gut she never expected, and she missed the work and the people. JoJo was disconnected from every positive thing she created for herself. It took all she had not to cry over all she lost only to become an incubator for a child who didn't seem like it was all that happy either.

Pregnancy did not agree with JoJo. She was sick all the time, and when she wasn't sick, she was ravenously hungry only to vomit it all back up. It was a smart thing Ray brought her back to settle where she had her mother. She could take care of JoJo and the baby. That would work. JoJo felt like Ripley in Alien. She felt like a cruel joke had been played upon her.

Pregnancy finally quieted its presence in her sixth month only to have her legs swell up so big she couldn't wear shoes. She couldn't wear slippers. She was genuinely barefoot and pregnant.

When weekends came and Ray was home, he went into full-on domestic mode. He wanted to hire a cleaning lady to ease the burden on JoJo. Ray rubbed her back; he propped her feet up above her heart. JoJo wanted to get up and move around. She wished when she told Ray she wanted to take a walk she insisted, rather than let him tell her no, she needed to lie down. It seemed no matter her idea Ray couldn't leave it be. If she had flowers she put the vase in the middle of the table, he would take them and put them in a "better" vase. If she put a few decorative candles out, he moved them to a different spot so they wouldn't be in the way. JoJo was too busy feeling like shit carrying this alien baby to fight it out with Ray over a pair of candlesticks.

These are the power struggles all married couples go through to help define the roles within the marriage that solidify the foundation on which to build a future. JoJo felt their marriage skipped this important step, but her life was out of her control, and she was too tired to challenge the forces that made it so.

She went with Ray at first to look at houses, but he found it annoying she wanted to buy every house they looked at. The two things she wanted, a good school district and to be located near her parents were simple enough to satisfy, but Ray felt they needed "more." He felt like he could provide more, and he did. JoJo's solid middle-class background didn't want more. They wanted enough, and if you wanted more you went out and got it for yourself and people considered you a showoff. Ray told her he could handle the house hunting and she should stay home with her feet up. JoJo was more than willing to let Ray buy a house. She asked him to rein it in. Not too much to maintain, she requested.

"You just put your feet up and prepare to be amazed," he said as he kissed her goodbye.

He picked a nice house in a good neighborhood in her chosen school district ten minutes from her parents. It had a first-floor master and bath, two bedrooms, and another full bath. It had an unfinished upper level with a bath, something for when they had teenagers and needed more room. It was exactly the kind of house a growing family needed. It was on a safe cul-de-sac where their future kids could ride their future bikes.

"You did good, Ray." JoJo sniffled and kissed him for his choice.

He had hired all the movers, and they would consolidate two households and bring it all back, and they'd have to decide things, but right now it was the bare minimum. They put everything in a storage unit and only used big things like beds, sofas, tables and chairs. Ray told her when she was no longer pregnant, she could take her time going through their things in storage to create the house of her dreams or toss it all out and start over. The house was a blank canvas ready for her to turn into a warm, inviting home.

****

115

CHAPTER EIGHTEEN

Julie explored a different path. She never did finish college. She was a nanny hired to create a sense of normalcy in the swamp of a rock and roll lifestyle for two small girls. The parents were chart topping musicians, constantly touring. The family adored her, but the girls were older now and going to boarding school. She still had her place in the family's New York apartment; they liked her to be around on holidays, but otherwise, there wasn't much need for her. They still had her on the payroll. She was excited JoJo had moved back home. Julie came home to hang around with her best friend and now sister or sister-in-law. Julie was in awe of JoJo's pregnancy and fascinated by every aspect of it.

"I can't believe you've got a baby in there!" she said as she poked JoJo's belly.

"Stop!" JoJo replied, pushing Julie's hand away. "You'll wake it! Don't wake the baby!"

"I can't believe you don't want to know what it is," Julie moaned. "What if it's a boy? Are you gonna call it Ray? If it's a girl, can you name her Julie?"

"No and no." JoJo laughed. "Have your own baby."

"I can't believe you married Ray! You'll probably have a whole bunch of ginger babies!" Julie teased.

"Can't happen. My Italian trumps your Irish any day."

"I'm trying to remember tenth grade biology. Is being a redhead a dominant or recessive trait? Besides, you're only half Italian."

"Don't bother, Julie. You skipped most of tenth grade biology. You skipped most of the tenth grade."

"Speaking of school, I can't believe you didn't go to the reunion. Alex Burton said to tell you hello."

At the mention of Alex's name, JoJo burst into tears. Even if it wasn't love, it was good. JoJo couldn't believe she could still feel him, hear him, taste him after all these years. She cried at mushy TV commercials. The memory of Alex on his mission to rehab her was one she held onto tightly, inside where nobody knew, but tears popped out at the thought of him. Plenty of times when she felt low, she would think of him, his kindness and his belief in her.

JoJo was embarrassed she was so needy and felt like she let him down. Alex took her as far as he could, and JoJo never went any further alone. She felt like she was such a failure. JoJo knew Alex would tell her she was full of shit, that she was perfect the way she was, and stop thinking that way.

"Oh, JoJo, oh," Julie wrapped her arms around her oldest friend. "It's okay, it's okay," she said soothingly. Julie felt JoJo relax into her. She calmed herself and sniffled. She pushed back but didn't pull away.

"Man, these pregnancy hormones are one wild ride." JoJo exhaled.

Since it was the weekend Ray was home and doing his chores. JoJo used to help him by finding all the tools required and prepping everything, he'd come and pound the nail in and then leave. She'd pick up and put away the hammer until the next time. At this late stage in her pregnancy, she took up more space than usual but wasn't any more help.

Ray was putting together the crib, and she felt the least she could do was listen to him carp about it. JoJo sat in the rocker, a gift from her mom. She included one of those hemorrhoid pillows. Ray said it was proof positive her mother was nuts.

"No, my mother is proof positive that there are people still paying attention to you and you can count on them to get you what you need. Your mother gave us Mackenzie Childs light switch faceplates. To each his own. But if your hemorrhoids bother you, don't even think about my pillow. Sit on those switch plates. I bet they're real comfortable." JoJo paused. "Sorry. That was so rude. You can use my pillow," she told him.

"Not that I need it," he said, "but thanks."

"I didn't mean to imply that you did, Ray."

"I need a screwdriver. No, the other kind. Just sit there JoJo, I'll find it. Sit," Ray ordered. "Now where's that fucking manual?" Ray cursed his way to completion, but it left her ears sore from the barrage of information. She felt like she was auditory assaulted. Or at least auditorily violated.

****

They decided if it was a girl, she'd pick the first name, he the middle name. If a boy, the reverse. Abbey Road Anderson was born after an unmedicated twenty-four-hour labor with her very last effort, the very last push. JoJo pushed so hard she was surprised her tonsils didn't follow the placenta. She found if she bought into the breathing part she learned in childbirth class, it was pretty effective. JoJo wanted to appreciate childbirth from the medical side.

It was pretty cool, she thought afterwards, the whole birth process. It was when they put the baby on her bare chest and the baby let out a good forty-five second yowl and didn't stop for the next three months. JoJo cried inside as the tears rolled down her cheeks, she was struck by the monumental task in front of her. This slippery, skinny baby was her responsibility for the next twenty years, *or longer if I fuck it up,* thought JoJo.

JoJo picked Abbey's name primarily to fulfill Ray's penchant for oblique references. "Only Beatles fans will get it," he told JoJo.

"You can explain your rationale to her when she's older."

Ray stayed home with his two girls for two weeks as a "hands over" dad, not a "hands on" dad. The one thing Ray did consistently was get up, get the baby and hand her over to JoJo for care, not the same as doing it for her. JoJo tried to nurse, but the baby wouldn't latch on. JoJo tried and she tried. They had a lactation specialist work with them, but Abbey would not cooperate. JoJo felt like such a failure. The most wholesome, healthy thing a mother could do with her child ended with both parties in tears.

Abbey cried constantly. Ray kept telling JoJo she wasn't trying hard enough. JoJo cried constantly. Her nipples were sucked raw. Mrs. Montgomery came over and sent Ray on an errand. As soon as he left, she opened her bag, took out some formula and warmed it up. She took her screaming, beet-red faced, miserable granddaughter and shoved the bottle in her mouth mid scream. Sudden silence.

JoJo looked at her mother with shock. "Ray doesn't want her bottle fed."

"When Ray's tits spill milk he can have a say. If he says anything, tell him the hospital sent it, and you gave it to her because, now memorize this, you were afraid the baby had 'failure to thrive.' I'll get the case I brought out of the car and put it in the pantry. Nobody wants to hear the words failure to thrive, honey," her mom said and went out and got the formula from the trunk of her car. She put it in the pantry.

Her mother became more of an ally. When she was younger, JoJo thought her mother was a leftover from a prior era. Nothing she had gone through could translate into JoJo's experience. She couldn't relate, so JoJo dismissed her, but the older she got the more she learned about her mom she realized her mom was no slouch.

Mrs. Montgomery was by nature quiet. JoJo chose to equate that to weakness on her mother's part, but she couldn't be further from the truth. JoJo's mom would rather carry a big stick. She was quiet but alert, absorbing what went on around her. When shit hit the fan, that's when Mrs. Montgomery was at her strongest.

She didn't ride in on her white horse to save the day, quite the opposite. Nothing happened, but soon the source of the threat was disarmed and rendered useless. When JoJo asked her how things got done when her mom didn't seem to be doing anything, her mother smiled and patted her hand.

"I know people," was her mother's answer.

JoJo and her mom needed a common issue to bond over and they found in Ray a big one.

It was Ray and his controlling ways that brought them together. If he thought he would gain ground because JoJo was busy, he was wrong. He was going to have to go through his mother-in-law first.

JoJo thought she understood now why she was named after her Gramma. There's nobody better to pick up the fight if you don't have the strength to do battle yourself than your mother.

She would have loved to honor her mother if only her mother's name wasn't Antonette. If you have a DeLuca woman in your corner you can't fail, and if you do, you'd certainly be terrified to go home to one.

Ray went back to work and never noticed she stopped breastfeeding. JoJo felt bad monopolizing her mother's time. She did her tour and wasn't at this spot in her life to raise grandchildren, but Toni knew inside what a difficult baby Abbey was but was afraid JoJo would lose her shit if confronted with it. Abbey never slept more than two hours at a time and JoJo was run ragged. Then Ray would take care of Abbey, who was no trouble for him, and JoJo would take care of Ray.

JoJo exhausted herself, and Toni had to confront Ray about it on her behalf. She told him the baby needed someone to come in four days a week from three to eleven p.m. If Ray couldn't be there, he needed to pay someone to help. JoJo needed someone, and since he was on the road all the time, he had to hire someone. The situation couldn't go on any longer, her mother told him. Ray dutifully found a private agency nurse to provide some relief for her.

The pediatrician told JoJo all kids were different, and she was just unlucky in that her baby was 'fussy' or colicky. Her marathon crying jags that went for hours she would gradually outgrow. In the meantime, it was okay to place her in the crib and leave the room if it was necessary for JoJo's sanity. Between the lack of sleep, the anxiety of being a new mom, her husband never being home, thrown in with some postpartum depression, JoJo was never far from a full-blown meltdown. Even the first baby nurse quit after a week, the reason being Abbey was just too difficult. JoJo knew intellectually it wasn't her fault her baby was inconsolable, but emotionally she took it hard.

The only thing that comforted Abbey was a warm bath. Maybe it was a sensory issue that made her so fussy, and the bath soothed her. She was still small enough to fit in the kitchen sink, and she loved splashing the water with her hands. She also enjoyed when a cup of bathwater was poured on her, any-place except her face. Abbey practiced her fine motor skills by playing with the cup. JoJo put a washcloth over her face and called out, "Abbey? Has anybody seen Abbey? Abbey?"

Until Abbey had the coordination to pull it off JoJo's face, JoJo would pull it off slowly from the bottom, so her face gradually appeared. "Boo!" she'd say, and Abbey would laugh. This amused Abbey for hours. *She spent so much time in the water the first couple of months she should have been born with gills,* JoJo thought.

She loved her baby, she really did, and she knew her daughter wasn't doing it on purpose, but it was killing JoJo inside. One day, Abbey was in her swing, screaming as usual, JoJo took the trash out. She was outside and could still hear her. She pitched the trash in the can and in her hurry to get back inside, she knocked over the stroller that leaned against the wall. JoJo had to get out of that house, or she'd go nuts. She went, got Abbey, put her in the stroller and pushed her down to the mailbox. Abby quieted down. JoJo pushed her a few houses and Abby started to wail. She was going to cry no matter what, JoJo decided she needed a walk and Abbey could cry through it. Off they went, Abbey scream-ing her head off, and JoJo in desperate need of a shower.

JoJo pushed and cried, she pushed and the baby cried, and cried some more, but JoJo stopped. She couldn't expend the energy. She went past the house where the teenage son and his gear-head friends always had their heads under the hood of some car in their driveway. JoJo walked by them again on the way home. As she passed one of them looked up and said, "That baby been crying this whole time?"

"Yes," she answered.

He said, "That sucks."

She yelled back, "This is why you should always wear a condom."

She laughed. Someone finally acknowledged the struggle was real. Her struggle was real. Abbey did outgrow this crying phase about four months. They walked all over anyway. Most of their neighbors were older, with grandchildren living elsewhere.

JoJo thought they must be as lonely as she was because it seemed very convenient, they were always out front when they walked by. JoJo enjoyed talking to them and looked forward to running into someone, too. Some neighbors watched for them to come by and tried to time their meeting at intersections as happenstance so they could have her stop and let them admire the baby. Abbey was blessed with curly auburn hair and blue eyes ringed with black lashes. She was a little stunner. Their interaction was something the baby looked forward to as well.

****

In the summer all the old gardeners gave her produce. Beautiful tomatoes, cucumbers, and zucchini. She came home with Abbey in her stroller, buried among the beautiful fresh vegetables to use for dinner. JoJo unloaded the produce first. She noticed little teeth marks on the zucchini and other squash. JoJo squatted next to her daughter. Abbey had a beautiful, red, ripe tomato in her hand. She slowly turned the tomato around and examined it from all angles. Abbey bit into it, and the tomato burst its summer goodness into her hand. The only place the juice from the tomato could go was down Abbey's arm, which Abbey didn't like, and she shook her arm at JoJo, whimpering. JoJo needed to act quick to avoid a crying jag.

"What's the matter, sweetie? Is this too juicy for you? Here, let Mommy fix."

Abbey started with the "Uh, Uh, Uh" noise she made when she was about to cry. JoJo looked for a towel or tissue to wipe her arm but found none. To stave off the crying fit she took Abbey's arm and licked off the dripping juice. She licked it until it was gone. Abbey laughed and held out her arm to JoJo.

"You have more?" JoJo licked the imaginary juice off. Abbey laughed again and waved her arm. JoJo licked and Abbey laughed. JoJo took the offending tomato and held it out to Abbey. She shook her head no.

"Abbey, look!" JoJo said. She took a huge bite out of the tomato. Juice and seeds squished out, covering JoJo's face and hand. Abbey laughed as the juice dripped down her face.

"You think messy Mommy is funny? Do you, little girl?" Abby pointed at the juice that ran down JoJo's arm. She held her arm out and Abbey licked it and laughed again. JoJo licked her arm again to Abbey's amusement.

"Silly girl," JoJo said as she made faces and jiggled the stroller. "I guess you like the sloppy Mommy best, don't you? That's good because Mommy is always sloppy." Abbey laughed and laughed. JoJo brought the rest of the vegetables inside, wiped herself down, and went out to get her daughter.

Her mom stopped by around three to see if she needed help with dinner. She stayed to eat, and the next time she brought her dad. Abbey had a thing for men, so her visit with Gramps gave both women time to cook and talk. It was a rare moment they had, not being concerned with the baby. *What a gift it is to be here for this,* JoJo thought. *Didn't the Bible say something about the happiness of ordinary times? Or did I read it on a bathroom wall in some dive bar?* JoJo couldn't remember.

Everyone worked their segment of the puzzle, Julie took a piece, too, so no single person bore the whole burden of Abbey. Abbey seemed to outgrow herself. The more she was able to move, the happier she was. She smiled and giggled and started to toddle. JoJo didn't need the help anymore, but she sure needed the company, so things continued a bit longer.

It was a rare morning Abbey let them sleep in when Ray reached for her. He rubbed his hard-on between her legs, and she started to rock against him. He stopped to sync her motion with his and then continued. He used his fingers against her so lightly she wasn't sure he touched her, forcing her to push and thrust her hips in search of something to rub against. He rolled her over on her back and took a good look at her. He saw the girl he knew years ago when she was asleep. Ray looked at JoJo like the trophy wife he wished she was, but JoJo didn't like getting pushed around and trophy wives were supposed to be benign.

He had feelings for JoJo for as long as he could remember. She was Ritchie's punk sister, always chewing big wads of gum. JoJo once sprayed him with the hose while he stopped by on his way to work. He had to go home to change into dry clothes and got yelled at for being late.

She just had this pull on him. Once she reached high school, he figured she was almost old enough to lust after. He kept his eye on her and watched her become a woman. He watched her internal struggle to make peace with her feminine curves. It took a bit for her to accept her breasts, she would try to stand with stooped shoulders with the least emphasis on them as possible, but she eventually stopped worrying about them.

Ray deliberately passed the job lead on to her, hoping she would take it so they would bump into each other occasionally. Things progressed slowly forward. That she was his, his dream came true. He enjoyed the newlywed battles they used to have, and he loved the sex they would have afterwards. It was like surrender wasn't in her vocabulary. He pulled the sheet off her and exposed her naked body. She bounced back physically or maybe it was all that walking, but she looked good.

Ray knew if he wanted her buy-in it was about fifteen minutes of foreplay. He figured five was all he could give her, so he went straight to the source of all her pleasure. He kissed her neck and nuzzled her, and she started to giggle. He stroked her and touched her until he could feel her wet and pliable underneath his fingers. She rocked against him. He licked up one side of her throat and then along her jaw. It ended when his warm breath echoed in her ear.

"I'm trying not to lose it you are so fucking hot," he said, pushing against her. "Really?" JoJo whispered. "That hot? She pushed her pelvis into his.

"The fact that I'm in agony doesn't help." He moaned into her neck, made moist by his begging. "You are so far out of my league it doesn't matter how big my dick is."

"No. It's what you do with it," she said low in her voice.

"Oh, I know what to do with it. I'm going to show you right now," he said and got between her legs and moved down.

"This is how a girl like you needs to be fucked," he said and entered her, taking her by surprise with the way he drove into her. "This is how. God, I love you JoJo. I don't deserve you."

She was sure he orgasmed somewhere in there, too. He collapsed next to her, sexually sated.

"A girl like me needs to be treated gently with respect. Don't just ram into me again. I don't 'need' to be fucked. I need to be loved. If you can't do that, don't bother trying to do something else," JoJo told him, irritated by his presumption that he could do that to her.

Ray reached over and pulled her into his arms. He squeezed her and gave her a kiss. "You are absolutely right, JoJo. I do love you. I love you so much I forget how kind and sweet you are. A woman like you should not be manhandled, she should be caressed with love and tenderness. I'm the luckiest guy in the world that you chose me."

"Thank you, Ray. I can't help being soft. I'm a girl. We like being told how special and wonderful we are. Too much aggression turns me off."

****

It was at Abbey's first birthday party and the whole family was present for cake and coffee. JoJo ate a piece of cake and turned to vomit it up in the trash. She turned around, wiped her mouth and said, "What?"

All the women said as one, "You're pregnant."

"No. It can't be. Give me a minute to do the math," JoJo said.

"You don't need a fucking accountant to figure that out. Congratulations," Julie said.

"You got to be kidding me. Jesus. I have to lie down now. I feel ill," JoJo said and left the party. She came back ten minutes later, still a bit green but composed. She waited until the party was over to tell Ray and started to cry.

"I finally got the hang of this and now I have to go backwards," she cried. "I don't know if I can do it again, Ray. It was so hard."

"We can do it, JoJo. I know the kids will be close in age, but that will be good when they're older. We can hire someone. Maybe a nanny for Abbey, so you only have the baby. It'll be all right. Your mom can help get us out," Ray assured her.

Baby Frankie. Sweet baby Frankie. He was a smooth delivery and cried once to satisfy the doctor and resumed his silent observation of the world. He was a quiet child. He loved the outdoors. Worms. Turtles. Rocks. Fossils. *You never*

124

knew what you would find in his pockets. You have to remember to empty them before they go in the washer, JoJo thought.

He let Abbey help him sometimes. He would start off in the morning roaming the woods and creek beds and be gone for hours. Abbey went every so often, but the bugs bothered her. Abbey and JoJo would draw bugs on the driveway in chalk. Sometimes Frankie did, too.

****

A few years later came Ray's carbon copy, Denver. A redhead that freckled from the sun.

JoJo had her tubes tied. Ray bragged he had super sperm, but no contraceptive could keep them down. JoJo wasn't going to argue. She had three babies. *I'm done being a broodmare, now I have to just survive motherhood,* JoJo thought.

After having two what JoJo considered reasonable babies, she thought about Abbey. She was tough, and not in a good way. Her colic almost drove three adults over the edge. Even when she outgrew the fits she threw, JoJo swore she suffered PTSD from being her mother.

When the kids were small, they were very involved in soccer or lacrosse. Ray coached and drove and was the snack dad. As the kids evolved into more organized school-level teams, Ray's involvement faded away. He used to make time to attend games, but each year less and less. JoJo went to all the home games it would have been nice if Ray went to an away game once in a while. The kids graduated and made plans. Frankie liked his job, Abby worked for a lawyer at an insurance company, and Denver was looking for an opportunity.

Life suddenly opened up for JoJo. She had gaps of unstructured time. She wanted to reconnect with Ray. So much energy and time consumed by those kids were now open to her. She tried hard with Ray, but it seemed he lost interest once she birthed him a son. Ray, who was into her for so long now, was content with a peck on the lips. Having three kids, thirty years pass, saggy boobs and a marshmallowy stomach rendered her unattractive to Ray.

JoJo tried. She tried when they were in bed and the lights were off. She tried to seduce him with candles and sexy lingerie. He enjoyed her efforts, but it was always at her initiative. When she married him, she knew he had a thing for her long before she was interested in him. He was obsessed with her. He couldn't get enough of her. That lessened over time. During their marriage, she handled the domestic things, and he rode in at the eleventh hour looking like the hero.

One day when she wasn't paying attention to Ray, she couldn't put him at the center of the universe because it was occupied at the time by a little boy with a bloody nose. Ray decided he loved his family and enjoyed being a family man, but the husband part was getting old. Even JoJo, he still loved her. She was still his crowning achievement, getting her to marry him was the smartest thing he ever did, only this older, tired version of JoJo didn't fit his vision.

He was a healthy male who still had all his hair, he worked out when on the road. He was still physically fit, he had moved up the career ladder; he was successful, and he was married to, well, a housewife.

JoJo could read Ray like nobody's business. She knew he was losing interest in not just her but their life. She invested her soul in this family, in Ray and his success, in their future. If he thought now when all the hard work was done, he was going to change his mind, he had another thing coming.

And then a drunk driver changed everything.

****

CHAPTER NINETEEN

It happened the way most accidents happen, with no warning to prepare or react. JoJo had the green light and went through the intersection as a dump truck with a drunk driver ran the red light and hit JoJo in the driver's side door. The dump truck smashed her and pushed her car into oncoming traffic only to be hit again. JoJo broke her back, shattered her pelvis, and a number of bones in her leg. She ruptured her spleen and suffered internal bleeding. JoJo spent six months in a rehab facility learning how to walk again. She felt like Humpty Dumpty. She'd bet in the OR while they rodded and screwed her back together when they finished there were a few extra parts left, unsure of where they actually came from, just like Ray whenever he tried to fix something.

JoJo reached the end of the road medically. They did what they could surgically. There were no more exercises to try. She couldn't see what shape her back was in, she knew there was a big scar up the middle. They needed to use long rods and screws to stabilize her spine. JoJo had a big scar on her stomach from the surgery to stop the internal bleeding. It required plates and screws to fix her ankle and a rod in her thigh. JoJo walked with a slight limp that got worse when she got tired. JoJo had crutches to use if she felt unsteady. She thanked Ray every day for buying a one-level home. JoJo had her Physical Therapy exercises, but she preferred to walk in circles in her cul-de-sac. When she got tired of going one way, she reversed. It was as much physical therapy as mental therapy. She was going nuts fighting with her body, trying to will it into submission when she finally reached acceptance. She was as good as she was going to get.

Time to move forward, JoJo thought, *even if I have nowhere to go.*

****

Abbey grew tired of her mother's ongoing medical drama and stopped coming around as much. If Abbey only knew how everyone else was sick of it, too, but at least JoJo made progress. Slow but steady progress. Every once in a while, she would wince. It would flash across her face so quickly it was like it almost didn't happen, but pain sometimes spiked to the top and broke through the surface, piercing her facade.

Frankie stopped by during his lunch break. Julie came over at least once a week, her parents came every few days. She had people come 9-12 for the chores, and her husband on weekends, JoJo had plenty of help. She was glad as time passed the traffic decreased, mostly just Frankie stopped by at lunch. Her parents were older and didn't need to come over as often. She worried about them worrying about her.

Julie had met someone while living the rock and roll lifestyle. She went to all the big festivals, and when backstage at one she met her own rockstar, a drummer by the name of Sledge. On stage, he was a beast. Off stage, he was a sweetheart. His real name was Russell, and he was based out of Nashville where he made his living as a session or gig player. He had eight years of sobriety from all substances. He drank tea and did yoga; he had his own line of herbal teas and wellness products. It was so successful he could give up his musical career. Sledge loved drumming so much he became a sought-after session drummer and rarely toured. He figured he aged out of life on the road but not out of the recording studio.

If somebody was going on tour, he sometimes signed on, but the money had to be there.

Sledge was surprised at how much he was worth on the road. He chose his gigs carefully; he didn't like to be away from his kids that long.

It didn't matter if he was hot as fuck; he was, though. He walked up to Julie and said, "My name is Russell, and I think I love you." She went on the next two tour dates with him and came back to her parents when the band went on to Europe. Jaded little globetrotter Julie chose to pass on Europe and go home.

She loved to go home. Julie loved seeing her family, and she loved seeing JoJo. She could be home for a month or six. She was happy at the consistency of life there. They made chili in the winter and cooked ribs on the grill in the summer. Julie thought it so funny that Josephine Montgomery was somebody's mother. JoJo laughed at that.

JoJo asked her mother, "Was I as difficult as baby as Abbey?"

"No. You were a perfectly normal baby. You became difficult after you started school and said it was stupid, and we paid taxes and didn't get our money's worth." Her mom recalled. "You used to get your father going on about the taxes."

****

The wonders of technology allowed Julie to speak to Russell anytime, and she would step away and talk. When he got back, Julie planned to meet him and his two kids, boys aged twelve and fourteen in Nashville. When JoJo found out about Julie being a stepmother she laughed and laughed. Boys. They'll probably fall in love with her and be little angels.

Julie returned from her phone call and sat next to JoJo on the floor. She was floored when Ray left. *He must have mental problems to walk away from his family like that,* Julie thought.

"What's the plan?" she said to her best friend. "Hear from Ray?"

"No. I don't expect to, either. He left the dog, the fucker. He only had her for one week, he must not have had the chance to bond with her yet. At least she's housebroken, but I need to give her a new name," JoJo said as the big black dog sat next to her on the floor. "What does she look like?"

"I'm not sure. Is it a German Shepard? It's all black. What's her name now?"

"Gladys. After Gladys Knight."

"I can't believe my brother is some kind of racist."

"What? No. It's not because she's black. He listens to the R&B station when he's driving. The Power Hour featured artist of the day he brought her home was Gladys Knight and he listened and sang to her all the way home. Although If I gave her a name because of her blackness it would have to be Oprah." She laughed. "That's terrible. No, it would be something regal, like Imani."

"Imani? That's pretty," Julie said.

"Yeah, I'm not sure. Ray said the kids who had her called her 'Furry.'"

"Furry? There are worse names. Maybe a little kid named her. It makes sense, then. I can see the name Furry. 'What's the name of your dog? Furry.'"

"Well, maybe she's got a chip in her or something."

Julie went with JoJo to the vets for company. The vet found a number tattooed in her ear. The vet informed them the dog was registered to the US Army. She was about five years old. Dr. Harper looked up the number.

"Her name is Fury. She was in the possession of a Sgt. Alonzo Dawson," the vet said.

"Huh. Fury," JoJo said. The dog sat at attention. "How cool is that?" They moved to the door and Fury remained behind. "Fury. Come," JoJo command-

129

ed, and the dog came. JoJo clipped her leash and they went back home to further investigate. Unfortunately, Google turned up Sgt. Dawson's obituary.

"Look at this, Julie. He was a decorated vet, served in Afghanistan, and died from cancer.

"Survived by one sister, several nieces and nephews, and Fury, the bomb-sniffing dog with whom he served."

"Where did Ray say he got her? What city was he in that day?"

"Driving distance, I know that much," JoJo said. "Yeah. The obituary said he was from Hillsboro. That's about driving distance, isn't it? Far, but doable. His sister might still live there. Google that." JoJo pointed at the screen. "Here she is. She's probably old enough to still have a landline. I'm going to call her."

JoJo dialed the number and it rang. She let it ring a few extra times in case the lady was old, and right when JoJo was ready to hang up an elderly voice said, "Hello? Hello?"

"Hello? My name is JoJo Anderson. Is it possible to speak to Mrs. Beverly Greenfield?"

"Hello?" the frail voice said. "Hello?" JoJo listened to what sounded like someone fumbling on the other end.

"Hello?" said a much stronger voice. "Who's calling, please?"

"Ma'am, my name is JoJo Anderson. I'm calling because I'd like to speak to Mrs. Greenfield, please."

"In regard to what?" Her voice remained icy.

"I have in my possession her late brother's dog, Fury. I was wondering if perhaps there was some mistake and she got loose or something. I'm a little over three hours east of you. My husband bought her off of a couple of kids on a corner."

Suddenly, the lady on the other end broke into heart wrenching sobs.

"Fury. You have Fury." She continued to sob. JoJo and Julie just listened until she calmed down.

"Oh, I'm sorry. I didn't mean to cry, but I was so worried about her. She was in Afghanistan with my brother. He was her handler. He got sick over there and had to come home. Leukemia. Fury was his dog, I guess they trained them together because the army didn't want her without him. His platoon figured out a way to get her here avoiding the government paperwork, if you know what I mean.

130

"She helped him so at the end. Fury never left his side. When he passed, one of his military friends brought Fury to the service. Fury sat at attention the whole time and followed his casket with the pallbearers. She sat at attention during the burial, and when they played 'Taps,' she stood. She knew she was saying goodbye. Fury came here and only left his room when she needed to do her business."

It took JoJo a minute to compose herself. "I have her, and I'll drive her to you right now." The sobbing began again.

"You don't understand. We couldn't afford to keep her. There's barely enough for the family to eat. I have three kids and my mother is here with me. My husband works, but he's got some health problems. We can't afford the vet bills. My son overheard, so he and his friends decided to sell her to get some money. When I found out, I went out to look for the man who bought her. I worried she fell into the wrong hands, but he was gone. I hoped he was a good man. He gave them more money than they asked. The boys wanted $100.00, and your husband told them she was worth more than that and gave them $300.00, so I prayed he was a good man."

"Your son picked a good man, Mrs. Greenfield. Are you still unable to keep her? Because if you like, we can keep her. She'll be safe and well loved," JoJo offered.

"You would do that? For a stranger's dog?"

"Ma'am, she's a US military veteran. I'd be honored to keep her, and if you like, when she passes, I'll pay to have her buried next to your brother, where she rightfully belongs. With her handler."

JoJo and Julie had to hold the phone away from their ears, she started crying again. After a few minutes, she stopped. "Excuse me. This is just so unexpected," she said.

"Well, Mrs. Greenfield, sit down. There's a bit more."

"I don't understand," she said, confused.

"I've looked into buying a retired military dog," JoJo told her. "It costs about twenty-five grand to train them. Being such highly trained dogs, even at the end of their careers, you can't find one less for less than ten thousand. I hope you don't find this insulting, but I'll pay you five grand for Fury."

"What?" the lady said. "You want to buy Fury for five thousand dollars, even though you have her?"

"Yes," said JoJo. "If that's all right. Here, talk to my friend Julie. She'll fill you in." She handed the phone to Julie.

"Hello?" Julie said. "Which branch? Tomorrow, we'll see to it in the morning, we'll let you know. Yes, goodbye." Julie ended the call.

"So. You now have a dog."

"I think Frankie may take her if I don't want her," JoJo said.

"Yeah. Do you even want a dog? I didn't know you wanted a dog or researched getting a retired combat dog. I hope you're happy because you now have a dog," Julie stated. "You just agreed to pay some lady five grand for this dog." She looked at Fury. "A dog named Fury. They really cost that much?"

"I have no idea. She didn't sound like the kind of person to accept charity. This way, she saves face and still gets the money. I just felt like she needed the cash and Ray can afford it."

"Ray already paid $300 for the dog."

"So, they got a bonus." JoJo shrugged. "They need the money. Ray can spare it. What good does it do anybody in the bank? Not that I knew I missed anyone but she's good company. Maybe I'll keep her. Alex always said I needed to let go of shit to make room for different shit. So, I let go of Ray and got Fury."

"Now might be a good time. I have someone to mop the floor now. I never wanted a dog because the floors would get all dirty. Fury doesn't seem that dirty. She needs to be brushed, but that's okay. Maybe Ray left to make room for the dog." JoJo said.

"Admit it. You want the dog because of its name. Fury. You feel like a badass with a dog named Fury. An ARMY dog named FURY. Forget the crazy old cat lazy. Watch out. It's that nut Mrs. Anderson and her attack dog Fury."

"Am I so transparent?"

"What if Ray wants her back?"

"I'm sorry, he gave me everything but his retirement. That means this dog is now mine," JoJo said.

"He's so dumb. Why did he get a dog and then leave it?" Julie said. "What do you want to do for dinner?"

"Let's go buy a bunch of burgers and go downtown under the bridge. There are homeless people. Let's bring Fury. Maybe she could give some comfort to the people there. Maybe find some homeless veterans or something. You always hear about them. Let's go serve our fellow man. Get some points on the plus side from the man upstairs. You've been living a rock and roll lifestyle. I'm sure there's a few things you need to atone for."

****

They bought twenty hamburger meals, drove downtown, and parked the car. "Are we going to do this? Really?" Julie hedged. JoJo looked at Fury. She was looking out of the window for a purpose. "Who's going to know if we chicken out?"

"Nobody," JoJo said. "There's one thing. If it looks like broken gas or syringes on the ground, we aren't letting Fury walk on that shit. If it's gross, we just give the burgers to the first guy we see and book it," JoJo said.

They walked over and noticed a van and some people unloading to-go boxes. They added the burgers to some boxes and discovered these people run a food bank and deliver here often. There were a few Vietnam War vets and a lady pointed one out. The girls looked at each other. They looked at the ground, and they looked at Fury, tall and alert.

JoJo exhaled, "Let's do this," and approached the guy.

He was pretty far gone as far as his faculties went. He was leaning against a cement post trying to light a cigarette, but his hand shook, so he couldn't hold it still long enough for it to catch.

"Here, let me help you," JoJo said and took the lighter out of his hand. She held the lighter still and cupped her hand to block the wind so he could catch the flame. She gave him back his lighter.

His name was Ed. He didn't want to talk about Vietnam. He started rambling, making no sense. Julie started to get nervous and backed away, but JoJo went about five feet from Ed with Fury. Ed stopped and eyed the dog warily.

"Fury. Ready," JoJo said, and the dog snapped to. She sat on her haunches, locked and loaded. She sat perfectly still, her nose twitched with the wind her only movement.

JoJo said, "Fury was in Afghanistan, Ed. She's a vet, too. This is how she says hello." Ed started to cry and said she was the most beautiful dog he ever saw. The food people came over and Ed couldn't stop talking about how beautiful the dog was. JoJo, Julie and Fury helped the volunteers pass out meals. Fury allowed anybody who wanted to pet her. A few had dogs of their own. JoJo saved a few burgers and gave them to the dogs.

133

The two of them walked car, both of them all watery-eyed and on the brink of tears; Fury twitched her nose.

"Let's only bring Fury to the hospital," Julie said. "That was the saddest thing I ever saw."

"Maybe like the Veterans Parade. That guy made me cry. Makes me want to call my Congressman and bitch slap him," JoJo said, a hard edge in her voice. "That guy needs help and someplace safe to live. He's a veteran for crying out loud. Doesn't he deserve better? Look how far he's fallen. Like he was eighteen years old in the military, he probably had dreams and shit. He got drafted and was going to do his tour and get it over with so he could come home and get on with his life, and something derailed him big time. He's an alcoholic, he's missing teeth, and he just exist to drink so he doesn't get the DTs. He lives under a bridge. What the fuck kind of life is that?" JoJo said, her voice caught in her throat.

"Apparently, the one he prefers," Observed Julie. "Let's stick to parades."

"Maybe if there's a military funeral," JoJo said.

"No, parades only at least while I'm in town."

"Here, I know something you like. Let's go shopping for dog stuff. She needs a new bed and toys and stuff. Let's go to the store on the boulevard. They let you bring the dogs inside."

****

It was a rare morning of no traffic in JoJo's home. It was blessedly silent, Fury sat alert at her side and followed JoJo from room to room. She was silent and barely a whisper came from the dog. *Maybe I'll take her to the canal for a walk,* JoJo thought.

She was in her closet looking for her sneakers when someone yelled out, "Hey! Mom!"

JoJo ran into the kitchen to find that Frankie had come through the door only to be stymied by Fury. He knew Gladys as a big black dog. In front of him sat a dog who was determined not to allow him contact with his mother. Not a step. He leaned against the wall.

"What are you doing?" she asked.

"The dog."

"What about the dog?"

"She won't let me in. What happened? Did you find some switch or barcode to turn this dog on? She's not that dog dad brought home, is she? Because that dog is actively guarding you. It's scary."

"Oh, her," JoJo said. She looked at the dog and said, "Fury. Good girl. Get in your bed," and pointed towards her dog bed. In two leaps, she was in her bed chewing on a toy, obviously paying no attention to the body language of the humans in the room.

"What's up with THAT?" Frankie said. "That dog looked like if I moved, she was going to rip my face off. What's her name? Gladys? I don't think so. Maybe Smith. Or Wesson."

"Gladys, that's not her name. Her name is Fury. She used to be in the army, and her original owner couldn't care for her," JoJo laughed.

"How'd that happened?" Frankie took a banana out of the fruit bowl and peeled it. JoJo told him the story.

"Well, it's a damn shame about her brother, no two ways about it. Young guy like that. Cancer. I think her elderly in-laws live with her, too. It sounded like when Grams used to answer the phone. Her voice sounded so spidery. Anyway, I think she needed the money. She was grateful to find out what happened to Fury. 'He was my brother's best friend, he's gone, now she's gone,' the lady said. She's good, this dog. She's always on alert. I think she's happy to have a job, I believe she thinks I'm lame and it's her job to protect me."

"That's not a bad idea since you are here alone," Frankie said after he ate the banana. He threw the peel in the garbage.

"One more thing. I've prepaid her burial. She's to be cremated and buried with Sgt. Alonzo Dawson, her handler. I want to see if I can get her a military funeral or at least a bugler to play taps. All the paperwork is in the safe. I'd like her back where she belongs, with Sgt. Dawson," JoJo informed him. "If I'm unavailable that's where she'll go."

A few weeks later JoJo got a call from the bank, a package came for her. She brought Julie with her to see who would send her a package care of the bank. It was a box from Beverly Greenfield. JoJo sat down before she opened. She had no idea what it could be, but sadness emanated from the unopened box. JoJo knew whatever it contained would make her cry, she was tearing up before she even touched it. She passed it to Julie.

"Would you open this, please? I can't. I'm going to cry even if it's just a bunch of dog treats."

"Sure." Julie opened the box. "Oh my God, I'm going to cry now." She held up Fury's government issued combat vest with her name stamped on it. Also, a thank you note to JoJo for helping her, Fury's future weighed heavy on her mind. A picture of Sgt. Dawson and Fury in Afghanistan in full gear had been included. He was down on one knee, his hand on Fury's back, smiling a big smile for the camera. JoJo started to sob, and Julie joined in. The bank manager as well as a few of the tellers watered up as well.

"Well," JoJo sniffled. "I know exactly what I'm going to do."

She went to a photo place and had the photo enlarged on canvas. JoJo had it manipulated from a color photo to a sepia print. The size of it with the color gradients took it from a photo to almost art. It even looked like sand, considering where it was taken. She ordered two. JoJo wrote Beverly a card saying, 'I'm doing ok. I like these people; I think the lady needs my help. I thought you might like to see me every day, so you don't forget what I look like. The lady has one too. It's by my bed so I don't forget either. Signed Fury.' JoJo got Beverly's address online and sent it to her house. It had no return address and their contact stopped.

Fury was good company. She kept JoJo's secrets, and she provided JoJo with a sense of security. She slept at the foot of JoJo's bed on a dog bed. If JoJo got up to pee Fury got up on watch. Once JoJo was in bed Fury settled in for the night.

JoJo enjoyed her mornings. Just the paper, the dog, and coffee. Sunlight slanting in the window created a Fury sized spot and the dog lay in its warmth. JoJo put the rest of the paper aside and picked up her pen. The Monster awaited her, the crossword puzzle featured in the Sunday edition. She had a fresh cup of coffee like in those TV commercials, the steam wafting in circles above the rim. She looked for where she left off when her peace was interrupted by a knock at the side door. A man stood there and looked at her. She looked back and he exaggerated the time by pointing at his watch. She looked at the notebook she kept, and she was supposed to have an appointment with her attorney. *Shoot. That must be the guy*, she thought.

She unlocked and opened the door to let the gentleman in, but he didn't move.

She looked at him puzzled. He pointed to Fury behind her and shook his head no. JoJo said, "Fury. Get in your bed, girl," and pointed to her bed.

Fury stood up and looked at JoJo as if to evaluate JoJo's competency to detect danger or not. She decided the man at the door was safe and went to her bed, staying on watch.

"C'mon in," JoJo said to the man. "Fury's okay now."

The man held his briefcase close, between Fury and his body. "That dog's a lawsuit waiting to happen," he told her.

"You definitely are the lawyer. I don't think we've met before. I'm Josephine Anderson." She smiled at the man, half in apology for Fury. "Please come in and sit. Can I get you a cup of coffee before we start?"

He placed his coat over a chair, sat down, and told her he preferred his coffee black. She placed his coffee in front of him. He quickly picked it off the paper. "Something wrong? Do you need cream? Sugar?" JoJo asked him.

"The puzzle," he said reverently. "You don't want to spill on it. You do it in pen." JoJo looked at the puzzle, surprised at him. "You like the puzzle, too?"

"Oh, yes," he said. "It's the only reason I have a subscription." He cleared his throat. "Ahem. I'm Robert Bennett. Forgive my manners, your dog, she surprised me."

"Oh, Fury. I think she makes people nervous because she watches them," JoJo said. "No, I think it's because she's a huge, black, scary German Shepherd named Fury, of all things. The way she's tuned into you. She watches you."

"We are getting used to each other. I just got her. I feel safer with her in the house. She's a working dog, I feel bad I don't have any work for her to do, so she mostly decided her job is me. Eliminating threats to me," JoJo explained.

"What kind of work does she do?" Mr. Bennett wanted to know. "She was in the ARMY. She's now retired."

"Well, that's quite interesting. Ahem," said Robert Bennett. "Don Hessel usually handles your affairs, he forwarded my name on because I'm a divorce lawyer, and I wouldn't be a very good one if I didn't think that's why you wanted to talk, correct?"

"Yes. A divorce," she repeated.

"Why don't you tell me a little about how you arrived at divorce as the solution," he asked.

"The short answer is he came home, said he wasn't happy, packed a bag and left," JoJo said. "He told me I could keep everything but his retirement. I told him if he left it was for good, and he left. So that's that. Sign the papers."

"Are you sure you don't want to try mediation or even counseling first? Your anger may be what's driving your emotions, you may think about it differently after you have some time to cool off."

"I don't want to think about it differently. He started it. He deserves to have it finished. He's done. So am I," JoJo made her mouth say, "I want everything but his retirement. Write it up. And he can't have this dog. She's mine."

JoJo handed him a piece of paper. "This is his daughter Abbey's number. She is the one most likely to speak to him. Try her. Or here's his business card. Try his office, but I'm not taking his calls. Any communication I have with him will be through you, so you figure it out."

"Oh. I have a questionnaire about marital assets and such."

"I don't have the figures. Don Hessel can give you the names. I had a significant settlement, and Don knows who's in charge of it. How to find it."

"I hope things continue as smoothly as this," he smiled as he pushed the pile of papers over to her. "When a couple's married, as long as you two, there are considerable assets and things always arise."

"A while ago I was in a terrible accident; My car was T-boned by a dump truck owned by Altman Construction, driven by James Altman, the owner's son, returning from a liquid lunch.

"He was charged with DWI, and he got in a lot of trouble. It wasn't the first time. He had a suspended license and numerous charges, quite a long history of such behavior. The problem of liability occurred when it was determined his dad knew he wasn't allowed to drive but assigned him the job anyway. They paid a lot of money to keep things quiet.

"That's what Don did for me. He set up trusts and things. A lot of the financials are already established, and Don can direct you. I don't need my husband or his money. I don't know where my husband is. I don't care. He wants to wipe 'the slate clean?' So be it. Fuck him, Mr. Bennett, excuse my language," JoJo said.

"Robert, please." He touched her hand. To his hand hers was warm and soft. He always heard you can tell a woman's age by her hands. They get work done on their faces but not on their hands. He looked at hers. Her nails were short and oval, bare of color. Her knuckles were smooth, the skin unwrinkled and absent of age spots, the tendons and veins invisible under her skin.

He pulled his attention back to her. "I just had a thought. Pardon me, Mrs. Anderson. It's just always sad when a couple who have been married as long as you two divorce. If you're sure, I'll start it."

"I've made bigger mistakes," she replied. "I'll regret it later if I need to. More coffee?"

"No, thank you." He looked down as he shuffled her papers. "I'll get working on this. Shouldn't be too complicated. Divorces without small children are much easier. Divorces, like those with little kids, are terrible to witness. Yeah, you shouldn't be married, no doubt about it. But to totally destroy the other person in front of their own kids? Unconscionable."

"You must see all kinds of things," she said as she showed him to the door.
"You have no idea."

"Thanks," she said. "It should be cut and dried. I don't see him coming back anytime soon. In fact, the longer he stays away, the happier I'll be."

****

CHAPTER TWENTY

A few days later JoJo was in the garage looking for the battery that operated all the equipment. She thought the next time one of the boys dropped in she'd ask him to trim the bushes. *Damn it, Ray. You talked about how great this thing is, one battery runs five pieces of power equipment. One battery. That's if you can find the battery. A charged one? Yeah, right,* JoJo thought, annoyed. She was wedged between metal shelving and a couple of spare tires.

"Hey, hey," a voice said to her. "That looks like it hurts. I'd help you but your dog's not very welcoming." JoJo turned and looked at the source of the voice. It was Mark Elliot, of Elliot Brothers Painting. A short guy, his face showed what thirty years without sunscreen looked like.

Permanently red, his face had deep grooves where most people had regular wrinkles, and his face showed a lifetime of living. He'd been a high school friend of Ray's. He lit a cigarette and waved in the direction of Fury.

"That's quite a dog. How long have you had it?" Mark asked her.

JoJo called Fury over and said, "Oh, about a week or so. Her name is Fury. Fury, relax."

She relaxed entirely and sank into the lawn, gnawing on a chew toy made out of Ray's socks. "Hey, Fury, nice to meet you," Mark coaxed. JoJo hoped Fury wouldn't get triggered by a garbage truck or something and take a chunk out of his palm. Fury approached slowly, smelled his fingers and hand and determined him to be friendly. She walked forward and let Mark scratch behind her ears. After a few minutes, she returned to her spot in the grass.

JoJo, in a fit of childish pique, took a bunch of Ray's socks, knotted them into a ball, and gave it to Fury to gnaw on. JoJo was pleased Fury enjoyed it so much.

"That's a nice dog," Mark said. He had run into Ray somewhere; Ray hired him to paint the house, and they were ready to start.

"Mark, have you seen Ray lately? He moved out a couple of weeks ago. I have no way to contact him." JoJo felt stupid saying that. "I didn't plan on having the house painted."

"No. He took care of this over a month ago. Let me see if I can get a hold of a copy from the office." He took his phone out of his pocket and made a call.

"My brother will bring a copy by. I have to give an estimate not too far from here, so I'm going to stop over there while we wait."

"You have a brother?"

Mark pointed to the side of his truck. The logo, "Elliot Brothers Painting, Commercial & Residential, We've Got You Covered!" was painted on the door.

"I didn't know you had brothers."

"I have two, I'm the youngest. Why would it say Elliot Brothers if it was just me?"

"Marketing?" JoJo said, and thought, *I've been married to Ray for way too long.*

"Nope," he said and got in the truck. "I won't be long." He pulled out and left. JoJo went back inside.

A little while later, a white van with the Elliot Bros logo on it parked in her driveway and a man different than Mark knocked on her door. She waved him in.

"Mrs. Anderson?" the man called. He was Mark Elliot if you put him in a taffy pulling machine. He looked similar but long and stretched out. He had a nice pair of khakis and a polo shirt on. *Typical front office. It looked like he couldn't cut an edge to save his life,* JoJo thought.

"Mrs. Anderson?" he asked again.

"Not for long." JoJo looked at his bewildered expression. "Yes, but you can call me JoJo."

"Hello, JoJo. I'm Harry Elliot, Mark's brother. I brought a copy of the bill for you." He looked down, visibly startled. Fury was standing between them. She slid in like a shadow. "Oh, that's my dog Fury. I got her for protection. We're just getting acquainted."

"I'm usually pretty good with dogs, but she's not like most dogs."

"No, she is not," JoJo said, scratching behind her ears. "But she's a good girl, aren't you, Fury? Go to your bed." The dog laid down but kept her eyes on JoJo's guest.

"Odd choice for a name, isn't it?"

"Not if you saw her mad, Mr. Elliot."

"I hope I never do. I have a copy of the signed contract and the canceled check your husband signed." He fumbled looking through his pockets but found the paperwork in his back pocket. He unfolded it and handed it to her. "What seems to be the problem?"

141

"Well, Mr. Elliot, my husband doesn't live here anymore and didn't say anything about having the house painted. I find the whole thing curious, but he did sign, and everything's in order. Maybe it's a parting gift to make him feel better about walking out and reducing this home to just a house."

He thought about his choice of words. "That fresh, huh? Sorry to bother you with this," he said, shoving the papers in his pocket. Harold recognized that look of stunned disbelief in her eyes and knew the look of saddened acceptance that would come, but it was the pain and hurt that existed in the space between them could almost bring a grown man to his knees. This he knew.

JoJo looked up and tried to blink the emotion away before she looked at him but didn't answer.

"I'll just be off, then. Is there anything I can get you before I go?" Harold asked JoJo gently.

"Thank you, but no. If you see your brother before I do, tell him he can start anytime. Nice to meet you, Mr. Elliot.

"Please call me Harry."

"I like Elliot better. Harry sounds like a dweeb."

He had no answer for that and let himself out.

****

"Morning, JoJo," Mark Elliot said into the open garage. He heard rather than saw somebody knocking around in there. "Can I help you find something in there?"

More rumblings, and out came JoJo. "Oh, hi, Mark. What was I looking for? I knocked over some recyclables and got distracted. You know, I forgot. I'm going inside. I'll yell out the window when it occurs to me."

She walked over to the side door and waved at him as she entered the house. *Ray was really off his rocker. He paid someone to paint a house he walked away from. Maybe it was a parting gift from his guilty conscious,* she thought.

It was a few days later, JoJo sat on the front steps and played fetch with Fury. She sat ready. When JoJo gave the command 'get' she took off so fast you would think she threw a hunk of prime rib instead of a ratty tennis ball. Their game got interrupted when a white van labeled 'Elliot Brothers Painting, Commercial & Residential, we've got you covered!' pulled in up the driveway.

The van door opened with a creak. JoJo figured it was Mark but saw it was Harold.

He walked over to her and stood in front of her, only Fury wouldn't let him near JoJo unsupervised. Fury sat facing him, away from him a few paces, but not far enough that Fury couldn't close the gap and rip his arm off in seconds if needed.

He stopped and asked she wanted to go for coffee, taking her by complete surprise. "I don't need to go for coffee. I have some in the house."

"Great!" he said and held out his hand to help her up. "Let's go, then."

Fury appeared without a sound. A sound from deep in her throat rumbled her presence. "Fury, down," JoJo said. The dog turned and stood behind her.

"That's amazing," he said as he walked with her to the door, Fury creeping behind. "Ah, geez, that dog. She just sneaks up on you."

"Ignore her. She feeds off your anxiety, just like my soon to-be-ex."

Fury went to lie in her bed and take a nap; she decided he posed no threat that required constant vigilance.

"Here, sit. I can make coffee," he said. It had been left out on the counter. Indeed, he could, and they soon sat at her kitchen table across from each other. He didn't say anything.

"I don't know where Mark went," JoJo told him. "Sorry, I can't help you."

"Confession," he said, smiling. "I came to see you."

"Uh, hi. Mission accomplished. You can leave now. I never should have let you in the house." She curled her lip as she spoke, and Fury suddenly sat on alert besides her.

"It's not like that, he explained. "Don't be so hostile. I haven't lived here in almost forty years. I was looking to connect more with someone my age, not to be rude. I outgrew sitting on a barstool years ago. I'm too young for bingo, at least I think I am. I could manage a bonfire if you know of any. My brother told me about you, how pretty you are, and your newly single status, so I thought I'd say hello. He forgot to tell me how mean you are, and you use that dog to repel people."

"I don't use her to repel people. She does that herself," was all she had to say.

"So, you don't deny being mean."

"Not at all."

"Then *what's* wrong with you?" he asked her as he rose. "I try to be neighborly and look at what I get in return. Anyway, if you see my brother tell him to call me."

"Uh, Mr. Elliot?" JoJo called after him. He stopped and turned around.

"It's Harold, Mrs. Anderson."

"Harold. Harold, two things. First, use your phone and call your brother. Second, I suggest you go and find a hot chick with daddy issues. You'll have better luck. Goodbye."

He waved as he backed out. *Interesting,* he thought. *Mark was right; she was pretty. She's also kind of rude and mean.*

****

Everyone has one story where sex was a weapon, even used against yourself once in a while when the vanquished felt lucky to be used in such a manner. It usually went like this: The wounded suffer a wrenching heartache. To reconcile the fact that you were wronged, someone you thought you knew was as exposed as a big fake, you break up. If it's the trifecta, broken heart, betrayal, and grief, she's looking for affirmations of her physical worth. The man didn't reject her because he found her repulsive, because of data to the contrary. Look at the guys lining up. A smart guy takes the woman, worships at her altar, fucks her brains out, and leaves never to see her again, but his desire for her validated whatever she needed, and he got laid. And that's that, Harry decided.

JoJo had one herself, following a cheating boyfriend. She reached for the validation of a stranger when she felt at her lowest. She did not find his desire for her life affirming, she considered it mechanical. His desire was gross and sloppy and smelled like cheap beer. She felt sleazy and took a shower as soon as she got home.

****

She was in the garage looking at things again when Mark and his crew pulled up, got their supplies readied, and started. He stopped to talk to her.

"Remember what that was?" he asked her.

"What?"

"What you forgot last time you were out here."

144

"No. Now it's two things I've forgotten. That and what I was looking for today. You're such a distraction," she teased. "Have you talked to your brother? He was looking for you."

"My brother? Harold?" he picked.

"Yeah. Him. Is the third brother a better choice?"

"Dave hasn't been back here in years. Harold's back. He's enough. He lives in Boston. Or, lived. Now he moved back here a few months ago. I don't know why. But he lives here now."

"He came over to say hello," JoJo told him.

"What did Fury think?" Mark asked her.

"She wasn't impressed." They both laughed at that.

"Goodbye, JoJo. Back to work," Mark said and walked off towards the crew. The work on the house finished, the new paint refreshed the look of the house.

There was a knock on the side door. Fury sat alert at activities yet to be un-folded. JoJo looked out the window and saw the paint company van. She looked out and saw Harold. She unbolted the door and pulled it open. She went to the kitchen table and sat down. He came in behind her, the dog stayed in her bed but looked at Harold with laser beam eyes.

"What's the matter? My husband wrote a bad check?"

"For what?" he sounded confused.

"Why else would you come over here? I know he stiffed you. He had to," she said. "No problem with it that I know of. Here, I brought some donuts. Some bagels, too."

"You came with donuts? *And* bagels?"

"Yes. Do you have coffee? I couldn't carry it all. I'll make it when Fury relaxes."

"She's fine. She's just keeping you honest," JoJo told him. "Yeah. I guess you're welcome to bring breakfast anytime. The coffee," she slid over and pointed. "Up there."

"Okay, let me think about it. Just cream?" he sounded almost convinced himself. She nodded yes. *I knew it.* He said to himself. He passed hers over and fixed one for himself and sat at the table. He looked at Fury, watching him. She stared at him, expressionless. She might want a treat or rip a chunk out of his ass, it was a toss-up.

"Um," Harold started, "I like dogs, and they usually like me, but I can't read Fury. She's a big, solid black Shepard with the name of 'Fury.' Her name leads one to assume she might be, ah, capable of wrath and devastation."

"You're not supposed to. She's an enigma. Until she's not. Then you better run."

"What does that mean?" he asked her.

"She's like a radio, tuned to a station we can't hear. She's always on alert. Paying attention to a frequency people don't get, so I don't know what will set her off. Something dangerous miles away we cannot detect, a truck or a car backfiring. A shift in the gravitational pull? I haven't had her long enough, and I don't know her history. She could have a wicked case of PTSD. Put your palm up. Fury, come." She grabbed his hand and brought it to her nose. Fury sniffed it a few times and licked it. She turned back to her bed. "I think you're okay now."

He looked over her shoulder at the dog. The dog looked back. Fury changed her mind and came over and decided to see her lady friend. She stood next to JoJo.

"Where did you learn about the frequency and all that?"

"That? I made it up. I thought it sounded pretty good." JoJo laughed. He watched her watch her dog. The dog stood there with its head in JoJo's lap, someplace he decided he wanted to place his head. Harold swore the dog looked at him and said, "Game On!"

"She's a beautiful dog, the black coat and all. Was she hard to find?" This required JoJo to spend time talking to him about Fury's origin. He asked pertinent questions and seemed actually interested.

"So that's her story. In the family room is a picture of Sgt. Alonzo Dawson with her over in Afghanistan." He stood up.

"May I?"

JoJo pointed to a doorway.

"Yes, it's in there." She stood and picked up their cups. He came back and sat down. "Where are you going? I'd like another cup of coffee," he said as he took his mug back. "And a donut."

She sat back down and passed him back her mug. "I might as well have another, too."

He handed her cup of coffee over to her as he sat down with his at the table. After she told Fury's origin story, she stopped talking and looked at him. He had a look of confusion on his face. He thought he might just have been fed the largest load of bullshit ever, but to see Fury that was the only way to explain her.

"That's quite a story," he said. "Please pass the donuts." She passed him the donuts. "You don't want a donut? A carb?" Harold mocked her.

"You don't want to leave?" JoJo pushed.

"Not yet. Tell me about you," he whispered.

"What? No. Here's the obvious. Three kids, one girl, two boys, all adults. Married to Ray thirty years. Best friend Julie. Separated from Ray about a month ago. Divorce proceedings are in the works. I should have left Ray at the altar, so there is no hope of reconciliation. That about sums it up."

"Don't you want the dirt on me?" he asked her.

"Only if you were six feet under it." JoJo smirked.

"I may have misjudged the dog, but not you. You are mean."

"We like to keep people guessing who has the worst bite. This is what I heard. You used to live in Boston, but you came home," she said.

"That's all?"

"That's more than enough."

She looked at him, there was something oddly sexually attractive about him. He was old. Well, older. He probably has his AARP card. He had a full head of hair, mostly if you don't count the thinning at the crown, the gray parts silver. He had a bit of a belly, but who was she to criticize, having a bit of a belly herself? Harold didn't look flabby, at least his arms and legs didn't. He looked like he golfed full time. Harold looked like money to her, not likely to be giving any away in her direction, so let some other fair maidens tame the dragon. In her experience, if you found a man you figured had money, it was his. He had no obligation to share it with you and usually didn't. That's why she always preferred to make her own.

He looked at her, she looked almost like a kid. He liked it when they actually made eye contact, a wink or a raised eyebrow in recognition was all that happened, but that was a big enough of a breadcrumb to keep her looking at him. She looked thin to him, and he wanted to take her to an all-you-can-eat buffet and shove food down her gullet, but he knew he'd get arrested for sure, so he tamped the thought down.

"I'm looking for my brother Mark," he said. "Have you seen him?"

"No. Not since he finished here," she replied.

"Would you be interested in having dinner with me?" he asked her.

"Thanks, but no thanks," she said.

"Drinks?"

"Sorry, no."

"Ice Cream?"

She hesitated.

"Ice cream it is!" he said and grabbed her hand. Fury stood up. "You won't mind riding in the van, will you?"

"No. Why would I?"

"Some girls are particular about things like that."

"How do those girls feel about walking?"

He laughed. "I knew you were different."

"Why? Because I'm not stupid?"

****

He offered to get her a cone and let her wait in the van. When he came back, she was leaning out the window talking to a young guy standing by a county truck. She introduced him to her son Frankie. He nodded, kissed his mother's cheek and moved on. They ate their cones for a bit before he spoke.

"Your son there, is he the oldest?"

"No, my middle son. My daughter Abbey is the oldest. Denny's the youngest. You?"

"I have two girls. Kerry is a flight attendant, and Ashley sells real estate. Both based out of Boston."

"Why'd you come back? What's here you couldn't wait to escape from forty years ago that you're willingly walking back into now?" JoJo asked him.

"It sounds exactly like what I'm doing." He laughed. "Things just worked out. I lucked out in the big internet sweepstakes and cashed out. Made some really smart investments. There was some talk about putting my mother in a home, and I'm here to stay with her to put that off as long as possible. A lot of resentment has been built up over the years around me not doing my fair share around here, so I'm here to do my fair share. My mom's old. If I don't spend some time now with her there may not be any time later. There's no reason not to be here. So, I'm here. I just wish I knew how to entertain her."

"Well, hope you get nice weather," she told him. "I need to get home now. You almost finished?"

"Yes. I'll see how it goes."

"Does she play mahjong?" JoJo asked him.

"I don't know. Should I know?" Harold asked her back.

"Why?"

"Find her stuff to do. Take her to the store. Girl things. Getting her hair done. Don't you have a sister or a girlfriend to tell you about this stuff? She's lived here all her life, she must have a routine. She probably mostly needs a driver."

"Can't you help me? Please? I don't know what to do with a ninety year old lady. I'll hire you two days a week as a lady's companion?"

"A lady's companion? Are we in a Victorian romance novel?" JoJo smirked.

"What else would you call it? Elder Sitter? Senior Minder? Senior Reminder?"

"The girl who helps with mom a couple days a week," she suggested.

"Girl?" he questioned her.

It took her a minute to realize he was referring to her. "Touché. Flunky. Fossil. I can do it two afternoons a week, but you have to do all the running, like coffee or lunch. Let me do a trial run on Thursday afternoon and I'll see how long I might want to commit. And Fury gets to come."

"Deal," he said quickly, as if afraid she'd change her mind if she thought it through. He had to pick her up for her Thursday afternoon visit. All she asked for was photo albums nearby, she brought a bag containing a puzzle and some playing cards.

Harold picked JoJo for her Thursday visit. She introduced herself as a lady who was home alone a lot, and she heard Mrs. Elliot was alone, too. "Maybe you could do me a favor," JoJo said, "help me pass the time if you don't mind."

"Why, of course," Harold's mother said, "but call me Helen. Harry, why don't you get us some coffee. Would you mind in the dining room, JoJo?"

"I'd love some coffee. The dining room would be perfect," JoJo answered. They spent a few hours going over all the pictures of strangers from another era.

Harold knew the pictures existed, but Helen knew the existence of each person. She told stories about people only she knew. Harold slipped out to get a haircut and stopped at the Ye Olde Used Booke Shoppe to wander around. When he got back, they were still at the table, almost through one album.

"Did you ladies have a lovely afternoon?" he said as he walked into the kitchen.

"We ladies certainly did. We did some online blackjack tourney thing, oh, and sorry, she spent your inheritance," JoJo said with a sad face.

"There was an inheritance?" he said. "I guess it's gone now."

"I like this aide. She listens to me," Helen told Harold.

"Mom, she's—"

"I like you, too, Helen. Why don't we get together again soon," JoJo interrupted.

"I'm going to bring JoJo home. I'll come back and we'll go for dinner." Harold told her. She opened the van door and climbed up with a wince. Getting into any car was hard for

To JoJo, SUVs were almost always impossible. He noticed the expression on her face and asked after it.

"Are you okay? You look like you hurt something," he asked out of legitimate concern. "Yeah. I was in a bad accident a few years ago. I broke a bunch of bones, and every once in a while, I have trouble hauling my ass up and over the wheel well to get in. It's not just the van. It's most SUVs," JoJo explained.

"Huh. I never knew that," he said.

"Why would you? You're like, way older than me."

"Was that meant as an insult?" he asked.

"No. The truth. Your brother Mark is Ray's age. Ray's two years older than I am, and you're older than Mark, so when I was probably graduating preschool, you were getting your driver's license," JoJo told him.

"I am three years older than Mark, so five years older than you. It's not that big a stretch."

He gave her a ride home and they laughed at Fury. She stayed on her feet, regardless of the paint can that came loose and rolled around the back there. They pulled into her driveway only to find another car parked there.

"Fuck. That's Ray. What's he want?"

"Do you want me to wait a minute and make sure everything's okay?"

"No. Ray's harmless." JoJo looked at him. "I enjoyed your mom. If you want me to go over and visit with her, I'll be happy to. Enjoy your dinner," she said as she opened the door and slowly got down. Fury followed.

Harold had his window down and wanted to catch a sense of the status of their marriage. Was it early on in the process, with brutal venom still hurled atop new or unhealed wounds, or late enough that they were fighting over the pen to sign the papers?

"What the fuck are you doing here, Ray?" JoJo greeted him unkindly. "What were you doing in that van? With him," Ray pointed at the van.   "Picking out paint colors, you asshole. What do you think we were doing?"

Harold pulled out of the driveway and laughed at Ray. She didn't need the help, but he might.

"I need to get a few things, but my key doesn't work," he told her.

"It won't. New locks. What do you want? You said you had all you needed, or you'd buy it on the road. There's nothing for you here," she remembered for him. "Send one of the boys over with a list."

"I'll take my dog, too," he said suddenly.

"Like hell you will. Fury." She came and sat next to JoJo. "Too late. We bonded."

JoJo pushed the door open, and the dog slipped inside. She stepped into the house, shut the door and locked it. "Send one of the boys," JoJo said through the glass.

****

A few days later, while she sat at the kitchen table, the door squeaked and announced the entry of her youngest, Denny.

"Hey, Mom, gotta take a leak I'll be right back," he said as he hurried to the bathroom. She heard the toilet flush and the water running. When he opened the door Fury wouldn't let him out. "Mom! This dog, Mom!" Denny yelled. JoJo told Fury to go lay down, she went to her bed and sat like the Sphinx.

"That's one strong dog," he observed. He kissed the top of her head and sat down. "How are you? Is it a good day?"

Denny was the one member of her family who recognized her positive reply when it wasn't a positive reply. He looked at her shoulders and hips to see how they lined up. If you watched her she would make these micro adjustments to her body, a shift in posture, move her foot, and fidget like she was trying to line up her vertebrae in an order that made sense to the rest of her body; these gave her away.

She still kept a smile on her face. Denver knew early on to read her movements. JoJo would not get into specifics it was all there, right below the surface.

151

Whether or not she was plagued by pain decided if it was a bad day. He hadn't seen her in a few days and his father talked to him as he gave him the list.

His father wouldn't shut up about the paint guy. She changed the locks and stole his dog. She stole his dog! And yeah, he paid for the painter guy to be there, he was there to paint his house, but what was his mother doing with him? Denny couldn't wait to get away from him.

"Hi, Mom, I'm sorry I haven't stopped by lately; things have been pretty busy at work.

Denver was doing a summer internship at an architectural firm downtown. They had projects everywhere, so he traveled quite a bit. The lifestyle suited him. He rented a room from Frankie for when he was local.

He still had two years of school left, but spending a summer interning for one of the biggest Architectural firms in the state was something he couldn't pass up. A friend of his father's helped get him in, he wasn't far enough along in his schooling to really qualify for an internship like this, but free help was free help, so they gave it to him.

Frankie was quite meticulous, and his brother much less. It was a good thing the arrangement was part-time for all involved.

"Denny, love, come hug your mother," JoJo smiled at her son, her rusty haired, freckled covered boy with the to-die for smile and blue eyes. He did and sat next to her.

"This is the dog Dad wants? This one?" He pointed at Fury. She looked at him and didn't break her gaze. He did and turned to JoJo. Fury transferred her gaze to JoJo and kept watch.

"Yes, her name is Fury. She's mine. The night he walked out on me I asked him if he was walking out on her, too, and as you can see, she's still here. He did a good thing taking her off the street. She has quite a story. Don't we all?

"I guess she can sense I'm a physical mess, so it's her job to protect me. Wait a sec," JoJo said and found the box with Fury's gear. "Here's her old uniform." She pitched the vest to Den. He held up the vest and looked at Fury. Fury was hesitant and looked at Denver because nobody was supposed to touch her things, but so much had changed since her time in the sand but her training kicked in and she emitted a low growl. Denny pitched the vest back to JoJo.

"Explains her name," Denny said. "The Fury is a famous tank from WWII. I'm surprised you haven't picked a more benign name now that she's retired."

"I decided to keep her when the vet told me her name. An attack dog named Fury. Who else has one? Nobody I know. She gets respect everywhere we go. That's a cool name, Fury. It kind of described my frame of mind at the time. Fury. Furious. I'm a bad assed woman with a bad assed dog. Anyway, I saw the movie about the tank. I love that movie. It starred Brad Pitt. If that wasn't a sign from God, I don't know what is."

JoJo got up and invited Denny into the family room.

"Want to see her in action? That's her handler, Sgt. Alonzo Dawson. He died from cancer. What a shame," JoJo told Denny.

"Yup. Everybody's got a story. I've got an update for yours." Denny tried to sound kind. JoJo went back to the table, sat back down, and thought, *I don't want to hear it, but it isn't fair to Denny not to let him deliver whatever it is from Ray. The kids should not be involved in any of this.*

"I think Dad misses you."

"You don't need to be involved. Did your father give you his divorce lawyer's name?"

"I think you need to slow down a bit, Mom."

"Slow down? How much slower can I get? The clock's ticking, Denny. I spent almost thirty years waiting for your father to pay attention; it was always 'one more client' and without you kids, this marriage probably would have imploded years ago. These plants have been dead for years, and now he decides to water them?" There was no hate or anger in her voice. "All I can say is this marriage died of neglect."

"I'm not sure Dad feels the same way."

"See, that's it. I don't care how he feels. He doesn't have a say anymore," JoJo told him, her face blank.

"We had breakfast the other day. I talked to him then, I think he might be having regrets."

****

Ray looked at Denver over a table spread with breakfast dishes. They always ordered too much. This included a meal for Frankie even though things were not to Frankie's dietary specifications, but they didn't want him to feel left out so they brought his home.

"So your mom's still mad?" Ray asked Denver, aware of their visit.

153

"I don't know. She wasn't pissed or anything, it was more get his shit and get it out of here. She didn't mention you once. Oh, that's not true; she said you paid to have the house painted."

"About that. You know the house painter. What's his story? I think he likes your mother." Ray pumped Denver for information.

"Mark Elliot? No way. He's married with a bunch of kids. He's super religious, he goes to that new church out on Rt. 217."

"That painter should have been done days ago. I don't know why he's there all the time. I drive by and see that truck there all the time. Any other news I should be clued in on?" Ray pried.

"No, she sometimes volunteers to sit with some old lady, but that's about it. Don't ask me for personal information about Mom. I'm not spying on her for you. Consider me Switzerland," Denver said.

He looked exactly like Ray did at that age. He was so young, bursting with cells dividing and hormones multiplying. Ray indeed named him Denver after the place he loved best. JoJo asked him why he didn't stay there, he loved it so much. He said it was a dream he fulfilled, and now onto other dreams like her. JoJo usually wanted to crack him in the head with a lamp, and then he would say something sweet like that, and she would forget why he made her mad. She was a sucker for a smooth talker, that much was true, and Ray was one smooth talker.

****

CHAPTER TWENTY-ONE

JoJo sat on her front step, waiting for Harold. She had plans to see his mom. She noticed a beautiful Mercedes pull on her street and drive towards her house and into her driveway. "What's Harold doing, Fury? He's got a new ride," JoJo said.

"Well, look at you, Daddy Warbucks. Very nice," she greeted him as he got out of his car.

He came over with a big smile. "See what you started."

"Me? I'm not in the market for a new car," she answered.

"No, but I thought about how hard it can be to get in those trucks for people like you or my mom. I'll be around a while, so I figured I'd lease something my mom would be able to get in and out of. You too."

She went over to her garage and pressed the code. As the door went up, it slowly showed the car she had parked there. It was a matching black Mercedes sedan.

"If you wanted to borrow a Mercedes, you could have used mine," she said, trying hard not to laugh. "Well, actually, it's Ray's trophy car, but it's mine now."

It seemed he was right next to her in two steps. He put his arm around her shoulder and squeezed her harder than a romantic hug. "Great minds," he said and took her over to his mother's house.

"Hello, Helen. It's me, JoJo. I'm back."

"Look, Harry, the nice aide is back, and her big dog, too." Fury had a soft spot for old ladies and let Helen pet her. She moved away and took a spot in the sun.

"Mom, JoJo isn't—"

"Why don't we finish looking at this album, Helen? We almost made it to the end last time. Would you like Harold to make us some coffee before he leaves?"

He brought the coffee to the table. He didn't feel like running errands, he wanted to watch JoJo. She was a natural with his mom. His mom was to the point where she knew things weren't right, but couldn't articulate her feelings, leaving her frustrated and scared. JoJo was so good with her when she got teary, JoJo just smiled and changed the subject.

He left they were pretty much ignoring him anyway. Harry did his errands and found himself back where he started, wanting to drool down JoJo's cleavage. He pulled himself together and went in to check on them. They were still talking when he called out, "Hello?"

"In here, Harry."

"Let me run JoJo home and I'll be back to pick you up for dinner," he told her.

"Oh, no, I think I just want to go lay down a bit," Helen said. "Take JoJo instead."

JoJo caught Helen's top lip curl in a smile. *The old girl isn't too old to meddle,* JoJo thought.

"What a great idea! Shall we, JoJo?" he called out to her.

"Oh, yes, let's!" she called back. "Come on, Fury."

They got in the car. He started the motor and looked at her. "Are you in the mood to eat dinner at four p.m.?"

"Actually, yes. I'm starving. We have to eat outside, though. Fury doesn't go inside."

"Do you care what you eat? I mean, we could go over the golf course and sit on the patio, but the menu's mostly pub food," he suggested.

"We don't care, do we, Fury? We just want a glass of wine."

"Let's do that," he said and drove the short distance to the golf course.

Fury looked funny, her big black head sticking out the window of the Mercedes. JoJo took her picture while Harold got them seated. He clipped Fury's leash onto her collar and escorted them to the table in the corner of the patio more out of respect for Fury and to keep her on the fringe of the crowd. Fury drew plenty of looks, but once she posed Sphinx-like, people admired her from afar. The waitress brought their drinks and left the menus. She came, took their orders and left. Harry was smiling.

"What's so funny?" she asked him.

"My mother. She fixed us up. That's funny," he said.

"I question her reasoning it might be dementia. She thinks I was your prom date. I'm a married woman. You've got no business here."

"I know. That's what makes it so much fun."

"Okay, your turn," JoJo said. "Tell me all I need to know."

"All you need to know is I like you. I have plans for you."

"I could turn into a crazy not-yet-divorcee who might be so bitter and angry I'll hate men so much I'll want to hang you upside down by your balls," she answered.

"At least I'll be naked."

"Yeah, but I won't. Look. Let me be honest. About five years ago I was in a bad car accident, but I think I told you that. I got hit by a dump truck. I broke my back and I had to have these long rods screwed into place. I have a rod in my leg because I broke my femur. I shattered my ankle. That's held together with more plates and screws. I probably have ten pounds of metal holding me together. That's just the inside. I have scars from when they operated on me for internal bleeding. Scars from broken glass. Look here." She took the hair from the left side of her face and held it up. "See this scar on my eyebrow? Follow it into my hair. It's about eight inches long. I almost lost my eye." She stopped talking to see what he had to say in response to her revelation.

He simply placed his hand over hers and looked at it. Harold looked at her with soft eyes. JoJo stared at his hand covering hers and lifted her eyes to his. He squeezed her hand, smiled and lifted his beer. He tilted his beer bottle toward her and said, "A toast. To you."

JoJo lifted her glass of wine and said, "Yeah. I'll drink to that."

Through the rest of dinner, JoJo learned the basics. He retired early and left Boston to come back here. His two daughters were in Boston. His was married to his ex for twenty years. His kids felt better if was the villain, so he was the villain. His marriage was like most, having periods of harmony or stress. It was during one of the periods of stress that instead of picking a fight with him and working it out, she let it go. She went to the gym, she went to the library book club, she went to the cafe. She told him she was thinking about going back to work; he fully supported her.

Harry thought by providing support, he was giving her what she wanted, independence and control over her life, when what she really wanted was for him to get mad and say no, he wanted her home to take care of him. She wanted him to get all Neanderthal and demand her, need her so she could have something to fight against, something that would make the failure of their marriage *his* fault, but that wasn't going to happen. She placed things that would cause him to trip and fall into her, he simply stepped around them, further increasing the distance between them.

Harold got mad and felt manipulated. As the story goes, she had met someone who appealed to her cruder desires, but she told the girls the marriage ended because he stopped loving her and pushed her out. He didn't dispute it. It hurt a lot, and it took a long time to reconcile the girl he loved with the girl she was. Even his kids. They weren't who he thought they were. It was one of the main reasons he left. He felt used and underappreciated, and figured he could plan an extended stay here and let them miss him for a while. His mother thought the sun rose and set on him, so here was good.

"As a result, among my mother and her friends, it has been determined I have the most eligible bachelor status. All her old lady friends know somebody that would be perfect for me."

"How's it going? Any princesses among the toads?" she asked him.

"So many toads, so little time," he said, and she laughed. They had another drink and talked late into the afternoon.

They got in the car, and he gave her a mint. "What's this for?" JoJo asked him.

"Your breath. It's awful." JoJo quickly popped it in her mouth.

"Sorry."

Five minutes later he pulled into her driveway and parked.

"Let me walk you to the door," he said, hopping out before she could say no. Fury was funny. She knew they weren't done, so going inside would be a waste. She sat in the grass and waited. The lady had keys out but leaned her back against the house.

He leaned close to her.

"Thanks for your time today," he said. "My mom sure likes you, but she likes everyone."

Harold leaned into her further. His lips were so close. "The breath mint. There wasn't anything wrong with your breath; I was afraid something might be wrong with mine. It was for this," he said, looking at her lips. The millimeters that separated their mouth closed, and all of a sudden, it was on. Harry recalled in romance novels, all the heroines end up being ravished, so he attempted to ravish her like the best of them. When they finally broke apart, she was breathing heavily and had her hand on his chest. He felt pretty ravished himself, and he kind of liked it.

"Huh," she said.

"Huh," he said back to her. Harry took a step back.

Fury got next to JoJo. She unlocked the door and went inside, the dog behind her. She looked out the window and waved at him. He waved back and pulled out of the drive. *Huh. She's quite a good kisser. Her husband must be an idiot to walk away from a woman who can kiss like that,* he thought as he drove away.

A few days later, JoJo started in Ray's office. JoJo hired her helper to spend the whole day boxing up his files. She moved them to the spot in the garage where he used to park his company car. Even the bookcases were bare. JoJo sat in Ray's, now hers, office chair. She spun around a few times to absorb the energy of the room. It felt light and airy. So nice, light, and bright. New space for new things.

"What? What did you do?" an overdramatic voice shrieked.

JoJo took the chair and spun it around until she faced her daughter. Abbey stood as if ready for battle.

"Why it's so nice for you to come over and visit your mother, Abbey," JoJo said non confrontationally.

"Where's all Dad's stuff?" Abbey asked.

"Packed nice and neat, all labeled in the garage. If he doesn't come get it, it's going to one of those storage units. I'll pay for three months and what happens after that is up to him," JoJo said as she spun herself around.

"Stop this!" Abbey screamed.

JoJo stopped and looked at her daughter, her beautiful, anxiety-ridden, perhaps eating disordered firstborn. JoJo stopped nagging her to eat years ago. Abbey being extremely thin was what she wanted; she had no respect for women who let themselves go. JoJo decided this line of thought came from Ray, and Abbey being his precious girl, would do anything to please him. He had no respect for women who let themselves go.

Maybe that's what this is about; Ray thought she let herself go. Could Ray be that shallow? JoJo asked herself, but she already knew how shallow Ray could be. The older he got, the more important the wrapping than the gift. *If that really was the reason, well fuck him, the ungrateful prick. I'm lucky I'm alive, and I know how to lose 185 pounds overnight. See ya, Ray, wouldn't want to be ya,* JoJo thought.

Maybe this was harder on Abbey, the dissolution of her parent's marriage, but not for the reasons most people think. Now it's the everyman-for-themselves mentality, and Abbey can't take center stage in her parents' drama if they've got a drama of their own.

She worked for a lawyer she met tending bar and swore it was on the up and up. If she wanted extra money, she could pick up a shift at the bar, so they outlived a financial crisis. A boyfriend crisis. The best friend crisis, and now the Daddy crisis.

"Have you talked to your father, Abbey? He might have some answers for you." JoJo tried to sound sympathetic but might have missed the mark.

"What did you do? What did you do to him, Mom?" Abbey rasped.

"Look. Ask him for the specifics. He said he was done. Okay. I'm done. I'm not gonna keep this place a shrine to him and hope he comes home. He can't come home. There is no home. He destroyed that from the inside. All I'm doing is dismantling the shell.

"I have to tell you, Abbey, that I want to be left alone, that men suck, and I deserve a shot with what's left of my life. I'm sick of being Ray's wife. He can come back as much as he wants, but it won't matter. I've evolved past him. I don't know what's next, but it sure doesn't include him. Don't look at me like that, Abbey. You know I didn't start this thing. It's in motion, and I'm working the angles that are what's best for me. I suggest you work on what's best for you."

Abbey cried as she watched the demise of her family. *Poor Abbey. Every holiday, all she ever did was bitch about having to go, being hungover and not hungry every year. Those Hallmark moments were the first to go, baby,* JoJo thought.

****

Ray's new life started out strong. He felt a second wind of youth. One day, he took the stairs and wasn't tired. He thought his posture was better. Getting old hit Ray hard. He saw the young bucks at work jockeying for his position or higher.

The young women entering the workforce were sexually advanced and so willing, it was a miracle he lasted as long as he did. One incredibly aggressive woman put him in a position to believe he wasn't past his prime or use by date, so he rushed before thinking about the impact leaving might have for the rest of his life.

He talked to the kids, he cut it clean with JoJo. He was free and unencumbered, ready to start anew, only to find it wasn't a shared vision. Those weren't freckles on his back; they were the stab marks of her stilettos on her way up the

160

corporate ladder, using his stooped shoulders and balding head as footholds to leap ahead of him.

He was so glad it was before he made any announcements as to his home situation. Ray was elated he had not let slip he was joining his lover. He needed to do damage control as soon as possible on his home life if he had a home to go home to. He wasn't sure, but JoJo suddenly seemed fearless, and oh God, it made him remember why he fell in love with her in the first place. As lame as life made her, she still swung for the fences.

How often do you even meet a person like that, let alone a woman? She allowed him in and built for him a nice, cozy home and gave him the three miracles of his life-his kids. He was one ungrateful son of a bitch. JoJo needed to know how sorry he was. They could build it again. Better. Anderson 2.0, Ray thought.

Ray couldn't help it he drove by their street at all hours. He needed aplan to get JoJo back. He saw the paint van there often, otherwise just his black car. He was driven mad by the idea JoJo replaced him just like that, with some guy who painted houses for a living, for fuck's sake. He could give her anything her heart desired, yet she'd choose a guy who came home with paint in his hair every night. What was wrong with her?

He would get Abbey to help. Upon hearing of the dismantling of his office, Ray thought he was having a stroke. Somebody touched his things. Ray thought of the painter guy. He touched JoJo. He just knew it.

"Geez, Dad, chill out. Mom's not doing the painter dude, at least not Mark Elliot. He's a born-again Christian, they don't do that kind of stuff," Denver said more than once to his dad. His father went to JoJo's house, and his mother wouldn't let him in. Ray cried in his car, but she shut the drapes. Denver saw a side of his mother he remembered before everything got so messed up. The "Badass-don't-fuck-with-me momma." It was good to know she was still around.

****

One afternoon, Helen, Harold, and JoJo decided after their visit to get ice cream. Harry went to get the cones, and JoJo leaned against the side of the car, talking to Helen, telling her about this being her first job. Harold returned with their ice cream. Fury stuck her head out the rear window, Helen sat up front, and they stood around eating their cones.

161

"Well, if it isn't Josephine Montgomery!" a voice off to the side said. She looked up and around and found the source.

"Alex! Oh My God! It's you! It's you!" she ran over and gave him the most enormous hug she could. "How are you? I can't believe I haven't run into you before! It's been years! Things go according to plan?"

"Hey Jo, not too much at once, okay?" Alex laughed. "My daughter's here for the summer. She has your old job. Maybe you could give her some tips."

"Hey, meet my friends." She introduced him as Alex Reeves, someone who had known her since elementary school.

"Really?" Suddenly, Harry seemed interested.

"Yes, but my name is Alex Burton, not Reeves."

"Tell me a story about who? What's her real name? What did you call her? Josephine?" Harry could tell JoJo was a little tense, unsure what memory he'd pull out of his hat.

"Well, there isn't so much something she did, she did lots of stuff and always got in trouble, but the way she walked. When the teacher would say, 'Josephine Montgomery, to my desk please,' she would get up and drag her feet like her shoes were stuck in cement. It wasn't possible to move any slower, and she always gave out this huge sigh when she got to the desk."

Harold laughed. "Tell me more."

"Before you stroll down memory lane, what's your daughter's name? I'll go say hello."

JoJo left them, went to the counter, and asked for Taylor. She told Taylor she scooped ice cream there over thirty years ago. The girl looked like it wasn't possible to care any less.

"Do they still call it Stoner Island?" That piqued Taylor's interest a bit.

"You know my dad?"

"Yeah. He's over there." She pointed to the group by the car. The girl did a quick glance and did a double-take.

"That's your car? Cool," the girl said.

"No," JoJo said. "But that's my dog. You can barely see her. That's Fury. Well, good luck to you, I'm sure I'll see you again." JoJo went back to the group.

JoJo chuckled to herself as she walked back across the parking lot. *Taylor's teenage ennui was at its peak. A meteor crashing into the Coney Island parking lot would get a barely an eyeroll.* Poor Alex. Teenage girls are the worst. She should know, she was one once.

Helen waved to her from the front seat, Fury's head stuck out of the rear one. JoJo waved back to Helen. Alex was there making small talk with Harold, Harold probably pumping him for high school tales of JoJo. Alex had many to choose from, JoJo hoped he kept it PG-13.

"Nice kid," JoJo said Alex. "How long are you in town?"

"I leave tomorrow. Are you free for coffee tomorrow morning?"

"Yeah, I'm free. I'd love to catch up. What did you have in mind?"

"Want to meet at that new café on Main? I'm kind of on a tight schedule. I have to be back for my son's baseball game. I coach."

"Sure. You're a man of all sports. Does he play football, too?"

"No football. My wife is afraid of him getting concussions."

"Is that what happened to you, Alex? You got your bell rung one time too many?"

"That might explain why I'm still friends with you," Alex joked.

"So tomorrow morning at nine sharp?"

"Won't Harold mind?"

"Harold? Why would he care?"

"Isn't he your—"

"In his dreams, maybe."

"Perfect." Alex had a huge smile on his face. "See you tomorrow."

****

It was a little after nine when Alex met her at the café. JoJo had an outside table because she brought Fury. JoJo waved to him. She got up to give him a huge hug and wrapped her arms around him just like she used to. He covered her arms with his and returned the squeeze. They luxuriously embraced in the familiarity of each other. Alex felt the way he felt all those years ago, strong and sturdy. He was a little softer in spots, which made him more comfortable with her. If he felt the same as he did when he was a teenager, she'd run for her car because she sure didn't. She had some downright squishy areas.

"Ah, JoJo. You fit in my arms just like you used to."

"I can't tell you how good that felt." She reluctantly pulled away. "You're like water to a man lost in the Sahara." JoJo felt the swell of tears and fought them. Being with Alex after all these years caused a jumble of memories and feelings to rise to the top. JoJo wasn't sure she could keep a lid on them all. "I can't believe it's you. And me. And so much happened so long ago. I can't believe it's hitting me this hard. So much time has passed, but so little has changed. Once, you were one of the most special people in my life. That hasn't changed. You still are."

"Stop that, JoJo. You're embarrassing me." Alex looked at her and smiled. "I can't believe I'm sitting here with you. We have so much history between us and not enough time to get into it. I have one thing to say about it, and that's why I feel the same way about you. So, we'll let sleeping dogs lie. Now, on to the present. Have you ordered yet?"

"They don't like the dog inside, so I figured I'd snag the table." She gave him her order, and he came back shortly with their drinks.

"Careful, it's hot. JoJo, I can't believe I'm here with you. You look wonderful."

"Thanks. The years have been kind to me, I guess if you don't count the last five or so."

"Yeah, I heard about your accident. It was pretty bad, wasn't it?"

"It's better now, or as good as it's going to get. I manage. How are you?"

"Me? No problems. It's all good."

"Then why is Taylor here? Nobody comes here voluntarily." Alex shifted in his chair, sipped his coffee, and looked at JoJo, a grimace on his face.

"It's my wife; she's a very religious woman, and Taylor committed an unforgivable sin in the eyes of the church. She was caught kissing a girl on her soccer team."

"Are you as religious as your wife?"

"On Sundays. Otherwise, I go with the flow."

"So, I take it your wife isn't comfortable with same-sex couples?" JoJo inferred that not only was she not comfortable, but she wasn't very tolerant, either. "What's your take on it?"

"Mine? You know me. I'm pretty laid back. I don't care. I mean, I do care for my wife's sake, so I have to support her. But Taylor is a great kid. A wonderful kid. If she's gay, she's gay. I'll love her regardless and let the Lord judge her. My wife, you met her. Kate. Remember? You gave us free ice cream?

"Anyway, it must have been a slow news day because the gym teacher caught them. It spread from the entire school to all over town. My wife is mortified; it being the talk of the town and all. Someone even confronted her at the grocery store.

"If Taylor is gay, my wife has two choices. Accept her or turn her away. If my wife is the Christian, she thinks she is, Taylor should be accepted and embraced. Like I said, the only one fit to judge is the Lord. In the meantime, she wanted to send Taylor to a heavy-duty bible camp in an attempt, I guess, to pray away the gay. I was against this camp, so I brokered a compromise; come here until things settled down and give Taylor some room.

"You wouldn't believe how cruel so-called Christians can be; the people in my wife's Bible study group are some of the worst. Taylor is here to do some self-reflection, get a job, and avoid the prying eyes of our 'Christian fellows.'"

"You know, kids at that age are trying to figure out who they are," JoJo said as she took a sip from her coffee mug. "Maybe she has to kiss a few girls to figure out that's not how she's wired, and if she is, that's how God made her. I'd challenge those holy rollers with the argument if she was made in God's image, well, God must be gay."

"I knew this was the right move." He smiled at JoJo. "I told her to look you up if she gets lonely and needs a friend. I imagine hanging around with her grandparents will get old fast."

"I'll keep my eye out for her. She's welcome any time."

"How's Ray?" He still couldn't believe JoJo ended up with him. He looked her in the eye and waited for her answer.

"Ray?" JoJo frowned when she said his name. "He's the same Ray he's always been. We are no longer together. He walked out on me, on us. He better be careful if I see him. Asshole."

"How did you end up with Ray? I still can't believe you married him."

JoJo bristled at his question. It was valid, and he had the right to ask it. "I wanted more than just Ray. I was lonely, approaching thirty, and nothing in front of me. I decided I wanted a family and a home. I wanted holidays and bloody noses and skinned knees. I wanted baseball and soccer games. I wanted a life bigger than my own. It seemed Ray outlasted everyone else.

"He was the last man standing, so in order to get the life I wanted, when Ray asked, I said yes. I built us quite a nice life, and he walked away from it. From me. I took Ray and shaped him into a decent man, a decent husband, and a decent human being; and for all my efforts look where it got me. He's the same selfish prick he always was."

"I wish I didn't have to leave. It sounds like you could use a friend to talk to." Alex stood up and pointed at his watch. Alex held out his arms to her, and JoJo stepped into his embrace. They hugged again.

"Walk me out to my car, Jo," he said. "If you think about it, you got just what you wanted. You got three great kids out of it, and you didn't miss one chance to be their mom. I bet you had more skinned knees and bloody noses than you can count. You had a chance to watch pretty much every gthe game they ever played. You had a nice home with plenty of Christmas mornings.

"So, things change, regardless of Ray. Your kids fly off and start lives with new people and you can't ever get that Christmas morning feeling back. There's always going to be someone missing. So you had a whole thirty years of it. That's a pretty good run."

They walked together to their cars, both smiling.

"Now, what did I tell you all those years ago? Let go and make room for something else." JoJo looked at him.

"It sounds good, but it looks kind of dark and lonely over there."

"There is that. I'm sorry, JoJo. I'm sorry I couldn't be the one for you."

"What one?"

"The *one*. The one that could have made your dreams come true."

"That's okay. I understand why. You married Kate because that's what you wanted in a girl. She's the girl for you. I was a bit too much. I know that if you were my boyfriend, that's all you'd be. You'd be thinking about me when your focus should be elsewhere. So you married the right girl for you. I married Ray.

"But you're right. I did get the family I wanted. If Ray's the price I had to pay to have them, it was worth it. I worked so hard to love him, and in the end, I did. I mean, what the fuck? The years I spent investing in him to finally get him to the point where he's worth it, and he leaves? Anyway, don't you need to get on the road? I'm sorry to take up your time when you need to get going." She gave him one last squeeze and let him go.

"Would you be upset if I told you I love you? Not in a sexual, romantic way, but in a best friend kind of way? I haven't seen you in forever, but I'm so happy I ran into you. It's like all the years disappeared, and we're kids again."

"Not at all. I love you, too. We have a bond that can't break. Hanging out with you that summer was one of the greatest experiences of my life. I'll always consider you one of the best friends I'll ever have. But you're right. I have to get going. So goodbye, Josephine Montgomery."

"Goodbye, Alex Burton. I'll keep my eye on Taylor for you." He laughed.

"It only took forty years for you to get it right."

"What's that?"

"My last name. Bye, JoJo." He kissed her on the cheek and got in his car.

JoJo put her hand to her cheek and watched him drive away. "*Bye, Alex,*" she said to herself.

****

Later that day, JoJo got in the car, but Harold didn't start it. He looked at JoJo and back to his mother. "Hey! Mom."

His mother looked and said, "Yes, dear?"

"Mom, what's JoJo's name?"

"Why, it's Josephine, after her grandmother." He looked back at her. She was nodding. *She's lived a whole life without me,* he thought sadly.

What a diva, JoJo thought.

He brought his mother home and left JoJo in the car. He wanted to talk to her alone. After he settled his mother inside, he came back and seated himself. Harry turned and faced her.

"What? Aren't we going anywhere?" she asked him.

"He loves you. That guy. Alex." Harold told her. His voice was low and deep.

"Yes, I know. I love him, too," JoJo said. "So? What of it?"

"When were you going to bring him into the mix?" he asked her. "Any other guys going to pop out of thin air and join the party? Fall out of the sky with a bouquet of roses?"

"What are you talking about? I haven't seen him in over thirty years. Thirty years ago, he was one of my best friends. We drifted apart after high school, but at that moment we were really close. It was obvious we were never going to be together forever, but yes, we were extremely close.

"Not so much 'I know this is gonna blow up but WTF' lovers, but true best friends. He had other plans, and I would have been a huge impediment, so he went down his path, and I went down mine. It's like a fossil preserved in stone.

167

It's not being in love or ever being in love. It's the noun love, versus the verb *love*. It's a relic from the past. I've never denied him being in my life or how much he meant to me, and I never will. But it's caught in the past and of no use to anyone now. I don't know how to explain it better than that."

"I don't know what to say to that because that wasn't what I expected to hear."

"You better start with an apology," JoJo told him. "Look. You've been around a while. Isn't there someone from your past that stuck out? Wasn't there a girl who helped you, let you copy her notes, studied with you and dragged you through some class, one you would otherwise have failed without her help? Don't you have a soft spot for her? Or a girl who would let you sleep it off in her bed? You only showed up when you were lonely, or hammered, and she was smart enough to recognize it for what it was and let you in anyway?

"When were you going through your divorce? No secretary who didn't cover your ass a number of times by prepping materials for meetings ahead of time because you were too shell-shocked by the unpredictable happenings in your life to get it together. Not even in high school, Mrs. Weathersbee in the front office, who let you use her copier and sometimes helped you out with lunch money? Not even her?"

"Who's Mrs. Weathersbee?" he asked.

"The lady who worked in the front office. See, you can't even remember her name. How self-absorbed are you?" JoJo asked him.

"No, Weathersbee wasn't her name. I'm sure of it."

"Never mind. You only need a handful of people. I'm sure you could pick out one or two over your whole life, you're pretty old. You're retired."

"Can I consider you one? Only one of the ones you might want to say, 'WTF lovers since it's gonna blow up anyway?'"

"No. Find your own people. You're too old to need people. Events have transpired. Either there were people who helped or who didn't. You're at the point in your life where you can be somebody's people. Use your time now to help someone else."

"Will you be my people?" he asked her sweetly. "Can I be your people?"

"Not right now. I have a very messy marriage to clean up," she said.

"You may need some support, there," he said. "I'll be your people for that."

"Thanks, I guess," she said. "I'm so confused."

"Don't worry. You've got people to help. Just make sure you call me first."

****

It was a few weeks later. Kathy, JoJo's cleaning lady/girl Friday, had just left JoJo's house fresh and clean. She was at the table, on her laptop searching the web, when the door opened with a squeak. JoJo looked up. It was Ray. JoJo stood up and yelled at him, "You don't live here anymore, Ray! You just can't walk in."

"Oh, JoJo, please don't be angry! I miss you so much! I was wrong," Ray pleaded. "I love you. I'm sorry, so sorry. I love you!"

"Stop it, Ray! Quit crying! You couldn't get out of here fast enough. What's the matter?

Washing your own clothes do you in?" JoJo sneered.

"Don't be mad. I made a mistake, a horrible, horrible mistake. Please forgive me. We've been married for almost thirty years. We have three beautiful children. Look at this wonderful home you created. I want my family back. I want a turkey on this table! A tree in the family room! I want it back! I want it all back! Remember, we were such a good team? We are so good together. Don't destroy everything we built. Please, JoJo, don't ruin the future for our kids! Our grandchildren!" he cried.

She looked at him. The father of her kids. Right here, the culmination of her whole adult life. Abbey. Frankie. Denny. Was she overreacting? A lot of men go through midlife crises. Did she have the right to wreck everyone else's future because she felt slighted?

Was her own pride and ego going to ruin it for her kids? She had been mad at Ray plenty of times in their marriage, sometimes even-hide-the-cutlery mad, but she always forgave him.

Couldn't she forgive him one more time? Should she? Seeing him cry, looking so lost, so small and old caused her to start tearing up. In spite of herself, she put her hand on his shoulder. He covered it with his own. He wept silently, not letting her have her hand back.

"Ray. Ray. Come on. It's okay," she said, holding back her tears. He stood up and enveloped her in a tight hug.

"Please, JoJo, please take me back. Please," he sobbed.

"Look, Ray. You have to go. You have to," she told him.

"Please tell me you'll think about it. Don't destroy our family over my foolishness."

169

"I'll think about it, I will." She walked him towards the door. "It's okay, Ray. It's okay."

"Please, please, promise me you'll think about it. Don't make me lose everything I love over my stupidity."

JoJo put her hand on the door and turned the knob, angling Ray to push him out. She turned her head and he grabbed her and he kissed her like he wasn't kidding. It shocked her still for a minute, her inaction he interpreted as permission, and he went in deep. JoJo pushed him off her and said he had to go, shoved him out, and remembered to lock the door after him.

She opened the fridge and found a barely touched bottle of white wine. That whole scene with Ray left her emotionally spent. She poured herself a nice glass and went into the family room to watch some TV. She felt like binge-watching *Intervention*, the only show that could make her feel like someone else's life was worse off than hers.

She sat on the floor, put the wine on the cocktail table along with her phone and channel surfed her options. She had another glass and then one more. Before she knew it, she was sound asleep on the floor next to Fury.

Harold called JoJo's phone twice, it went directly to voicemail. The third time he called her the phone clicked and all he heard was Fury barking. He was alarmed, he never heard Fury make a peep, let alone bark.

He drove over to the cul-de-sac and pulled into her driveway, jumped out and pounded on the door, no answer except Fury barking. He looked at a sticker with an emergency number in the corner of the window and called. Her son Frankie answered. He was right around the corner, and he'd come right over, but gave him the override code so he could get in immediately.

He punched the code and went in, was met by Fury, who brought him to JoJo. She was slumped between the coffee table and couch, sound asleep. He looked at Fury and then JoJo. Her son entered and looked at his mother, and the empty wine bottle. Frankie looked at Harry.

"You got this?" he asked Harry.

"No," he answered. They laughed. Frankie went into the kitchen and got him a pot. "You might need this if you wake her up." The two of them laughed at JoJo. The sound woke her, and she was totally confused with the whole situation until she moved, her brain went one way and her stomach the other. JoJo felt her guts come up, and she grabbed the pot and puked.

"Well, looks like you've got a grip on things here," Frankie laughed. "Dude. It's still the gentlemanly thing to do, holding a girl's hair while she pukes," he tutored Harold. When she brought her face up, she saw the two of them looking down on her.

"Jesus. Fuck," she said and up came some more. The guys sprang into motion at the sound of her hurling.

"Bye, Mom, drink some Gatorade, see ya, dude, good luck," Frankie said as he exited. Harold looked at JoJo, slumped against the sofa, propped up by Fury. For the first time, he saw Fury express anything other than high alert. She was relieved. She showed in her eyes she did what she was supposed to, and it worked. JoJo was okay, Fury wasn't alone, and the rest was up to Harold.

Harold did the first thing that came to mind and grabbed the remote. He turned the channel. Golf was on. He looked at JoJo. He decided to get her on the couch and let her sleep it off, and he'd watch TV for a while. He gently lifted her onto the couch. He was worried, he knew she hurt, but didn't know how or where, so he handled her as gently as he could. Harry propped her up on the end, using the arm of the couch for support. He looked at her, her head back and her mouth ajar. He thought she was going to drool or snore soon, he looked at her lap and recalled how happy Fury seemed with her head resting there.

Harold sat on the couch and put his head in her lap. Fury was right. He took her hand and put it on his cheek. Her touch was warm and dry. Harry put her hand in his hair. She stirred, and absent-mindedly started to stroke his head, petting him like she would Fury. When he died, he wanted to come back as Fury or her next dog.

God, he couldn't remember the last time something purely sensual as her touch happened to him. He didn't need to start or finish anything, and neither did she. Harry just luxuriated in her touch and shut his eyes. He stayed that way until he felt her stir and sat up. Harry got up and laid her down on the couch, sat on the floor with Fury, and watched golf.

After golf, he started watching some dumb movie. He questioned his sanity. She was married. Unavailable. By the time she was a tree ready to be climbed, he wondered if he'd be a weak old man who would rather have a cup of tea thaen fuck her.

He had been divorced a long time and been a plus-one more times than he could count, but he preferred to sleep alone. He wanted to be at his place with

171

his things and was required to communicate nothing more than a grunt. He wanted to walk around with his dick hanging out if he felt like it.

Women cramped his style. He lived with three women for a long time. He loved his daughters, he did. He loved them the hardest he could; maybe his tight hold on them is why their relationship was so fractured now. He adored them. When they were little, he was the giant in their lives, able to slay dragons and chase away the monsters under the bed. They were the cowgirls, and he was the horse. Harry crammed his six-foot-tall frame into child sized furniture for tea parties. They painted his fingernails like a rainbow.

He went to an important business meeting like that, accidentally, it helped him win the bid.

The women on the committee thought that the big man letting his little girls paint his nails automatically weighed heavily in his favor. A committee member commented on it, and he said, "Oh, no! I don't have any lipstick on my teeth, do I?" and they tittered at his cleverness.

Then they grew up. Playing cowgirl or tea parties became dumb. They spent most of their free time with his wife, shopping, salons and whatever else they did. He wanted dinner as a family at night, but the three were obsessed with calories and food.

There was never anything to eat at home, so he ate out alone. He found they minimized his role as a contributing member of the family. He wasn't Dad, he was their father now. He was so taken aback by their shallowness, that he was flabbergasted when he realized he had overlooked the source for so long it was cemented in their collective psyches, his wife.

Caitlin was a stunning brunette who worked in a coffee shop. She was sweet and friendly. She made an ungodly amount in tips. He was captivated by her charm. She flirted with him shamelessly. Harold pursued her. It was early in his career. He had stamina. They had such fun. She traveled with him. It was on a trip to Vegas they eloped. Life was exciting and new. After a while, they bought a place, new and bright.

Ashley was born, and two years later, Kerry. Caitlin was home where she wanted to be, taking care of the little girls she always wanted. He went out and earned a living, allowingher to stay home as well as have nice things. Even though money wasn't an issue, her attitude about it concerned him.

She would get the girls outrageously expensive outfits and plan elaborate birthday parties he felt were unnecessary, but he loved those girls too, so he let alot slide. The tea parties and pretend games weren't enough. Her desire for more meant he was gone more, worked more and more time between connections. If he had home more, he might have seen how much his wife had changed from his fun partner into an accumulator of things. Expensive things. How many shoes did she need? Frivolous purchases most of it, and he was not going to allow her to waste money on crap.

It came to a head when the kids were teenagers. They, like all kids, flocked to the latest and greatest electronics. He was going through the credit charges, and he hit the ceiling when he saw the bill for the Apple store. He took Caitlin's credit cards away for a month, and she stopped talking to him. When she got them back, she went on a tear and bought as much as she could. She had been waging a behind-the-scenes, *your father doesn't want you to be happy* war, when his point was things aren't what make you happy. Harold said he wanted personal financial responsibility for each, alone. He would sit down with each of them, figure out expenses, figure savings, and most importantly figure budgets.

If they refused to do it with him, he would get an accountant, and the last option was it would be done for them without their input. Any change could be negotiated. He also wanted one afternoon a week, together or separately, spent with him on an urban adventure. Someplace new to both of them. Museum, gallery, restaurants.

Caitlin threatened, "You do that, and you better find a new place to live."

He signed a lease for a year and got a divorce lawyer. Most of his money came in after the divorce, so she lost out there. It took six months for his kids to get the message shit was real, and his weekly afternoon visits consisted of non-confrontational enjoyable things like just getting ice cream or walking around local parks. His kids came around and realized you can't fill a void in your soul with stuff, but it was seductive to try. They understood their mom needed them to endorse her behavior; their participation helped to justify it. If it wasn't in their nature to accept certain things as truths, or what may be one person's truth may not be yours, it was okay to pass. "You see what you see, and nobody can say otherwise. Make up your own minds," he told them.

****

173

CHAPTER TWENTY-TWO

Later that afternoon, JoJo sat up on the couch, her head woozy. She saw the empty wine bottle. She remembered Ray's visit. Her mouth felt gross. She needed to pee. JoJo put her feet down and went to stand, not realizing Harold had fallen asleep on the floor. He had been spooning Fury, but Fury disengaged when JoJo awoke and stood at the ready. Poor Harold. When JoJo stood, it was on top of Harold's soft belly, who immediately rolled and brought JoJo down on top of him. Fury looked ready to leap on top but changed her mind when JoJo screamed.

"Oh, no!" she yelled. Harold tried to roll in the direction of her fall so she didn't land on the floor, she would land on him, and he would break her fall. She landed face down she rolled off him in what was a gentle landing.

"What the fuck? Why are you here? Why does this keep happening to me?" she said, face-first into the carpet.

"Hey!" Harold yelled. He fell asleep on the floor, and Fury curled up next to him. He had a nice nap spooning the dog and was unaware JoJo was awake until she stepped on him. Harold rolled over with an "Oof" and broke JoJo's fall. She laid face down with no attempt at moving.

"JoJo! Are you okay? Did you hurt anything?"

"Only my dignity and self-respect," she answered into the pile.

"I won't tell anyone," he consoled her. "Do you need help getting up? Or at least rolling over?"

"Would you mind helping me rollover? I'm not ready to stand. I don't feel so great."

"It would be my pleasure; it will help you breathe better. Now let me know if I'm hurting you." He gently rolled her over on her back. "Is that better?"

"Yeah. She brought her knees up to allow her to put her feet flat on the floor. "I can't lay flat on my back for too long, but this is okay for now. I can't believe this. How did you get here? What happened?" she asked him.

He explained everything slowly as she nodded along.

"What time is it?" she asked him.

"Almost seven."

"Seven in the morning? I've been here all night?"

"In the evening, JoJo."

"Oh. I'm sorry, Harold. You don't need to get caught up in this. Can you roll me on my side?" she asked him.

He rolled her, and it was his turn to spoon her. He wanted to have Fury lay on the other side and create a JoJo sandwich. Harold put his hand on her hip. He could feel her receding into her own head, and he didn't want her to shut down and not talk for a few days, her habit when she got overwhelmed. He figured he needed to shock JoJo back to reality.

"Are you hungover?"

"Surprisingly not."

"That's probably because the alcohol wasn't in your system that long. You threw most of it up. Nice boy, your son. He made sure you had a pot to puke in and reminded me to hold your hair back when you do."

"Yeah, they're good boys. I can't believe I did that. Oh. Yeah. Fuck. Ray," she moaned. "I need to get off the floor now and take a hot shower."

"Stay put," Harold said. "Let me get up." He tried to do so without groaning, but if she had difficulty, he could understand why.

"Here," Harold said and extended his arm. JoJo got up, and he made her sit a minute on the couch in case she was dizzy. She felt able and got up. "I need a hot shower to loosen up. You can stay if you like. I can explain then," she said and went towards her room.

Oh, I'm staying, he thought. *This, I gotta hear.*

She came back, twisting her damp hair. Harold had ready for her some toast and tea. "You did this for me? You didn't have to, but thanks," JoJo said gratefully and took a sip. "This is just what I needed."

"Care to tell me how we got to this point?"

"No, but probably I should. After Kathy left yesterday the door was open, and Ray walked in. He cried and begged, saying I'm ruining the family, I'm destroying the holidays in the family home. Ray begged and pleaded with me to take him back. He made a mistake, I can't punish the whole family, why can't I forgive him, blah blah blah. The only way I could get him to leave was promised to think about things." She rubbed both of her temples with her fingers, trying to decide what was worse, thinking about Ray or her liquid lunch. JoJo

175

decided both were giving her a headache, and she decided she wanted to avoid thinking about either.

"I felt sad and mad and found the wine in the fridge and told myself just one, and then I said fuck it and I'm not sure I even used a glass. I'm sorry I missed it, hearing Fury bark and all. I can't believe I slept through that. I wish I slept through Ray's bullshit. That's my weak spot. I've been conditioned all my life to help people. I have such guilt. I want to turn it off and walk away, but these people follow me and suck me in."

He remained quiet.

"Any thoughts?" she asked him.

"Since you asked. Can I get on the list to be sucked in?"

"See? That's what I mean," JoJo said. "Why can't you suck me in? Why do I have to do everything?"

"Because we don't like leaving if we get in. And some of us wait years for the invite, so you better mean it."

"You're crazy. After you divorced how often did you see each other?"

"Never. I never wanted to see her again. We were civil and respectful, or I was. It was only after a while we had to get near each other at the kid's things we knew we had to for their sake let it go. The girls were teens. I still wonder how they could expect the very worst from me. I love them. How could they think so little of me? They were learning all the wrong things from their mother. I realized it was so good in the beginning because we traveled a lot. She got to fill her spot with experiences. After the kids she filled it with stuff, expensive stuff. I didn't fill that spot. It took a long time to accept that I wasn't enough. She had a void inside I couldn't fill. I would always come up short. She'd never get enough, and she'd always be looking somewhere else. So, I left," Harold said.

"Ray comes over and says I'm ruining everyone's holidays. Our future grandchildren's Christmases. Why can't I forgive him? Why should I? Fuck him. Then I feel guilty. Ray wants to say, 'oopsy' I made a mistake, and hit the reset button. Why am I the asshole because I can't forgive him? Poor fucking Ray. He thinks he has time to think it over and change his mind. He didn't have time. He chose. It's over. Get over it. Oh shit. Abbey. She'll be pissed I won't forgive him she wants us back together. She'll be miserable. Oh, the boys. What would they want?" she rambled on.

"JoJo," he interrupted. "It's a lot. Slow down. About the boys, they're fine. Neither expressed a desire to see you back together, and they left you alone with me, so they approve of your choice in men. Frankie could have told me to go and called Ray. What do *you* want, JoJo? That's the important question."

"I want my family back. I made a nice home for a family," JoJo said. "I enjoyed that."

"What about Ray? Do you still love him?" Harold asked.

"Do I still love Ray? No. Absolutely not. I never did, at least not like that."

"Wait, What? If you didn't love Ray, why did you marry him?"

JoJo gave a sharp laugh, so sharp it could slice a sandwich. "Nobody else asked. I was living alone. No prospects. I was almost thirty. My brother had a couple of kids, and they were happy, so I looked at it like, 'I could be happy like them,' and Ray was interested. I convinced myself I loved him. I *wanted* to love him. It would be so convenient to marry Ray. It sounds dumb, but we had a good enough life. We got along fine. We have three great kids. I built that life on purpose. That's what I wanted. So, what one piece of the puzzle was Ray? I worked with him and made him into a decent husband. I do love him, but not the way I should. I don't, um, *hunger,* for him."

"Does Ray know this?"

"No. Of course not. There was no reason to tell him. If I go back to him, what am I going back to? My creation of this Norman Rockwell/Martha Stewart's illegitimate love child's fantasy? It's not real, but does it matter if the memories and traditions are real?"

"Yes, they are real, wonderful for a family to have; but your kids are adults now. That whole waking up to the smell of turkey is nice if you're nine but old at nineteen. I think you accomplished your goals. You created a nice warm nest for all of them, Ray included. They grew up with a great mom who taught them well. When the world kicked them around, they came home to milk and cookies and their mother's love. To a wonderful home with memories. Maybe it's time to change things now everyone's all grown up. Doesn't one of your kids have a house? Let him entertain his family. Make new memories."

"Frankie. He'd let you use his house but probably not show up. How do you handle who hosts what?"

"Easy. We go out. Neutral territory. So, what if my ex-wife brings her new boyfriend? What do I care? I'll always love the mother of my girls, but she's not around. She's frozen, stuck in the past, and she can stay there. Anyway, I think this is the real Cait. She's still looking to fill that hole. I couldn't do it, a family couldn't do it. I don't know if she'll ever be content with what's in front of her. Luckily, the damage to my kids was minor, I hope. I was there when they were small and involved as much as I could be right through high school. I never trash talked their mom, ever. I did my best. I hope it was enough, that's all I could do. It's all you can do."

"Huh. I'm old or older. I'm getting tired. I just want what I want. When's it my turn?" she asked him softly. "I'm going to hire someone to travel with me, then I get to go where I want when I want. Maybe even—"

The door slammed open and in walked her eldest. She was such a gorgeous girl. Abbey's thick, auburn hair caught the light and lit up her face. Her blue eyes were big bright spots in the planes of her face. The freckles that Ray and Denny were cursed with only sprinkled across her nose and cheeks. Her smile of straight white teeth and full lips only emphasized the beauty of the rest of her face. She was stunning. Only when she opened her mouth she ruined everything.

"Mom," she said crossly. "What's wrong now? I heard from Dad. Why are you being so difficult?" She stopped and took a breath. She looked at Harold. "Who is this?"

"That's my friend Mr. Elliot. Why?" JoJo's temper flared. "You don't just get to come in here and start ordering me around. You're a guest in my home. Act like one or leave."

Abbey's eyes widened in shock at the sharpness of her mother's voice.

"I was at Frankie's, and they were talking about coming over here and finding you passed out on the floor. You should be embarrassed," Abbey lectured.

"You should shut up, Abbey. Mr. Elliot, my daughter Abbey. Abbey, say hello to Mr. Elliot."

"Hello, Mr. Elliot. Nice to meet you." Abbey said with flared nostrils. "I'm not sure why you're here. My mom is not in a good spot right now, there's a whole lot on her plate. I need to make sure my mother doesn't do anything she might regret. She's in a vulnerable position, and we need to know nobody's taking advantage of her. My father just moved out and she's a married woman. It's too soon for her to be involved with anybody, and she shouldn't be hanging around with a single guy."

"Who said he's single?" JoJo asked. JoJo looked at Abbey while sitting at the table drinking tea. It had been a ridiculous day. The last thing she needed was a pile of crap from Abbey.

"How many times do I have to tell you your father left *me*? What happens next is up to *me*."

"Why can't you forgive him?" Abbey said, looking at Harold. "I can't believe you are being such a bitch about this. You're being selfish. Dad had a midlife crisis. Is that a good enough reason to destroy the rest of us? You're being ridiculous. Why does his one mistake have to ruin everything? If you forgive him, we can go back to the way things were. I wish you would look at the big picture, Mom. Our future is at stake."

Harold stood. "I think you might want to talk about this in private, so I think I'll go now," he said as he moved to the door.

"Sit down, Harold," JoJo ordered. "See, I don't want to talk about this in private. I don't want to talk about it in public. I don't want to talk about it at all. You can't un-ring a bell, Abbey."

"God, I hate when you say that," Abbey moaned. "Mom, he's human. He indulged in a delusion. He was stupid. It's not like you never did anything stupid. You can't forgive him? I—"

"Go, Abbey. You're stressing us out. Even Fury. If there's nothing more you need to say, then go. I love you but *go*. You're embarrassing me in front of the paint guy."

"Oh," Abbey said, an edge in her voice at being dismissed. "Excuse me. Mom, I'll catch up with you later." She picked up her things and left.

"Maybe you shouldn't come around. I mean, for your own sanity," JoJo said to Harold, "but I have a confession to make. Your van, Elliot Bros. You drove it here a few times. Then Mark shows up and paints the house, so it's his truck here but with the same logo. He leaves, and you park the van here a few times. Ray is convinced I'm having an affair with the paint guy because the truck's been here so much. I don't think anyone realized the & Bros. was back in town. The paint guy to him is your brother Mark Elliot. That's the only Elliot Ray knows. Abbey's going to tell him the paint guy was here again. Your poor brother."

"My brother Mark? He thinks you're fooling around with Mark?"

"That's what my other son says. Ray accused me of doing the paint guy."

179

"But he's some kind of Jesus freak."

"I prefer a devout Christian. But still." They both had a good laugh at that.

****

CHAPTER TWENTY-THREE

A few afternoons later, Fury and JoJo were on the front lawn playing fetch. JoJo wished she could open her shoulder up and give her some range. *Maybe I'll do some physical therapy,* JoJo thought. *Fury was so kind to get excited about my measly throws. But she was happy to play with her.* JoJo noticed a girl ride her bike into the cul-de-sac. She had the choice of three homes. She picked JoJo's first because of the welcoming flowers and landscaping.

For Mother's Day each year they landscaped her yard. Frankie's latest girl is a landscape architect, but she's always working. That's enough for Frankie. She helped a lot with the front beds. She came to water them twice a week for a while. Then Frankie showed up, and then both of them. He had no idea she watered them, and they met over the garden hose; both coming at the same time one night. He decided this was the girl for him.

Her name was Crystal. She was strong; she tossed around big bags of mulch with ease, which excited Frankie. She wore Timberland boots and cut off Levi's, showcasing her muscular legs.

Crystal loved the work and harmony of gardening. She watered clients' gardens to establish the roots strictly for the plant's benefit, even if the homeowner didn't pay for it. Frankie loved that she revered Mother Earth. She probably didn't shave her armpits, JoJo figured, but she grew her own vegetables and canned her own tomatoes.

****

JoJo was out front admiring the flowers and tossing a ball for Fury. It was hot out and Fury went into the shade and chewed on a stick. She watched a young girl approach her house.

The girl looked familiar, she looked hot in her all black attire, especially the denim. She was just a little wisp of a thing. She pushed her bike up the walk and looked at JoJo.

"Is this where the big black dog lives?" she asked.

"You mean Fury? She's over there, chewing on a stick."

At the mention of her name, Fury popped her head up and trotted over. She sat and looked at the girl.

"Have a seat. Take your gear off," JoJo said and sat back down. The girl sat down next to JoJo but stayed with her gaze in front of her. JoJo knew her, she couldn't place her. She had dyed her hair pitch black and must have cut it herself judging by the hack job. The sandy eyelashes.

Just like her dad.

"Taylor Burton," JoJo said.

"Yeah, that's me."

"Fury. Come," JoJo said, and she snapped too. "Here. Say hello to Taylor." Fury came up, and JoJo took Taylor's hand. She spread her fingers open and let Fury catch her scent.

"You're in her database on a non-threatening list. You can scratch behind her ears now," JoJo instructed her.

"Why'd you name her Fury?"

"I didn't. The Army did. They give them names like Slaughter or Chaos. Play head games with the enemy, I guess."

"She was in the Army? Cool. She looks like a real badass."

"That's what they say about me," JoJo told her.

She scratched behind her ears and Fury leaned on Taylor's legs. JoJo could feel the girl start to lose whatever nerve that got her this far. She placed her arms around the dog and started to sob. JoJo rubbed the girl's back, gently like she'd soothe a toddler. Alex secretly hoped JoJo was able to connect with her on some level, catch her before she was too far away to save. He knew JoJo had a hard time in high school. Taylor was having a hard time, too.

Fury, with the patience of a saint, or a Saint Bernard, allowed the girl to comfort herself in her fur. JoJo went into the garage and grabbed a box of tissues. She remembered the copious amounts of snot a teenage girl could produce. After a bit, Taylor settled down. JoJo handed her a wad of towels.

"Did that help at all? I often find a good cry wash away some of the stress. You might want to wipe your face really well because she sheds big time. If you like Fury, you can come over whenever you want. You can walk her too. Did you come over just to see Fury, or did you want to talk to me, too?"

Taylor started sobbing again. JoJo reached out and pulled her over in a big hug.

"Did your dad tell you to come talk to me? I used to be a teenage girl once. I think he remembered how tough a time I had growing up, but he helped. I think he thinks maybe I can return the favor."

"I don't think so. It's hopeless," she cried.

"Why don't you run it by me and let's see."

"I think I'm gay. My parents caught me making out with a girl. My mother wanted to send me to some sort of Christian re-education camp all summer, but my dad was able to talk her into sending me to my grandparents, and I had to get a job. So here I am, trying to figure this out on my own. I don't understand. It's like my body is stronger than my mind. I want to be good, but I can't help it." She sobbed.

"Hey, hey. It's okay. Stop telling yourself there is something wrong with you. And any religious bullshit is answered by the fact if you believe in God you have to believe God doesn't make mistakes. Anyway, I'm not sure you're one or the other. That's all growing up is, finding out who you are and your place in the world.

"I think that's okay you kissed a girl, but did you want to, or did you do it to rub your mom's nose in that fact that she's losing control? Have you ever kissed a boy? Maybe you might like that too. Maybe the right person will decide what your preferences are for you. Lots of questions, growing up, but look at it this way. You can do most of it here outside the prying eyes of people back home. You may not get any answers, but at least when you leave, you'll feel better about who you are, and you're capable of handling what comes your way.

"I'm not sure, though, how your mother will feel if she realized instead of bumming out in your Gramma's attic as punishment, you're hanging around a bunch of fucked up old people. It doesn't get any better just because you get older. You still have to scoop two nights a week on top of that. I'm glad you don't mind hanging around. It's nice to have a fresh perspective. If you want to walk Fury sometimes, I'm sure she'd be grateful."

"What about that guy in the Mercedes? Where does he fit in?" Taylor said.

"One piece at a time, Taylor. I have no idea. He's a wild card," JoJo told her.

"A wild card. Sounds exciting." Taylor's voice echoed JoJo's.

"We shall see.

****

Taylor became a fixture at JoJo's. JoJo laughed and said she was Fury's aide.

"Maybe you can use it on your college application. You spent your summer taking care of an old lady named Fury, who was a real dog."

"Maybe I'll become a vet," Taylor said.

"See that, Taylor? You mentioned the future, as far off as that may be. That's healthy."

"Yeah. I guess." Taylor sounded less than impressed. "Do you mind if I bring her for a walk into town? There's this old lady who feeds the ducks and likes to see dogs. She always stops people to pet their dogs. I bet she'd like Fury."

"That's a great idea. Just watch her paws on the hot pavement. Tell Mrs. W. I said hello," JoJo added.

"Who?"

"The lady who feeds the ducks. Her last name is some long Polish name, so I just call her Mrs. W." Taylor looked surprised. "Small town," offered JoJo.

****

JoJo asked Taylor if she wanted to do a few errands with her, and she said she would. JoJo hit the button, and the garage door lifted.

When Taylor saw the car she said, "Why do you have that old guy's car?"

JoJo laughed. "I had mine first. He copied me. It was Ray's, but it's mine now. Another parting gift."

"Cool."

JoJo brought Taylor to the local thrift shop. She pointed at the heavy, wide-legged jeans and said, "Your shirts I can live with, but we have to do something about your jeans. That's way too much material, and it's way too hot out. I hope you're not offended by the store, but you can get cool things here, I got this snakeskin jacket here once. You look like the kind of person who likes to treasure hunt. I can take you to Hot Topic after."

"Hot Topic? No, thank you. Let's go score something," Taylor said and turned towards the door.

JoJo followed her into the store. *My people*, thought JoJo. They were able to find her some black jeans she could cut off and an oversized Levi's jean jacket, faded and worn.

"It's a classic," JoJo said. She also found a black broomstick skirt, perfect should she decide to wear it to a music festival. And a few tees with band logos

JoJo had never heard of on the front. It was a start. Taylor had a few pairs of jeans she wanted to cut off into shorts. All in all, it was a productive visit.

****

Harold came over with Helen; she wanted to have lunch in the park and invite JoJo. She took Fury and ran into Taylor at the bottom of the street, so she piled in, too. His mother was excited, it was a beautiful day for a picnic. It was decided Helen and JoJo would wait with Fury; trusting them to pick out a good spot. He would wait in line for sandwiches while Taylor ran into the grocery store for drinks. He took a wad of cash out of his front pocket and gave it to her. "Here. Go." They split up at the plaza and went in different directions and planned to meet back at the park.

They all sat around a wooden picnic table and enjoyed a pleasant afternoon. Helen had a good time. She enjoyed Taylor because "kids keep you young," she told Harry.

"Oh, it's too late for Harold," teased JoJo. "He's already old."

"You're right behind me, don't forget," he teased back.

After a while, Taylor announced she'd be taking off, she had to work. Her grandparents lived a few blocks away, it was a short walk home. She thanked Harold for lunch, kissed Helen's cheek goodbye, and gave Fury a good scratch behind her ears. She told JoJo she would see her soon. They watched her walk away. She was wearing a black wife beater, black cut-offs, and her Doc Martens. She was a tiny little thing.

"What a delightful child," Helen said.

"She seems happy enough," Harold observed.

"I think she's okay. She hasn't opened up to me yet, though," JoJo told them.

It happened a few days later. JoJo knew something was wrong when Taylor came in and headed to where Fury lay on the family room floor. She laid down next to Fury buried her face in Fury's fur and started to cry. An unfortunate combination of shedding dog and tears made a mess of her face. JoJo grabbed the tissues, went back and sat on the couch. Fury looked at her, but she shook her no, so the dog stayed put.

"Hey, Taylor. Did something happen today?" JoJo probed gently and gave her the tissues.

"I don't know. I guess so." Taylor said, hiccupping and wiping her face.

"What?"

"Remember how I told you I got in trouble because of that girl?"

"Yeah."

"Well, my parents have been put in the position of having a kid who the whole town talks about. Some lady called my mother a name and called me a slut in line at the grocery store again. I thought things would blow over, it being summer, but no."

"Small town, small minds. I'd like to help you," JoJo said. "I think that's why you're here, but the only thing I can offer is support. I was a teenage girl once, and I survived. I think I know what your dad is hoping I can do. I can tell you my story, and we can talk about that. JoJo forced herself to revisit that painful period with Brandon and spoke honestly.

"I'm not sure if making out with a girl is so bad. Think about this. What if you fell in love, real love, and that person was yanked away, put in prep school, their parents up and sold their house and moved away? Because of a seventeen-year-old girl? Because of you? It felt like I was on a plane and the door opened and sucked everything out. I was lost. He said he would love me forever. And then he was gone." The pain she felt back then was still visible on JoJo's face.

"One day we were giggling on the couch, the next day, I couldn't talk to him. The phone number is no longer in service. I thought he went to tennis camp, but I think they took him somewhere and brainwashed him because when I saw him, he looked like he was going to have a breakdown. He would have cracked if I put any more pressure on him, so I let him go. How could love be bad? How? It took almost a year to accept what his parents did, not even whether it was right or not. I was clinically depressed. Emotionally checked out.

"Anyway, your dad helped me focus on what was in front of me. He was a good friend when I really needed one, he was my best friend and kept his eye on me.

"I think he's worried about you, so he sent you here, to show you it's okay. I think he's trying to tell you that you are just fine, the same message he gave me. You are just fine, it's other people who have the problem. You can't let one event define you, and you are who you are. Just because you're gay doesn't mean you are exempt from life's shit list. You still have stupid people you have to deal with. They're not stupid because you're gay, they're stupid because they're stupid.

"Go back to school. I'm sure there's some new drama to take the heat off you. Or ask if you can live with your grandparents and go to school here, if you need to. It's only one year. Just use the time to do things explore everything. Then, when you get to college, maybe love will present itself, and you'll be a little more prepared, or at least you'll be more likely to recognize it. Your dad saved you from Christian Bible Conversion summer camp, didn't he? You know he's in your corner, right?"

****

After her talk with Taylor, JoJo thought of Brandon Bridges. She turned the thought of where he was over and over in her mind. Where was he? Was he married? Was he happy? It was so long ago it surprised her how she felt the same hurt she felt back then.

That was over thirty-five years ago, and she could still feel the pain. It faded from an agonizing ice pick through her heart to a dull ache in her chest, but it was still there. JoJo did some googling and found out he joined the Navy and went to Annapolis. She couldn't get the thought of him out of her mind. What happened to him? Was he happy? Did he have a good life?

What was she supposed to do? Call up the Department of Veteran Affairs and say she was trying to stalk her old boyfriend? Would they mind looking him up for her?

JoJo heard he went to Mid-State Prep in Connecticut; maybe he was mentioned in their yearbook. JoJo found the yearbook online, but the only mention of Brandon had him listed undergraduates. There was no senior class photo of him in the yearbook.

JoJo knew his parents' names and found them easily, but she wouldn't go near them. She remembered he had a sister named Rebecca and googled her. There was a Rebecca Bridges living in the same city as his parents. She was a realtor with a local company. JoJo couldn't help herself, she called the office and asked for her.

"Rebecca Bridges speaking. Let's start looking for your dream home today."

"Hello, Ms. Bridges, my name is Linda," she looked quickly around for a last name, her eye caught the desk, "Linda Woods. I'm with the Mid-State Prep

Alumni Association, and I was hoping to update our contact information. Would you be able to provide us with current contact information regarding your brother Brandon? We seem to have lost track of him since he joined the service. The mailing address or even a current email would be enough."

"Sure. I'd be happy to." JoJo heard her smile through the phone. "Here, I have his email right here," she said, giving it to JoJo.

"Thank you on behalf of the Mid-State Prep Alumni Association."

"My pleasure. If you're ever in the market for a house, please consider me. I specialize in finding you the home of your dreams."

JoJo looked at the piece of paper with the email address. Forty years vanished just like that. She took that piece of paper and hung it on the refrigerator. She left it up for almost a week while she thought about what to say. What she really wanted was to rewrite the ending of their goodbye.

The image of him looking at her like an animal caught in a trap, and her yelling at his parents as she walked away, defeated and distraught, haunted her. He was her first love, and she hadn't felt love like that since. Her love for him was true. It was pure. She still held a piece of it in her, that love was the yardstick she used to measure other love. Nothing ever came close.

Maybe nothing ever could match that first love. Every other love was now tainted with the stain of the hurt and pain that came with the risk of being in love.

JoJo sat at her computer and started to type. She had no idea what to say or if it was worth saying. She started to type:

Dear Brandon,

I think you may be surprised to hear from me. I hope not. I guess what I'm trying to say is I still think about you after all these years. You were my first boyfriend, my first love, my first partner. I guess being a girl these things stay with you. I want to rewrite our ending. There was so much good. It was beautiful. I loved you with my whole heart. If you ever do think of me, please don't think about the end. We were so much more. Think about something that makes you smile, like all those times I kicked your ass in tennis. Well, maybe not that.

I hope you're happy and having a great life. I wish you only the best. With love,
JoJo

Perhaps the first time you fell in love, ignorant of the risk of pain that comes with losing it; was why it was so special, she pondered. What if he forgot her? What if what she thought was so special was meaningless to him? There it is right there, the risk of adult love. Thoughts like this don't happen with your first love because you think it will last and go on forever.

JoJo sat for a bit and wondered what the fuck she was doing. What's the point of contacting him now? She's history. This served no purpose at all. She can't revise history. JoJo wondered if maybe she should edit it a bit. *Screw it,* JoJo thought, and hit delete.

****

Taylor was on the floor in the family room, scratching Fury when she heard the side door open. A man's voice called for JoJo. JoJo went to the door and inhaled deeply.

JoJo looked at Ray and said, "You're not supposed just to walk in here, Ray. Now get the fuck out. All communication will be through my attorney."

"You don't get it," Ray whined. "I'm dying without you. I can't believe you won't take me back. I'll spend the rest of my life making it up to you, JoJo. Please," Ray begged her. "I'm so lonely. I hate eating alone. I want our nice home again. I want my life back."

"I've had a while to think about it," JoJo responded, "and this is what I think. It takes a lot for a man to toss aside his life and his family. You had a nice thing going on here, people look their whole lives for something like this. You were fed, cared for, and had every need met because if you needed anything, I found it for you.

"You were gone all week and came home on weekends, and nobody bitched at you if the dishwasher was broken, to bring the patio furniture in from the shed, nothing. I handled it all, and you never had a complaint, so you must have had a good reason, which I have no interest in, to chuck it all and start over. Well, whatever it was supposed to be didn't work out, and now you're back here.

"What was it, Ray? What didn't work out?" She looked him in the eyes when she asked, but her face was expressionless. He looked at her. Little beads of sweat started to stick to his hairline, and he could feel the dampness in his armpits.

"Okay," Ray explained, "I had an opportunity to go into the home office in San Diego. It was a big promotion, a VP spot, and I just wanted a more significant challenge career-wise. I didn't think it was fair to uproot you from your life so I could take a risk, but the position ended up going to someone else." There. He got it all on the table except the part about Stephanie, the stiletto-wearing shark who used an older man's vanity and her sexual prowess to undercut him at work.

JoJo looked at Ray and narrowed her eyes. She knew there was something else going on, but she didn't have all the pieces. Would Ray really have the nuts to go solo in California? JoJo didn't think so. He needed an audience to appreciate his interpersonal skills. She would have bet money he was too lazy to have an affair.

She could see him being seduced by power and titles, having his own office with a brass plaque on his door, announcing him as Vice President of Internal Bullshit, or similar. That shit excited Ray. Sitting closest to the head of the conference table got Ray hard. Attending closed door meetings turned Ray on. JoJo knew the effect of power on Ray. He loved having it, and he loved being around those who possessed it, so she understood his desire for more himself. That part of the story she understood.

"Look, Ray, go away. Unfortunately, what you did had a significant impact on me. I'm not going to say, 'Welcome home, Ray,' and roll out the red carpet for you. I am royally pissed off at you, and I'm not ready to forgive you yet, if at all. So get the fuck out of my house right now, or I'll call the cops and get a restraining order. Leave." She went to the door and opened it.

"So you think you can forgive me? Because if you do, I'll treat you like a queen. I'll give you anything. I'll do anything. Please. Tell me. I'll do it," Ray begged. "I love you. There has never been anybody but you. She never came close. Please, JoJo! I love you! Forgive me, JoJo."

"I don't know, I really need to think about it," JoJo told Ray. She was so concerned about getting him to leave she wasn't listening. If she was, his words might have hit her harder, whoever 'she' might be. The comment sailed over her head.

"You need to go. Now." She pointed at the open door. He didn't move, but Fury did. She was suddenly next to JoJo's side. She looked at Ray and the opened door.

At the sight of Fury, Ray moved to the door. He looked at the dog. "Stupid dog, he doesn't even know who rescued him. I did, you ungrateful pile of fur." Fury looked at him and growled long and low in her chest. Ray moved quickly to the door.

"Please. JoJo, think about it. Let me come home. I promise to put you first. Forever."

"The dog's name is Fury, Ray. She's a GIRL. That's why she doesn't like you. GIRLS hate you, Ray," she screamed as she slammed and locked the door. JoJo sat at the table and folded her arms. "Fuck," JoJo said and laid her head on her arms.

A little while later, Fury came over and licked her leg, and somebody rubbed JoJo's shoulder. She looked up and saw Taylor with her hand on JoJo's shoulder, looking back at her. Standing over JoJo, with her hair growing out, her original sandy brown color was prominent, and her gentle brown eyes with the sandy-colored eyelashes and dark eyebrows looked so like her dad JoJo broke and grabbed the girl by the waist and just sobbed.

JoJo realized she lost it in front of some young girl who should not be weighed down by regular grown-up sucky-ness. She reached toward the table, and Taylor handed her the roll of paper towels. JoJo pulled off a chunk and sniffled her thanks.

"What you just heard is my husband begging me to let him move back in, and me in the middle saying no. So, what if he did something so stupid, I could hold it over his head for the rest of his life? I'd have my family back. My home-made cinnamon buns baking while we opened gifts on Christmas morning, and he'd look like he hoped a pit would crack in the earth beneath him and swallow him whole. What's so bad about that? That would make me happy, wouldn't it? Well?" JoJo demanded. Taylor shrugged.

"Please call your dad and ask him to speak to me for a second," JoJo said. "You cannot be put in the middle of this family drama when you have your own family drama." She hadn't talked to Alex in years other than coffee or in the parking lot of Coney Island, and this was what she had to talk to him about.

She got his voicemail and left a message. JoJo walked over to the sink and splashed water on her face. She grabbed the paper towels and wiped her face.

"The way we've been going through these, we should buy stock in the company," JoJo said and held up the roll.

Taylor's phone rang shortly thereafter, it was her dad. She handed JoJo the phone. JoJo put the phone on speaker. Her dad said tenderly, in a voice Taylor had never heard him speak before, "How're things, JoJo? You met my daughter; don't you just love her?" JoJo decided the phone on speaker wasn't needed and took it off.

"Yeah, she's quite a girl. That's why I'm calling. I know her purpose here is to right her own ship, but some of the people here are bad influences, like me. I'm a horrible influence. My husband left me. Now he wants back in. Taylor witnessed me go off on him. It's not healthy."

They had a lengthy conversation about Taylor and what she could handle. While JoJo may have disagreed with what she heard, Alex was the girl's father.

"Your dad is something," she said as she hung up the phone.

"He said I owe him big time, and he thinks his kid needs to relax and walk the dog, and I need to relax and let you. It's not news that Ray is an asshole. Everybody knows that. He wanted you here because it's the best place for you to get your soul back, I know what he's talking about and don't underestimate his little girl. Oh, and don't let you neglect your grandparents."

"Can I still come over here and visit Fury?" Taylor asked.

"You need to talk to her. She's old enough to pick her own friends," JoJo told her.

"What about you? Can we still hang out? I like your old people friends."

"Old people? I'll take it as you're referring to Helen. I'd like to take Fury over to the VA today. Put her vest on and say hello. It's a nice day, so we can go out on the patio. Fury likes it. She respects them. I don't know, being in the military must have been ingrained in her. She's among her peers."

****

JoJo had established a good rapport with the Activities Director at the Local VA. The scene under the bridge was a few levels above her skill set. Those vets people needed more in the way of social services, so the rehab part of the local VA worked out perfectly. Twice a month, they dressed her up in her desert camo, and Fury went and said hello. JoJo mostly picked out lonely patients and sat with them. She asked if they wanted to talk. Otherwise, she watched Taylor usher Fury around. As only young people can, she squatted so she was at eye-level with each patient, and she talked to these grizzled old men. Fury sat at attention for each of them. JoJo felt like crying, looking at Taylor. She had the patience of a saint and remembered details about these guys other people forgot, that time would have forgotten if Taylor hadn't been there to listen to it.

It made JoJo mad that someone dared to criticize Taylor, her own mother wanted to 'fix' her. She never met the girl Alex married, but she sounded pretty rigid. She can see self-discipline being a turn on for Alex, something he practiced all his life. It was his thing, he never got into arguments with people regarding different philosophies or methods. He just did it. It sounds like his wife embraced his habits as well, but decided it was a change she would apply to her whole family. Alex probably didn't notice, but there is only so much kale a child will eat.

JoJo offered to buy lunch after the visit, they went down by the park at this outdoor café. Fury sat at her feet. JoJo couldn't help but notice a group of kids Taylor's age playing frisbee in the park. She noticed that Taylor noticed them, too. Every once in her eye would glance at the motion in her peripheral vision. They had just finished eating, and JoJo asked her to walk Fury home through the park.

"By those kids?" Taylor sounded suspicious.

"Yeah," JoJo said. No more was mentioned about Taylor walking, but when they got to the car, she decided to take the shortcut across the park.

"Don't be too late and don't bring Fury anywhere. Call your grandparents and let them know where you are," JoJo yelled as she drove away. Taylor reaching out to kids her own age was a big deal for her, but Fury helped. She was the perfect ice breaker.

"A pure black German Shepard who was in Iraq, fucking named Fury. Cool," said one of the boys. There didn't seem to be the need to say more.

JoJo pulled into her driveway and parked next to the identical Benz. Harold was around here somewhere. He came from around back.

"Oh good, you're home. Happy hour's out back." He took her hand and walked to the picnic table, covered with appetizers. He poured her a glass of white wine and had her sit next to him on the swing. He rubbed her knee and told her "How good it was to see her. He missed Fury, true, but this way, at least, they could talk.

"Talk about what?" JoJo immediately withdrew.

"Why are you so spooked?" he asked her.

"I'm not. I just don't like talks. The last talk I had, I found out how babies are made and I haven't been the same since."

"Let me fix you a plate. We have lots to choose from."

"Crudité, charcuterie, petit fours, canapé, pate foie gras, caviar. Such sophisticated words for little things," she said.

"Hope Diamond, Mount Everest, Great Dane. Such small words for big things," he countered.

"I shall never win. Have your way with me, Mr. Elliot," she said offhandedly.

"Oh, but I will, Mrs. Anderson, I will. But not yet. Therein lies the exquisite point of why we endure all this foolishness for ten seconds of ecstasy," he said, with a kind of leering look on his face. "If we end up too early, we will have lost seconds of pleasure, or too late, and it's gone stale. You need to time it just right. If you can find a woman, or your woman, and you time it right, well, that's the Holy Grail, right there."

"Is that so?" she said.

"It is so," he declared. "That's what men look for their entire lives."

"I gotta say you make a convincing argument. I wish I could remember what we were talking about. Damn, I hate when that happens," JoJo said. She sounded hollowed out.

"Hey. Don't worry about it," he reassured her. "I have all summer to help you remember."

They sat and had a glass of wine and nibbled on snacks while they waited for Taylor and Fury. JoJo heard someone at the side door and called, "Out back!" Her three children came around the corner of the house.

"Wow! All three of you at once! What's up?" JoJo asked.

"Nothin,' Mom. Just stopped in to say hello," her youngest said. JoJo knew Denny wouldn't have ever spoken first unless his siblings put him up to it, so in an effort to teach them not to try to manipulate her, she would offer no help to steer this boat to see where they took it.

"You're just in time for happy hour. Grab a beer or a glass of wine and fill a plate," she looked at Harold, who, up to this point, had been silent.

"Oh, yeah. Frankie, Denny, meet my friend Harold. I think you already had the pleasure of meeting my daughter Abbey."

The men greeted each other with hellos, but they had met before. Everyone sat back and waited.

"Mom," Denny said, "it's good Harold is here. We'd like to talk."

"Hi, everyone. Excuse me. I brought Fury back. I'll fill her water dish and go," Taylor said.

JoJo told her to get a soda out of the fridge and fix a plate. "Denny, Frankie, and Abbey, my dog walker Taylor." They said hi back, and Abbey asked if Taylor was leaving, they had family business to discuss.

"Leaving? Oh, hell no. She comes over more than you do, Abbey."

"Well, if you don't mind our business all over the neighborhood, I guess she can stay," Abbey told her mother.

Taylor stood and said she'd be back tomorrow.

"Sit, Taylor, finish your drink. Let's hear them out. Maybe it's something exciting," JoJo said sarcastically. "Denny, you don't have to do this. Go home."

"No, Mom, I'm good. I'm a little worried, too."

"Worried? What? Why?"

They were silent. JoJo wasn't sure she knew where they were going until she saw Abbey's eyes dart to Harold.

"So, what's the problem with Harold? What about Harold? Is Harold too old for me?" His eyes widened at her question. "He's unemployed? Maybe he's just in the way. After all, it does make things harder for your father. He can't just walk in and out of here whenever he feels like it, seeing as Harold and I have the same car, he won't be able to tell if I have company or not. It should make it really easy for him to mind his own business."

Harold wasn't sure if he should stick up for himself or not, but the smile tugging at the corners of Taylor's mouth kept him quiet. Frankie, JoJo's calm amidst chaos, took a stab. He turned to Harold.

"Harold, we don't want to come off as ungrateful," Frankie said, "but our mom has had a lot of changes in her life recently, and, well, maybe we're being overprotective, but we worry about her." Dear Frankie. Direct and to the point.

"Thank you, Frankie, for being so honest, but I assure you there is nothing even remotely romantic going on here. It's not your mother, it's her dog," Harold said. He looked over at Taylor, who was looking at the floor. "If I could go anywhere in the world to pick out a dog, I'm afraid I wouldn't leave town. I'd just sneak over here and steal Fury. She's my dream dog," he finished and looked again at Taylor, who gave him a slight nod.

"She's not quite as pretty as your mom," Harry continued, "but she is a lot younger."

Of the six people seated, four of them were trying hard not to laugh. Harry was doing a good job selling it with a straight face, but Abbey got angry.

"It's not funny! How is Dad supposed to make up with Mom if HE's always here?" The smile fell from JoJo's mouth. She stood and leaned up into Abbey's face. "This is MY house, MY friend, and MY dog. Your father *chose* to leave. If this is uncomfortable for you, get out, Abbey. You are a child meddling in adult business, so walk carefully. Some things you just can't take back, don't you think, Abbey?" JoJo asked her.

"Okay, let's go," Frankie said and stood up, kissing his mother's cheek. He nodded to Harold. "Abbey, come on."

"We're not done, Momma," Abbey said and hugged her.

"I didn't think we were, sweetie." JoJo hugged her back.

"Well, good time for me to head out," Taylor said. "Bye, all."

"Here," Denny said to her. "I'll walk out with you. Bye, Mom, Harold." They left.

"Not the happiest of hours," he observed.

"There have been worse," JoJo told him. "Why are you still here?"

"I want to have dessert."

"What's for dessert?" she asked him.

"Here," he said. "Have a mint."

****

CHAPTER TWENTY-FOUR

Later that week, there was a knock at the door, and Taylor came in. She sat at the table with Fury's head in her lap. JoJo was looking at her list and realized Taylor was still there.

"Hey Taylor, what's up? Still scooping ice cream?"

"Yup, not much changed there. I wanted to ask you a question, if you don't mind."

"Ask away," JoJo reassured her it wasajudgment-free zone.

"The reason I was exiled here was because I might be gay, right?" Taylor said.

"Pretty much. Why?"

"Well, I might not be."

"Fill in the blanks, please," JoJo asked her.

"See, I haven't kissed all that many boys, or maybe any, with more experience than me, and I really didn't enjoy it much. When I kissed Rachael, I did enjoy it. But she's like two years older, so maybe that's why it was different. She knew what she was doing."

"That's a distinct possibility. Has any guy in particular caused this doubt?"

"Yeah, a couple of guys in the park seem okay, I mean, not heartthrob material or anything. Does Denny have a girlfriend?" Taylor asked her.

"Oh, Taylor, Denny? I know he's perfect, but he might be a little too mature for you."

"I know. I turn eighteen in January; I wouldn't be interested in anybody until I get my college situation settled. I might come back next summer. I'll be back anyway to visit my grandparents, so I'll be by to see Fury. I was just surprised the other night when he walked me home, I felt a little shocked, I guess, I sorta got butterflies from a guy. *Any guy.*"

Huh. That's why he left his truck here. He walked her home. Oh, Jesus, Alex is gonna kill me, JoJo thought.

"Have you decided about this fall? Where do you want to finish high school?"

"It would probably be easiest if I went home," Taylor said. "But I'm not really good at doing things the easy way."

"You never learn anything that way," JoJo agreed. "Or at least I never did."

~~.~~

JoJo decided she needed a little sit down with Den. Denny was his father's knock-off, looks-wise. When JoJo could see Ray in Denny's looks, she cut herself some slack, he was handsome. Denny was long and tall, taller than his father, slender with broad shoulders and a strong back. He always had a smile on his face and was quick to offer his if you were in need of one. He looked just like Ray if Ray had soul or a conscience. Denny's face was pure and untroubled, whereas Ray always looked to be plotting something, the real estate of his forehead always creased with tension. It was too hot for coffee, but a nice cold glass of lemonade was perfect.

"What's up, Mom?"

"It's Taylor; I'm worried about her."

"Why? What's wrong with her?"

"You. I think she might be developing, ah, developing feelings for you," JoJo told him.

"Yeah. So?" Den asked.

"You're a lot older, experience-wise. You're a lot older, period. She hasn't finished high school, and I don't want her to miss out on things trying to catch up to you. She hasn't started college, and you're almost done. I don't want what you're doing to influence her choices."

"I agree. Completely. That's why she's going back home. I like her. I walked her home the other night. She's funny, and cute. But way too young. *Way, way* too young. We both agreed on that. That doesn't mean we can't be friends. If she comes to visit, we might have coffee, but no more than that.

"I have some long-term goals I'm not going to give up for her, or any other girl. Who knows where she'll be in five years? She might not even remember my name. But she's a nice person. Both of us agree that neither of us is in a position to deal with a relationship right now. There's no reason we can't be friends, is there?"

"That sounds good on paper, Den, but when it comes to the heart of a teenage girl, well, it's located far enough away from her brain that the smartest thing to do isn't always front and center."

"Mom. One, she doesn't even live here. Two, she might be gay, so quit worrying. There is nothing to worry about. She's a cool chick, but that's where it ends."

"I understand *you* understand it. I worry about *her* understanding."

"Have this talk with her, if you want assurances. Nothing is or will be going on except friendship. I promise."

JoJo looked at her son and decided to trust he knew what he's doing. *Just because his dad is a lying sack of shit doesn't mean he is,* she decided.

"I will talk to her, just to make sure she understands your point of view."

"If you need to, go ahead. But I'm telling you, those feelings aren't there. In the meantime, I go bother her at work and make her wait on me about fifty times."

"Denny! Leave her alone. It's things like that that make a girl fall in love."

"I know," he said with a smile. "But I'm just joking. I don't do that. She's too nice a person to screw with her head. I only get ice cream when I want it, and if she happens to wait on me, I ask her to throw me in an extra scoop. She says, 'Haha. Nice try. Next!'"

****

JoJo lounged on her deck with a book marketed to be a page-turner, and decided the writer of the selected blurbs from random reviews was truly the creative writer. The level of interest the outer copy generated could not be sustained for not much more than the table of contents. She shut her eyes and tilted her face up to the sun. She could see the sun through her eyelids, hot pink, and little squiggly capillaries there.

Something suddenly crossed the sun and cast a shadow down, blocking her light. She opened her eyes. "Jesus, Ray. What now?"

"Talk to me, please," he said and tossed his jacket across a chair. He sat next to her by her knees, crowding her.

"What do you want now?" JoJo said crossly.

"Aren't you lonely? Remember, JoJo, we used to have such fun. Pick a place. I'll book it. We can go anywhere and do anything. Start over. Have the holidays here with everyone. I promise I'll be a better husband. Take me back, JoJo. Please."

"Oh, hey JoJo, sorry to interrupt," Taylor said as she came around the house. "I'll walk Fury now before work, and you don't need to worry about it." She attached Fury's leash and left.

"You should start charging that kid rent. Where does she live, anyway?" Ray said. Every ounce of goodwill and tenderness Ray had succeeded in adding to his plus column crumbled when he shot his mouth off, and he didn't disappoint this time.

"Jesus, Ray. When you see me, you should keep your mouth shut. Every time I think about us, I recall what a big bully you are, and thank God I don't have to deal with you anymore."

"JoJo! You think of us? Do you think about us getting back together? Really?" Ray said, with an edge of hope in his voice.

"Well, kind of. I miss my family. I miss my home, but I mostly miss feeling established, and entrenched in a life I created. It was where I belonged, but it was just a big joke to you."

"It wasn't, I swear. I didn't realize how important it was to you. I'll fix it. Just let me try. Please. Let me try. I'll make it even better."

"Look, Ray, I can't get over the fact you left. You just decided to leave. You never discussed wanting to leave. Whether you believe me or not, I don't care, but I invested all I had in this family, and when you left, you pretty much shat all over everything I valued.

"So now what? I get this empty bag of a life, and I have to start all over? I get to put things I love in it, only this time, I'm smart enough to look at the bottom to find the hole you ripped in it. It was hard enough once. I'm not sure I have the energy to do it again."

"Really? You might want to try to see if we can make this work? I'll go to counseling. I'd do anything for you to just give me a chance." Ray spoke excitedly. "A couples retreat? How about that? Would that make you happy?"

"Happy? Make me happy? That's another thing. You think that's what I want? You listen and then rearrange the words so they're what you want to hear. Anyway, you have to go. When Taylor comes back, we're going to the vet. Fury senses when I'm agitated, and I don't want you here because she might bite."

Ray jumped up. "I should go. I don't quite trust that dog."

"Me either," JoJo told him. "Sometimes she gets this look in her eye like she might go off. I wouldn't trust her if I were you."

Ray turned and headed to his car. "Think about us! Please! I love you, JoJo!" he yelled as he pulled out.

Taylor came out of the kitchen door with Fury. Fury looked pleased Ray was gone.

"I'm sorry, I didn't mean to eavesdrop, but I knew you were still back here, so we went in the front door," Taylor told her. "Is it true about Fury? Do you think she'd snap?"

"Gingersnap, maybe. No, I think she's fine. It was the only way to get rid of him."

"Would you talk to me a little more about love? I don't think I get it," Taylor asked. "How come, as much as you seem to hate him, he's always here?"

"Huh." JoJo mulled it over. "That's probably why he was so good at his job, sales. He won't take no for an answer. I try not to encourage him, but every once in a while, he catches me at a low moment, that's why he's here. He's waiting me out, to catch me weak. He's had years to practice it."

"But do you love him? It's one thing to chuck it all if you don't love him, and if you don't, why bother? He doesn't seem very lovable, or worth the trouble," Taylor observed.

"I agree," said JoJo. "I think about how he brought home Fury, and gave those kids extra money, and I think maybe I overreacted a bit."

"What else has he done for you? Besides Fury? He did that for those kids, so they'd think he was a big deal. That they'd think he was 'cool.' I don't think you crossed his mind. How about recently? Taylor challenged her. "Well?"

"Once the kids got to college, he sort of faded away. He put more effort into his job, but I was glad, that meant he wasn't here getting in my way. Then I thought I should try harder, but once again, lopsided. Here I am, chasing him in lingerie, and it's, 'Later, babe, the game's on.' It was really stupid trying to get his attention when I wasn't sure I wanted it. I wanted him to want me so I could reject him, if that makes sense. It floored me when he left. He was packing his clothes, but in his head, he was already gone."

****

201

CHAPTER TWENTY-FIVE

Abbey sat and waited for her dad to meet her at the diner for their regular Saturday morning breakfast. Her patience grows thin the longer he makes her wait, but he's always late. If he doesn't get there soon, Abbey's liable to go off on him and ruin breakfast entirely. This is the first time since he left her mother they had a chance to talk, and Abbey missed him. She would always be Daddy's little girl no matter how old or fat she got; he always made her feel special.

Abbey felt that if her dad wasn't happy with her mom, he shouldn't stay with her, but she never felt anything stressful or odd when she went home. Her parents had no pressing issues like financial trouble or marital strife that Abbey could see or feel; there was no indication whatsoever that her dad was unhappy. She didn't want to think or talk about why he left. *It is none of my business what's going on,* Abbey thought. *Let them figure it out.*

"Pumpkin, I'm sorry I'm late. I took too long at the gym," Ray said as he slid into the booth opposite her. "Have you been waiting long?"

"Yes, I have, but I'll let it go. Since when do you go to the gym?" Abbey said in disbelief.

"For a while now. Most hotels have a fitness center, and rather than go to the bar, I started going to the gym instead. I look good, don't I?" Ray said proudly.

"Yes, you do. Do you know what you want to eat? I'm starving."

The waitress, whose name tag said she was Susan, came over with the coffee pot, filled his cup, and topped Abbey's off. "Good morning. What can I get for you? I haven't seen you guys in a while, but you always get blueberry pancakes with a side of bacon, and you get the Big Plate Breakfast special."

"Yes, you do have a good memory. Yes, that's what I'll have. Dad?"

"I think I'll switch it up today. Egg white omelet, wheat toast, and the fruit and yogurt cup."

"Sounds good. I'll put the order in; it should be out shortly. Is your coffee good? Need a refill before I go?" she said before she walked away.

"Egg white omelet? Yogurt? How come you ordered that?" Abbey asked suspiciously. She'd never seen him eat yogurt in his life.

"I guess I'm on a fitness kick. There's no sense working out if I'm only going to fill my body with crap. So, how are your brothers? I stopped by there a couple of times, but nobody was home."

"Good, I guess. I haven't seen them either. Denny is traveling for his internship, and Frankie is just Frankie. You could find him eating dinner at the pub if you wanted to see him."

His phone rang, and he took it out of his pocket and set it on the table. It wasn't that phone, it was the one in his other pocket. He looked at it and said, "I have to take this. It's work. I'll step outside where it's quieter, but I'll be back before our food's out," he said as he slid out and headed for the door.

Abbey was curious why her dad had two phones. He never needed two before. She picked up the phone and looked at the screen, but it was locked. *He thinks I can't unlock it, but little does he know I could break into it in two seconds. I'm going to have it unlocked before he gets back here,* she thought. Abbey tried his birthday, October 20th. She entered 1020, and the screen unlocked.

Bingo! Abbey scores again! She was surprised to see a picture of a naked woman's body from the neck down. She scrolled through and saw a few more. There was even a dick pic. *Ew, I think I just saw a picture of my dad's penis.* Abbey scrolled through and looked at his texts and found the phone was dedicated for use with just one woman, a woman named Stephanie, who worked with him. There were a lot of lewd and sexual exchanges between the two of them. Her father is working out, watching his weight, and now visible proof of an affair. Abbey took out her phone and took a couple of screenshots as evidence. She heard him coming and closed his phone.

"Sorry, Pumpkin. I know this is our special time together. I'll get rid of these phones right now, and let's enjoy breakfast," he said as Susan brought their food. He put the phones in his pocket and picked up his fork. "Dig in."

Abbey sat back and looked at her father. *What a selfish asshole,* she thought. *What a liar. What a cheater. He lied to all of us.* Something inside her snapped—on behalf of her mother. Whether it was her X chromosome or some kind of girl code, Abbey was furious. *He betrayed her. He betrayed all of us. Our happy family was some big lie to him.* It took everything she had not to lean across the table and claw his eyes out.

"So, anything new going on at work?" she said instead.

Abbey ate her pancakes while he blathered on, her ears on alert for the mention of the name Stephanie, but there was none. "Have you talked to Mom lately?"

"No, it wouldn't do any good. Your mother refuses to be rational about things."

"Have you talked to a lawyer yet? Are you proceeding with a divorce?"

"There's no hurry for that. No need to rush things."

"If you're done with her; why not let her go?"

"Like I said, no need to rush things."

Abbey finished her breakfast and sat there looking at him while the words *liar* and *cheater* ping-ponged around in her brain.

"How about you, Abbey? How are things going at the bar?"

"The bar? I haven't worked there in months. I'm the office manager at the Barnard & Sheffield Law Firm."

"That's right. I remember you telling me about that. Going well?"

"Yes. I like it a lot. Listen, I hate to rush you, Daddy, but I need to get to the bank before it closes. Are you almost done?"

Her father put his fork down, wiped his mouth with a napkin, and said, "All set. Let me get the check, and I'll walk out with you."

They walked out together, and Ray walked her to her car. He kissed her cheek and told her he loved her. Abbey said it back but wondered if he really meant it. *Do you love me, Daddy, or is it another one of your lies?*

She sat in her car and watched him drive away. *Where are you going, Daddy? To hook up with Stephanie?* All her life, she had him on a pedestal; he was larger than life and could do no wrong. When things blew up, it was always her mother's fault. That was his opinion, and Abbey just parroted it. She swallowed everything her father told her without question. He was Daddy, and Daddy was always right, or so she thought. When she saw his phone, all Abbey could think was, *how could you, Daddy? How could you ruin all our lives? It wasn't just Mom. It's all of us, and you don't seem to give two shits about any of us.*

Abbey considered her mom or reconsidered her. When Abbey was little and suffered from nightmares, her mother was the one who always answered her cries. She was the one who got down on her hands and looked under the bed for monsters. JoJo left the light on the closet and closed the door, so Abbey could be sure no monsters could come in. She even sprinkled "pixie dust" around her bed to keep them away. It was her mother that cared for her when she was sick. When she dropped her father's expensive camera, the one she was forbidden to touch, and broke the lens, her mother said she did it, so Daddy didn't get mad at her.

It was her mother who cried when Abbey had a flute solo at her fifth-grade concert. Her mom came and watched with tears in her eyes. That time she and her friends got drunk in the woods, it was her mother picked them up and didn't say anything. He Mother helped her with school projects. Her mom baked cupcakes at midnight for the next day's soccer team bake sale because Abbey forgot to tell her she needed them until eight p.m. the night before. She even let her best friend stay with them while the girl's parents went through a bitter divorce. Her mom did all the grunt work.

Maybe Abbey felt special when her father was there because he was rarely present, so to be the object of his affection meant everything to her. These Saturday breakfasts started because it was the only time, he could fit her in, and her mother encouraged her to love her dad. Her mom never once trash-talked her father, even though he probably deserved it on many occasions. She never threw him under the bus.

Her mother was the foundation of the family, and her dad was purely window-dressing. As much as she pushed away from her mom to be her own girl, her mother her never held it against her. She knew it was about growing up. It took her father's affair to shock Abbey into reality. Her mom deserved so much better from her, but she was so busy chasing her dad's affection that she ignored her completely. Abbey felt ashamed and guilty for being such a little snot to her mother, whose only sin was to love Abbey enough to forgive her time and time again.

Abbey went to see her brothers. She didn't know if they knew, but they would soon enough because she was unsure what to do with this knowledge and needed to find out what they thought.

Denny just got home from a business trip and was unpacking. He heard a pounding at the door. It was his sister, and he let her in.

"Morning, Abbey. What brings you by?"

"I just came from breakfast with Dad. I think the reason he left Mom was because he has a girlfriend," Abbey blurted out; she couldn't hold her father's secret any longer.

"You're crazy," Denny said.

"He even has this separate phone. Here, look at these." She showed him the screenshots. What does it look like to you?"

"Wow. Our father is cheating on our mother and lacks the balls to tell her. He's not only a liar and a cheat; he's a weasel, too."

They went back and forth over a cup of coffee, whether to tell their mom or not. Abbey was so traumatized by her father's behavior she could barely stop crying. The man who was supposed to love her above all else didn't exist. He pretended he thought Abbey was special in front of her. When he was gone, who knew if he even thought about them?

Frankie came in. They brought him up to speed about what happened at breakfast. Frankie said, "Huh," after he looked at the evidence of their father's infidelity.

"Should we tell Mom? Denny said no, but I think we should tell her. What do you think?"

"We stay quiet. Mom may already know; she's not stupid. If she knows we know, she might feel embarrassed. She still has her dignity. Let her hang on to it as long as possible," Frankie answered.

"But what if she takes him back because she doesn't know about this?"

"Then I'll tell him he has to come clean, he has to tell her. Or else."

"Or else what?" said Denny.

"Or else I'll tell her. That's why Cain killed Abel, y'know."

"What's that, Frankie? Half the time, I don't know what you're talking about," Abbey said.

"In the Bible, why Cain killed Abel. He caught him fucking around with his wife."

"Really?" asked Denny.

"Hell, if I know. I know that's what I'd do."

They decided to keep quiet and watch their parents' marriage fall apart, and only become involved if their mom needed back-up.

~~.~~

JoJo got a text from Harold. His mom was in the hospital so he wouldn't be stopping by, but he would let her know when he had more information. Taylor came in and had some lunch with JoJo, both concerned about Helen. Harold called and said they thought she had a stroke, and she was getting admitted. JoJo ordered flowers and signed the card from Fury.

Taylor left but came back with a jacket she found outside. JoJo recognized it as Ray's and tossed it on the couch. JoJo sat down and gave Fury a good brushing. She took a long time doing it; it was nice to see Fury look so pretty. JoJo was enjoying herself. When she was done, Fury's coat shone black and glossy. "Maybe we should move to Hollywood and see if you could get work. I bet you'd be the prettiest pup out there," JoJo scratched her, Fury responded with a satisfied tail thumping.

"Oh, no, Fury. I think I've been on the floor too long. I don't know if I can get up." JoJo figured the easiest way up was to get herself seated on the couch and go from there. She managed to get on the sofa with minor difficulty. She sat on something hard. She pulled the blue jacket out from under her and looked at it. Ray's jacket.

JoJo wondered if he left it on purpose, giving him a reason to come back. She wouldn't put it past him. She tossed it over the back of the sofa. It landed cockeyed, and a pill bottle fell out of the pocket. JoJo picked it up, looked at the label, and searched the rest of his pockets. She unfolded a piece of paper and read it. She looked at the pill bottle and compared it with the paper. Ray told her he was in Dallas. *Son of a bitch. Ray, you bastard.* It was a hotel receipt from the Chicago Marriot and the bottle was Viagra on its third refill.

****

JoJo put the pill bottle and receipt together on the kitchen table and poured a glass of lemonade. She looked at the items unsure what to do first. This was it. This iced the cake. All those big pieces of the puzzle suddenly shifted into place, Ray had or was still having an affair. For a while, apparently.

JoJo thought about putting a shot of vodka in her lemonade; she went to the cabinet and looked. She heard a knock, but JoJo didn't turn towards the door. Maybe if she pretended she didn't hear the knocking, whoever it was would go away. It went from a loud thump to being pounded upon. Someone was yelling her name. She turned and saw Harold. JoJo just looked at him, the vodka bottle in her hand. He yelled for her to let him in. She unlocked the door, turned, and went back to the table. JoJo sat and traced the condensation on her glass from little drips to big.

Harold shook her. "JoJo! JoJo! What are you doing?" he yelled at her and shook her again.

She snapped back and said, "What's the matter?" Harold took the vodka bottle away.

"Give me that. Why are you drinking alone?"

"Nobody else was here."

"What's that about? Are you a closet drinker? A boozy housewife? What?"

JoJo gave him the contents of Ray's jacket. She didn't watch his response but grabbed the vodka and put in a splash. Harold reached over to take it back. He grabbed her in a fierce hug and held her tight to console her, but tears didn't fall.

"I never guessed, I didn't know," she kept repeating. JoJo pulled back. "I forgot to ask about Helen."

"I'm sorry, Jo. She died this afternoon. That's what I came to tell you." She reached out and hugged him as hard as she could, poor Harold.

JoJo had him sit in the recliner and sat on his lap. She held him and let him cry into her neck. She rubbed his back and made soft, soothing sounds he felt in his chest. It felt so good not to be alone. He was glad he came here. Harold knew he should be strong for JoJo, and he would be. Soon. Right now, he wanted to cave into her softness and allow her warmth to envelope him.

JoJo offered him that. They missed Helen together. Even Fury lay at Harold's feet, her detail to say goodbye to Helen and cover Harold's flank.

****

After a bit, she got up and grabbed a box of tissues. She pulled out quite a few and gave what was left of the box to Harold. "I'm sorry about your mom, Harold. I didn't know her for a very long, but I think she enjoyed herself right until the end. We had fun, and because of you, she was able to stay right where she wanted."

"Thank you, JoJo. I know you have your own troubles. Losing my mom, I can't believe how much it hurts. It's not your job to make me feel better, but I didn't know where else to go," he admitted.

"Well, your mom was my friend, and she'll only die once, but Ray will be a prick forever."

"I should go now, JoJo. I've already ruined your evening."

"You don't have to if you don't want to," she offered. "I'm not extending anything other than a warm, puffy body to sleep next to, but if you don't want to be alone, it may be enough."

"Are you serious? Because I could really use a warm, puffy body to cozy up to."

"I'll let Fury out, and then let's go lay down and watch TV." She found him a toothbrush and met him in bed. They giggled and goofed around a bit, eventually settling down to watch TV. She fell asleep on her side, facing away from him. He tried to tuck himself around her puffy, warm body. She wore a tee shirt and some underwear; he had on boxers. He curled up next to her and fell asleep.

His phone woke him around seven. It was Mark, looking for his van. Harold drove it home from the hospital, he was to bring it back to the house last night. He was supposed to have it back for Mark earlier this morning. Harold told Mark he had a few too many and stayed somewhere, but he'd forgotten and would bring it back now. He kissed JoJo's forehead. He told her he needed to return the paint van back to Mark, but she had the most comfortable bed, he'd give her a call later, and left.

Meanwhile, Ray was on cloud nine. He could sense JoJo was softening, she always did. He knew if he played it right, nice and contrite, she'd cave. She loved everything else about her life, and she'd get over Ray's mini mid-life crisis. He'd gladly serve out his sentence in the doghouse. He just needed a sliver of opportunity; he could jackhammer the rest of his way in.

Ray drove by his street as was his habit, and looked at his house, anxious to return. He saw the painter's truck pull out of his driveway and leave. This early in the morning? What was she doing? Ray was in, not some house painter. It was a mistake. *It was probably just a delivery,* Ray thought. He knew she wanted him. He could tell. Yesterday, he felt her thaw.

****

Taylor came over and sat at JoJo's kitchen table. JoJo told Taylor about Helen and held her while she cried. Taylor knew of people who died, but Helen was someone she *knew* who died. Just almost eighteen, Taylor did not have the exposure to or experience with death and didn't know how to process it. She hadn't known Helen that long. Taylor was surprised at how deep a well grief ran. Why did the death of some old lady upset her so?

"I didn't know her that long either," JoJo said. "But she was our friend. She was part of our clique. You had an odd group of friends here, Taylor. A ninety-year-old lady, a rescue dog, and two old people."

"I know Harry's old. Who's the other?" Taylor asked.

"Me," JoJo answered.

"You? You're not old."

"Is your dad old?" JoJo asked her.

"Well, yeah. Of course."

"He's my age."

"Oh. You are old."

JoJo laughed. "You think?" she said, and Taylor's voice caught on a sob.

"Why does it hurt so much? If you're old, and you're supposed to die, it shouldn't be so sad." Taylor said.

"Maybe it's sad when they're old because you have them in your life for so long, when they're gone, they leave a huge hole, and lots to miss. When I was in elementary school, a boy in my class had leukemia, and he died. What's sadder? Someone like Helen, who had a chance to do anything she wanted, or the kid in my class who never had a chance to do anything at all?"

The thought of a child dying was too much for Taylor, and she started crying like she wasn't going to stop. JoJo reached over and pulled her into her arms.

"I'm sorry, it shouldn't have told you about that kid. That doesn't happen too often anymore, but I guess it made it a little too real. There are no words, Taylor. Some things just suck, so you live every day and make it count.

"Like Helen. The only thing worse than losing Helen would be not knowing her at all, don't you think? We didn't even know her that long and look how much we miss her. Poor Harold. She's, his mom. He's really gonna miss her." JoJo pulled off her sweatshirt and gave it to Taylor to wipe her face and blow her nose.

"I wish you were my mom," Taylor said. "She doesn't get it at all."

"Hey, cut your mom some slack. It's easy for me to talk like this to you, maybe because you are a part of a bigger world to me. But to your parents, you *are* the world. Maybe what's suffocating to you is love to them. You're the youngest, right? Maybe your mom is figuring I have to get this one right, this is my last chance."

"Maybe," Taylor sounded unconvinced.

"If it makes you feel any better my daughter probably wishes I was your mother, too. She feels shortchanged, like when she was born, she came with a certificate from God saying how special she was, but I was such a slacker I set it on fire when I used it to light a joint."

Taylor gasped. "You didn't do that, did you?"

"Of course not."

There was a knock at the door. It wasn't locked, and her son Denny showed himself in.

Fury was familiar with the traffic in and out and only honed in on the unfamiliar, so she paid Den no mind.

"Hi, Denny. No work today?" asked his mom.

"Too hot. I was in the mood for some ice cream," he said, looking at Taylor. She turned bright red, even the tips of her ears.

****

CHAPTER TWENTY-SIX

Harold called to let JoJo know the arrangements for his mother. Cremation, memorial service, private burial and a luncheon afterwards. JoJo said she was going to the service, probably with Taylor, and she'd see him after everything settled down.

"No," Harold said. "Absolutely not. I want you, Taylor, and Fury up front with me."

"I don't think so," she replied. "You want Fury to go to church? Your family is going to be there. That's not our place."

"Oh yes, it is. My mother enjoyed her last days because of you guys. You brought her light and life right to the end. She adored Taylor, and Fury, too. You, she could take or leave."

"Haha. Regardless, I will attend in a minor capacity. Taylor hasn't really experienced this type of loss, but I know she wants to go. I think having Fury there will help her, and Fury does like to work. I'll be there, but in the background."

"Not if I catch you first. You're going to need my support. You are really going to require a lot more than you think. I'm not going to take my eyes off you. My mother would never forgive me," he advised her.

"Boy, your mother is good, meddling from beyond the grave," JoJo commented.

"Her son is better. I was her favorite."

"I'm not sure the other Elliots would agree," JoJo said.

****

Harold called the next morning and told her what time to be at the funeral home, but she told him they would see him at the service. JoJo said they would try to be early at the church. He sounded quite panicked, and his offer to comfort her was more apt in reverse. Harold wanted her to comfort him.

"Just hurry, please," he asked.

Taylor drove Ray's car, Fury's head stuck out the window. They parked on the side of the church, hoping to sit there and avoid the center aisle, but as soon as Harold saw them, he rushed over.

"Oh, thank—"

"Hey. Stop," JoJo told him. "Take a deep breath. Another. One more. Okay, Harold. We'll be off to the side, but we're going in now to see what's going to work for Fury. Deep breath. Good boy, Harold. Breathe."

They entered through the side. The organist was practicing, they determined the music was fine with Fury. Up in front was a pedestal, upon sat a fancy urn; Helen's remains, JoJo figured. Next to that was the biggest spray of flowers she had ever seen. It looked bigger than the ones at the Kentucky Derby. She heard Taylor, her voice trembling, say "Look," and pointed at the card nestled among the velvety petals, "See you at the Rainbow Bridge, xo Fury." JoJo wanted to cry. These weren't the ones she sent. These had to come from Harry.

"Okay, Fury, pick your spot," Taylor told her. She sat Sphinx-like next to the pedestal. Her coat glowed in the church light, and her ears, the size of a woman's foot, stood up. Taylor brought JoJo to a seat on the side, easy for Fury to spot if needed. People came in and saw the tableaux of dog, pedestal, and floral monstrosity and a murmur ran through the crowd how this was "So Helen."

Taylor left to find a whole bunch of tissues in the restroom, some she gave to JoJo, and she brought the rest over for Harold and his family. He grabbed Taylor and whispered, "Take me with you." She ordered him to sit and stay and returned back to JoJo. They could hear his brothers laughing at Harold as he obeyed the tiny girl who ordered him around. Taylor showed a great deal of poise for someone so young and out of her comfort zone.

"Fury looks like this isn't her first funeral," JoJo whispered.

"That's sad," Taylor said quietly.

The service ended, and Fury stayed until Harold came and picked up the urn. Fury stood at his side, left the church with him, and escorted her senior charge to the opposite side of the veil.

JoJo and Taylor met Fury outside, standing next to Harold. He grabbed JoJo and held her, Helen's urn crushed into her sternum. "Can I ride with you?" he asked.

"No. That's your car over there. C'mon, Harold. It's okay. We'll make Fury come. It's almost over, you'll be okay. We'll meet you there," she told him. JoJo walked back to her car.

Outside the side entrance, near where they parked, a peaceful little prayer garden had been constructed with a small marble bench, perfect to sit upon and reflect. JoJo sat on the bench and wanted a minute to say goodbye to her friend.

She wished Helen a wonderful afterlife filled with the love of those who went before her, comfort and peace to those she left behind, and then before she could catch herself, she remembered Ray's betrayal.

JoJo said a prayer for her sorry ass, the mess her life was in, put her face in her hands, and wept until the last car drove away. Taylor put Fury in the car, leaned against the door, and waited. She could tell by JoJo's defeated posture this was about more than Helen, something happened that brought her to her knees. She waited and hoped JoJo could find the strength to get to her feet. Harold was one of the last cars to leave, and he saw JoJo alone and crying. He almost slammed on the brakes and jumped out of the car to help her, but he saw Taylor and hoped she would call him if she needed back-up.

****

JoJo sat a bit, trying to pull herself together. She was digging through her pockets looking for a dry tissue and not having any success. Taylor came over and gave her some. She sat, put her arm across JoJo's shoulders, and hugged her.

"Are you going to be all right? I think this is about more than Helen." Taylor asked her.

"Taylor, I'm sorry," she said through her snot. "I can't really confide in you. You are too young to see any of this adult bullshit. You are supposed to have hope and optimism in your heart at your age, if you hang around with me, I'm afraid I'll poison you with ugly reality way too soon."

"Everyone talks about age. Too young for this, too old for that," Taylor said. "I could have a baby if I wanted one. I could have two, but I can't know why my friend is hurting or how I can help her. You have helped me so much, I wish I could return the favor, you know. Let me at least help you carry whatever's gonna sink you."

"Taylor, I'm going to tell you what's wrong, only because I need someone to run interference for me while I figure out how to get the strength to do what I need to do. I don't want this to get between Denny and his dad. I don't want *you* to get between Denny and his dad. Ray's been lying to me this whole time. He's been having an affair with someone from work. I think the reason he

214

wanted to come home isn't because he loves me and made a mistake, I think she dumped him, and he has nowhere else to go."

"Yeah, I know. I saw pills on the table."

****

Harold's two daughters wondered about the woman he seemed attached to, and the young girl in charge of the dog. They thought his return home to his mother was an act of childish defiance; the women in his life were too unwilling to make accommodations for him, so he went home to his mother to be nurtured and spoiled. He seemed no worse for wear, and he replaced them with not necessarily more attractive versions of them, but definitely kinder ones.

****

CHAPTER TWENTY-SEVEN

Ray approached his car later that morning, formulating a plan to win JoJo back. He couldn't sleep that night, combing his mind for little details he might have forgotten but communicated to JoJo how much he loved her. No detail was too small to overlook when it came to JoJo; she had a mind like a steel trap and unerring bullshit detector, so Ray needed to be extra careful. He neared his car and noticed a guy leaning against his driver's side door.

"Hey, buddy," Ray said rudely. "Watch the door."

"Raymond Anderson?" the man asked him.

"Yes? Please move; I'm in a hurry," Ray told the guy.

"This is for you." Ray grabbed the paper out of the extended hand. "You've been served. Have a great day," the guy wished him as he ran off.

Ray read the paper, and it was a punch in the gut he never saw coming. That bitch. She filed for divorce as well as an emergency temporary no-contact order against him, saying he had to stay at least one hundred feet away from her, her house, and that fucking dog. She's afraid for her safety because he threatened her over that fucking dog and wouldn't stop trying to break into the house.

JoJo and Taylor arrived at the luncheon with Fury. Depending on the crowd or room size, Fury might be more comfortable outside or at home. It was pretty crowded; half the place was a banquet room, and the other half a bar/restaurant. The Elliots were a local family going way back; plenty of people came to pay their respects, especially with an open bar. The family greeted people as they arrived, a lot of the locals stayed on the bar side. Frankie brought Crystal, the gardener, as a plus one. Denny was there, too. He kept telling his brother to bring a girl to a funeral didn't count as a date.

"Close enough," was Frankie's response.

JoJo and Taylor wandered through the room. Many people stopped Taylor and questioned her at length about Fury, but she performed as a therapy dog for Helen; JoJo decided Fury's prior military experience was omitted from her resume. She went around the room a few times, and Taylor took her outside. JoJo said hello to Harold. He was speaking to people, he saw her and said in front of everyone, "Oh, good, you're here. Let's go," and turned towards the door.

"No, Harold, you have to stay longer. I'll be around. I won't leave," JoJo told him and went over to the memory board and years of photo albums on display. She saw one that looked familiar and smiled at it, remembering how Helen recalled all the people and events it contained. JoJo heard voices next to her and looked out of the side of her eye at Harold's girls. They looked nearly identical and must resemble their mother because she could barely see Harold in them.

JoJo noticed they were side eyeing her as well. She flipped through the pages and stopped at a particular picture.

"Excuse me, my name is JoJo, and I volunteered during the week with Helen so your father could run errands. We spent a lot of time going through these old albums, and this one right here was one of her favorites."

JoJo pointed at a photo. It was a picture of the two girls as little kids helping Helen plant flowers. It took the two of them to lift a full watering can; water spilled all over, the girls covered in mud, Helen laughing at the studious expressions they had on their determined faces. It was a memory they both forgot.

"She loved this picture," JoJo commented as she walked away.

JoJo decided she needed a drink. She went to the bar side and took her place in line. The bar side was crowded; she stood on the side the wait staff used. JoJo wanted to move and give them room, but there wasn't any. They assured her she was fine, but she squashed herself against the bar to give them space as best she could.

****

Ray sat in his car and stared at the papers, but the words didn't change. He felt the sweat bead on the back of his neck. His face felt hot and then hotter still, and Ray was going over there to straighten this out once and for all. He went to the house and pounded on the door, but it was quiet. The dog usually looked out at him and taunted him, but didn't, so Ray didn't think she was home.

He called Denny and asked, "Do you know where your mother is?"

"Yeah. Mom's here at the Bellewood at Mrs. Elliot's thing."

He heard his father scream, "Elliot!" and his phone dropped on the floor.

"What was that all about? Who was yelling?" Taylor said to him.

"My dad. Looking for my mom," he answered. "I don't have a good feeling about this."

"Should we go warn her?" Taylor asked.

217

"I don't think so. Let's try to keep him away from here."

A black convertible late-model mid-life crisis came flying into the parking lot, tires screeching and gravel spewing as the car skidded to a stop.

"Too late," Denny said.

The car barely came to a halt, and out jumped his father. Ray saw the Elliot Paint Company van and almost had an aneurysm. He didn't bother to shut the car door and ran screaming into the restaurant. Denny walked towards him to try to stop him, but Ray shoved him so hard he almost went down. He was too busy trying to keep his balance to say anything, and Ray charged past him.

Ray yelled, "Where are you, you motherfucker? You stay away from my wife, or I'll kill you!" as he passed by. He flung the door open so hard it almost broke the hinges on his way into the restaurant.

Denny looked at Taylor and laughed. "That can't be good," he said and followed him inside, Taylor with Fury on his heels.

Ray flew through the door; the dark of the restaurant disoriented him after the blinding noonday sun. He didn't see JoJo; he ran right past her and located Mark Elliot on the opposite side of the room; he ran full bore and tackled him, still yelling, "Elliot! You motherfucker! Stay away from my wife! Give me back my dog, you sonofabitch!"

The room was stunned into silence by Ray's voice loud and clear. Suddenly, Frankie realized how involved he was, it was his father exploding in front of the whole place. Frankie grabbed Ray, pulled him off Mark, and threw him against the wall. He helped Mark to his feet while his father stood there and raged, still screaming, "Stay away from my wife, Elliot! Keep your hands off my wife!"

At JoJo's end of the bar, a large pitcher of ice water awaited the waitstaff to refill the water glasses. Ray continued yelling and cussing at the top of his lungs.

JoJo just reacted, furious he embarrassed her so. She picked up the pitcher of ice water and heaved it as hard as she could at Ray. It hit him square in the chest, soaking him with a face full of water, the plastic pitcher bounced harmlessly away. It was JoJo's turn to yell.

"Ray! You moron! Not that Elliot!" she pointed at Mark. "THAT one!" she pointed at Harold.

Frankie and Denny quickly escorted Ray, still screaming obscenities, outside to his car. He was baffled. Shocked. JoJo pulled the perfect end-around. She cut him off at the knees. He lost it all, and he was furious. *She's got a lot of fucking nerve thinking she's gonna get away with this!* Ray thought. *Who does she think she is, that bitch?*

JoJo followed them out into the parking lot, Fury right on JoJo's six and Taylor after her. "Do you know where your mother is?" Ray sputtered. "I can't believe she's running all over town with that Elliot guy. She's a married woman! This all her fault!"

"Dad, stay away from Mom," Frankie told him. "Leave. Get in your car and leave. Just go. Please." He was too late. His mother came up behind him and heard Ray's last remark, which only added gasoline to the fire burning in her gut.

"Looking for me, Ray?" she said. The tone of her voice could neatly cut a brick in half. "You've got a lot of nerve showing up here. I'm here with my friends, and you show up, causing a scene like that. I've never been more embarrassed in my life."

Denny looked at Taylor and shook his head. This was a side of his mother he hadn't seen in a while. His badass mother showed up.

"Yes, I'm looking for you! Talk about nerve," Ray yelled. "You're here with that painter, you're fucking that painter, and you're a married woman."

"Jesus, Dad. Shut up," said Frankie.

JoJo looked around. Abbey had joined them, and people from the party spilled out the door and watched the Anderson family go at it. JoJo swallowed. The thought of exposing Ray in front of his kids caused her to pause and almost hold her tongue. Almost.

I built this house, and I can wreck it to ruins if I want, JoJo thought. *Fuck it. Enough with everyone else's feelings. I'm going to go after Ray like a napalm bomb. He's not going to know what hit him, that lying, cheating rat bastard,* JoJo thought, narrowed her eyes and looked at Ray. She got right up in his face and pointed her finger at him, stabbing his chest for emphasis.

"Ray, you lying sack of shit! How dare you come here accusing me of running around. Well, guess what, Ray, you lying sack of shit, not only are you a lying sack of shit, but you're also a lying *cheating* sack of shit!" JoJo stabbed him with her finger right in his chest, harder with every adjective.

"You're busted, Ray. I know all about your affair; I know everything. The other woman. I know about you going to the Marriott Chicago instead of that sales meeting in Dallas. What I don't know is if I had a good time. You checked in as Mr. and Mrs. Ray Anderson, you moron. I know because I called thereafter I found the receipt. You know what else I know? You can't get it up any-more. I found your Viagra, Ray. I'd tell you to fuck off, but I guess you can't." JoJo laughed. "Poor Ray. He has a limp biscuit."

"Mom," Denny said. "Not here. Not now."

"Why not? He started it when he walked out on me. I'm finishing it. If it's a spectacle, so be it. I don't care who else knows your father is a liar and a cheater. He did this to himself."

Fury stood next to JoJo and emitted the fiercest growl, low and deep in her chest. It was almost a dare for Ray to start running and give Fury a reason to take off a good chunk of his backside. All eyes turned towards Fury.

"Easy," JoJo said. Fury quieted down but stared at Ray. No, she locked her eyes on Ray. She was like a laser ready to take down her enemy. Fury growled again.

"Make that dog stop," whined Ray.

"The dog's the least of your problems. Right now, the whole town knows you're a lying, cheating, rat bastard of a husband. A man who runs around on his wife because he thinks he's the smartest guy in the room, and his wife is too stupid to figure it out," JoJo spat out the words. "You weren't even smart enough to realize you shouldn't check in a hotel using your real name when you're out fucking around on your wife. Fuck you, Ray. You're such a dick. 'Mr. and Mrs. Anderson.' You know what? Keep the Anderson. I'm going back to Montgomery. I'm through with you. Sign the divorce papers, or I'll go after your 401K. It's over, you asshole. I don't ever want to see you again," JoJo said and walked towards the door.

Some of the braver guests spilled out of the doorway and watched the scene unfold before their very eyes. JoJo cut a path between the onlookers. "Show's over, guys. I won," she said, grabbed Harold by his tie and pulled him into the restaurant.

"Did they serve lunch yet, and what's a girl gotta do to get a drink?" JoJo said to Harry and went back into the banquet room. She hid in the corner. JoJo couldn't believe she went off on Ray like that in front of everybody. She didn't think about the kids or how her actions affected them. *I hope they don't hate me for going after their dad in public,* JoJo thought. Harold came looking for her.

"Tell me where you are if you want this glass of wine."

"Over here," she called from the darkest corner.

"Here you go," he said as he passed her drink. "Don't say it, Harry. Please."

"But it's too good not to: You were the very definition of Fury! 'Hell hath no Fury as a woman scorned,'" he quoted. "You were magnificent! You should rent your family out for corporate events; it was that good. What are you gonna do at my funeral?"

"Probably twenty to life," she confessed. "I'll probably be the reason you're in the casket."

"Is it premeditated or a crime of passion? Passion, please."

"It would be a mercy killing or a public service."

"I can't tell you how exciting it was to watch you take down Ray. I found it incredibly sexy," he told her. "I can't wait until it's my turn."

"Bitchslapping Ray gave me an appetite," JoJo told him. "Would you mind finding me something to eat, please? I thought there was supposed to be food here."

****

Taylor and Fury went into the dining room looking for JoJo. They found her with Harold.

JoJo ordered him back to the party, and to check on the food. Taylor said she'd sit with her. "Wow," Taylor said. "You nailed Ray right in the chest. That was a great throw."

"It must have been all the adrenaline. I doubt I could do it again," JoJo answered. "Where are the boys? Did I embarrass them so severely they can't show their faces ever again?"

"I think they're outside. What flipped Ray out like that?"

"He got served the divorce papers. I *told* him not to fuck with me. He has a bad habit of talking me out of stuff. He knows all my soft spots and uses them against me. I don't want him close to me because he'll talk me out of what I want, and I want three things. My dog. My house. And I want my name back. I want to be known as Josephine Montgomery."

"I haven't been around that long, and this probably sounds awful, but it seemed like no big deal to the guys. Just another day in the life," Taylor told her.

JoJo overlooked Fury, who came in with Taylor. She had placed her head in JoJo's lap, and JoJo absentmindedly scratched her neck.

221

"Oh, hi, girl," she said to her. "I wonder what she thinks about this. Her life has been one cluster fuck after another, but she seems to adapt regardless. She's been all over the world but having her head on my lap is her favorite spot. Isn't it, girl, isn't it?" JoJo scratched behind her ears.

"Mine, too," Harold told her as he handed her a plate of buffet food.

"Harold, would you please get me another glass of wine?" she asked him sweetly.

"Of course," he said. "If I take too long, are you going smack me around?"

"I may just for practice, Harold," she replied. "Hurry back."

****

"Taylor, since it's just us I need to talk to you before anyone comes. It's about Denny."

"Denny? What about him?" Taylor backed up.

"I talked to him about you. I wanted you to know that it wasn't a secret. Now I want to talk to you about him," JoJo explained. "I told him that you had a life to live, and I didn't want him to influence the choices you make."

"Like what?" Taylor wondered.

"Like going to school someplace because it's near him. Like not doing a semester abroad because you'll miss him. Like passing up an internship because of him, or he is the reason you can't do what you want. You have a choice you make, and if what you do isn't based on you, it's based on an 'us' that's just wrong. I think you're too young, and he's a lot older than you."

"Only five years," Taylor answered.

"Almost six. Anyway, a lot of growth happens at that time in your life. I don't want you to short-change your experiences because of a guy, even if he's one of my favorites. Like school. What are your plans for this fall? Have you thought about that at all?"

"Yes, JoJo, give me a little credit. Of course, I've thought about things. Denny and I are friends, but that's about it. I have no intention of getting involved with anyone. He knows I have plans; he wants me to have plans.

"I'm going home to finish high school, it's stupid to transfer now. I think for college, I want to do some sort of therapy with dogs. Maybe I'll look into law enforcement and work towards a K-9 job, a tracker, a drug or bomb squad. Maybe even the military, but I'm too sure about that. I know I enjoyed Helen

222

and the guys at the VA, so maybe old people therapy. I have a direction, now, at least to where to look. That's more than I had when I got here."

"What about the reason you were banished here in the first place? How are you going to handle that?"

"That seems so small and stupid. Maybe I'll start a rumor I'm into girls, so I won't have to deal with a boyfriend this last year. Any guys who give me shit I'll just say it's because I can score the hottest girls and they're just jealous. If I come back here, it would be to see my grandparents, not Denny. If I do see him, it's as a friend. He knows that, and he's cool with it."

"Yeah, Taylor, I do need to give you some credit. A lot of credit. You came into a completely unknown situation with a lot of stress and look at you. You have made friends, found some sort of bizarro pseudo-family, and not your average dog. Despite it being kinda weird, I enjoyed you. Your parents did a really good job on the last one, they should be proud of you. You came out above average."

"Thanks, I guess. I have to ask you a question, I hope I don't hurt your feelings."

"Didn't Ray tell you? I don't have any feelings."

"Seriously. Why doesn't my mother like you?"

JoJo looked at Taylor. She looked just like Alex, right down to his high-watt-age smile and his calm, rational outlook on life.

"I'm not sure why. I barely met her once, but I have an idea. It's like this summer. A lot of odd things happened, but it seemed normal until you told someone, and then it sounds all messed up.

"I had a summer like that with your dad. I was in a bad place, and he helped me out of it. A lot of random events all hooked together made it sound like more than it was, but I like him like I like you. Not romantically, but I consider you family. Maybe your mom would need to experience it in order to understand it.

"Or maybe your mom loves your dad so much she's not leaving room for the ghosts of girlfriends past. That's okay. If your dad has someone who loves him that much, he's one lucky guy.

"This is nice, Taylor, talking to you like this. You grew up this summer and sometimes acted like the most rational person in the room. I feel a lot better about you and Den, regardless of your five-year age difference."

"I could say the same about the age difference between you and Harry."

"Harry?" JoJo said.

"Did I hear my name?" he called as he returned to the table and took a seat next to JoJo.

THE
END

ABOUT THE AUTHOR

After retiring from Corporate America, she spent her free time volunteering until Covid-19 made those activities obsolete. Not one to sit around and watch *Days of Our Lives*, she decided to write a book. She wrote a couple, so depending on which one hits the shelf first, this could be her debut novel. She is an empty nester of two adult daughters. One husband, a dog, and a cat remain.

www.ingramcontent.com/pod-product-compliance
Lightning Source LLC
Chambersburg PA
CBHW032053020426
42335CB00011B/325